UNBOUNDING EUROPE

UNBOUNDING EUROPE

Bordering and the Politics of Mediterranean Solidarity in Sicily and Tunisia

Ilaria Giglioli

CORNELL UNIVERSITY PRESS   ITHACA AND LONDON

First published 2025 by Cornell University Press

Library of Congress Cataloging-in-Publication Data

Names: Giglioli, Ilaria, 1984– author.
Title: Unbounding Europe : bordering and the politics of Mediterranean solidarity in Sicily and Tunisia / Ilaria Giglioli.
Description: Ithaca, NY : Cornell University Press, 2025. | Includes bibliographical references and index.
Identifiers: LCCN 2024051486 (print) | LCCN 2024051487 (ebook) | ISBN 9781501782251 (hardcover) | ISBN 9781501782268 (paperback) | ISBN 9781501782275 (epub) | ISBN 9781501782282 (pdf)
Subjects: LCSH: Tunisians—Italy—Mazara del Vallo—Social conditions. | Immigrants—Italy—Mazara del Vallo—Social conditions. | Political culture—Mediterranean Region. | Mazara del Vallo (Italy)—Emigration and immigration. | Mazara del Vallo (Italy)—Ethnic relations. | Mazara del Vallo (Italy)—Social conditions. | Tunisia—Emigration and immigration. | Italy—Foreign relations—Tunisia. | Tunisia—Foreign relations—Italy.
Classification: LCC JV8139.Z6 M394 2025 (print) | LCC JV8139.Z6 (ebook) | DDC 305.892/76110458—dc23/eng/20250305
LC record available at https://lccn.loc.gov/2024051486
LC ebook record available at https://lccn.loc.gov/2024051487

*To all those who have the courage to cross borders
and bring down walls*

Contents

Acknowledgments

Writing is a collective endeavor. This book could not have been written without the intellectual, material, and moral support of family, friends, colleagues, institutions, and mentors. All the participants in this research on both shores of the Mediterranean were incredibly generous with their time and their trust. In order to protect their confidentiality, they are referred to through pseudonyms, with a few exceptions of public figures who accepted to be quoted directly. My hope is that this book will contribute to the creation of more just and equitable relations between people of European and North African descent and to the building of relationships of solidarity, trust, and friendship between the northern and the southern shores of the Mediterranean.

Gillian Hart, Jake Kosek, Mia Fuller, Paola Bacchetta, Michael Watts, and John Agnew provided invaluable support and advice on the research on which this book is based. Colleagues in writing groups at UC Berkeley, UCLA, New College of Florida, and the University of San Francisco offered extensive feedback on early drafts of individual chapters. In particular, suggestions by Sadia Saeed, Hugo Viera Vargas, Timur Hammond, Shaina Potts, Gustavo Oliveira, Angelo Matteo Caglioti, and Glenna Anton were extremely helpful. Camilla Hawthorne provided essential conceptual feedback and practical suggestions at multiple stages of the project. Conversations with Debora Del Pistoia and Montassir Sakhi allowed me to develop my critique of Mediterraneanism. Other scholars of Sicily–Tunisia relations and of migration to Italy were incredibly generous with their time and resources, in particular Naor Ben-Yehoyada, Pietro Saitta, Domenico Perrotta, Daniela Melfa, Leila Ammar, Antonino Cusumano, Maria D'Arrigo, Giuliana Sanò, and Valeria Piro.

Vito Pipitone supported my fieldwork by hosting me at the Institute for Biological Resources and Marine Biotechnologies of the National Research Council in Mazara del Vallo and by connecting me to his professional and personal network in the city. I could not have carried out the research in Mazara without his help. Interest and support from staff at the city library of Mazara del Vallo, the National Library of Tunisia and National Archives of Tunisia in Tunis, the Higher Institute of History of the National Movement in Tunis, and the historical archive of the Italian Ministry of Foreign Affairs in Rome were crucial to my work.

Funding from the Center for Race and Gender and from the Institute for European Studies at the University of California, Berkeley, made the field research for this book possible. Start-up funding from New College of Florida and the Faculty Development Fund from the University of San Francisco allowed me to make use of professional editorial support, and my editor, Steven Hiatt, greatly improved the flow and readability of the manuscript. The University of San Francisco's Faculty Development Fund also allowed me to organize a book manuscript workshop. The participants in this workshop—Reece Jones, Mayanthi Fernando, and Cristina Lombardi-Diop—provided both the feedback and the motivation for a final revision of the manuscript. This, combined with the comments of the two anonymous reviewers, allowed me to fine-tune my argument and better organize the narrative arc of the book.

Three chapters in this book are based on previously published journal articles. In particular, chapter 1 is derived in part from an article published in *Geopolitics* in 2017, copyright © Taylor & Francis, available online at https://doi.org/10.1080/14650045.2016.1233529 (Giglioli 2017a). Chapter 3 is derived in part from an article published in *Social and Cultural Geography* in 2021, copyright © Taylor & Francis, available online at https://doi.org/10.1080/14649365.2019.1601248 (Giglioli 2021). Chapter 4 is derived in part from an article published in the *International Journal of Urban and Regional Research* in 2017, copyright © Urban Research Publications Limited in 2017, available online at https://doi.org/10.1111/1468-2427.12544 (Giglioli 2017b).

Throughout the research and writing process, my family provided inspiration, support, and advice. My parents, Ann Frye and Pier Paolo Giglioli, and my brother, Matteo Giglioli, read drafts of individual chapters and provided feedback, logistical support, and—most importantly—encouragement during the decade I worked on this project. My partner, Ramon Quintero, introduced me to decolonial theory in 2010—the conceptual backdrop to this project. He has also been extremely supportive intellectually, professionally, and personally. My mother-in-law, Beatriz Arredondo, took care of my children on multiple occasions, allowing me to work on the manuscript. My children, Lucia and Leonardo, gave me the balance and joy that I needed to finish this book. I am profoundly grateful for all of the support that I have received from my professional and personal network, though of course any errors and omissions remain my own.

Note on Transliteration

In citations from the French and Italian colonial archives, transliterations from Arabic were left as they appear in the original document. In the references, transliterations from Arabic follow the rules adopted by the US Library of Congress.

Introduction

THE POLITICS OF MIXING IN MEDITERRANEAN BORDERLANDS

> The Mediterranean represents . . . an environment where the domi-
> nant values have always been hospitality, solidarity and dialogue. For
> over a millennium, Sicily has played the role of a meeting place and a
> bridge between cultures and civilizations. I believe this is one of the
> vocations of this land.
>
> Bishop of Mazara del Vallo, February 2014 interview

In the first quarter of the twenty-first century, fortified borders have become a fact of life. Throughout the world, the rise of border walls and the increased surveillance of maritime borders have been matched by the hardening of symbolic ones. The Mediterranean represents the epitome of this trend. Transformed from a sparkling sea to a secured boundary through the fortification of Europe's external borders in the mid-1990s, since the first decade of the twenty-first century, it has become one of the most dangerous border-crossing sites in the world. At the same time, rising right-wing nationalist forces across Europe, such as the Italian Lega or Fratelli d'Italia and the French Front National, organize around restrictive programs of who should be part of the national community. They express their anti-immigrant sentiment through expression of economic grievances—such as attributing unemployment to labor competition by migrants or blaming delays in accessing health care or public assistance on "swamping" of the system by migrants—thus drawing a symbolic dividing line between the deserving poor within the national community and the undeserving external poor who are challenging that border. They also draw on rhetoric from the early 2000s war on terror to cast the Mediterranean, in Samuel Huntington's terms, as a "bloody border" in a broader "clash of civilizations" (Huntington 1993).

In this pervasive political landscape, it is tempting to search for locations that may disprove these theories, places where subjects rhetorically situated on opposite sides of the Mediterranean "civilizational divide" interact as neighbors, colleagues, and friends, and consequently a place where a different type of politics may emerge. According to critical geographers and cultural theorists, borderlands often represent such spaces, thanks to their rich web of cross-border connections that allow for questioning of the material and symbolic borders of the nation (Chambers 2008; Dear 2013). Sicily, the southernmost region of Italy, is a classic example of a Mediterranean borderland. Currently an entry point for migrants into Europe, its diverse architectural and culinary fabric testifies to millennial histories of interconnection with the southern Mediterranean. In addition, in both Sicilian popular speech and political discourse, it is quite common to define the island's culture and identity as a mix of European, African, and Middle Eastern heritage. A diverse range of actors mobilize this trope politically, from migrant-rights activists advocating for freedom of movement, to Catholic figures celebrating the Mediterranean as an epicenter of religious dialogue, to local government officials attempting to brand their region as a strategic site for cross-Mediterranean cooperation (Ben-Yehoyada 2011, 2014; Kutz and Giglioli 2021). Despite the diversity of their aims, they converge in their "Mediterraneanist" rhetoric: the celebration of long-standing interconnections between Europe and the Middle East/North Africa region, the framing of local culture as a hybrid result of long histories of exchange, and the rejection of Huntington-style notions of the Mediterranean as a bloody border.

If Sicily represents the prototype of a Mediterranean borderland, it is also an internal periphery of Italy. Economically marginalized since Italian unification in 1861, its inhabitants have long been racialized by Italian government officials and northern scholars as "backward" and more culturally and racially similar to Arabs and North Africans than to other Europeans. Thus, both in Sicily and in Italy more generally, there is the assumption that Sicilians' history of marginalization has made them less racist than other Italians and Europeans. Since the second decade of the twenty-first century, Sicily (alongside other EU peripheries such as Greece) has borne the brunt of post-2008 financial crisis economic restructuring, and has thus also been the object of reemerging deficiency tropes at the national and EU level concerning the inability of its political class to institute sound financial management (Carney 2021). Histories of economic marginality, exacerbated by the more recent climate of austerity, have meant that this region is hardly a site of economic opportunity for migrants, with Sicilian agriculture and other productive sectors depending on the exploitation of underpaid and undocumented migrant labor (Corrado et al. 2016). Not surprisingly, the current moment of economic austerity has led to heightened labor competition between Sicilians and migrant workers.

Do these precarious economic conditions mean that borderland "third nations" (Dear 2013) are simply an intellectual fantasy, imagined spaces of coexistence with little correspondence to the actual daily relations between people of

European and North African descent in Europe's southern peripheries such as Sicily? What opportunities of political, social, and economic inclusion do these peripheries offer to racialized populations of non-European descent? And, finally, to what extent do Mediterraneanist politics emerging from these locations have the potential to question material borders and to dismantle symbolic ones?

The town of Mazara del Vallo represents an ideal location to explore these questions. Located in Trapani province on the southwestern coast of Sicily, its economic, political, and migratory connections with North Africa date back more than a century. In the late 1800s, as the Sicilian economy was stagnating following the region's incorporation into unified Italy, significant numbers of Sicilians from the area migrated southward to colonial Tunisia and settled there, taking advantage of the opportunities offered to European settlers under the French Protectorate. In the second half of the twentieth century, following Tunisian decolonization, the migration flow changed direction, as in the 1960s Tunisian migrants began to head northward to work in Mazara del Vallo's growing fishing sector. Thus, Mazara del Vallo hosts one of the oldest North African communities in Italy and is often mentioned as an example of "integration" between people of Italian and North African descent. The city of Mazara also depends on cross-Mediterranean connections for its economy. Its main economic engine, the fishing sector, could not have boomed without fishing in Tunisian territorial waters and without the employment of significant numbers of Tunisian crew members.

The centrality of cross-Mediterranean connections to Mazara del Vallo's economy have long made the city an epicenter of Mediterraneanist politics, and the city's elected officials and its economic and intellectual elite have repeatedly engaged in initiatives of cross-Mediterranean diplomacy to protect the interests of the fishing sector (Ben-Yehoyada 2018). As the fishing industry entered into an irreversible decline, new forms of Mediterraneanist politics emerged in the city. In an attempt to relaunch the local economy, municipal authorities embraced Mediterraneanism as a regional development project, branding the city as an exotic yet safe tourist destination and a cosmopolitan hub of cross-Mediterranean cultural and economic cooperation—a perfect site for national and EU funding for cross-border cooperation. At the same time, Mazara's Catholic institutions—as well as some secular voices—embraced Mediterraneanism for their own multicultural projects, celebrating Mediterranean coexistence as a response to the presumed difficulties stemming from people of different national, cultural, and religious backgrounds sharing the same spaces. According to this narrative, Mazara del Vallo represents a model of multicultural Mediterranean coexistence that could serve as an example for other parts of Europe with stronger identitarian boundaries.

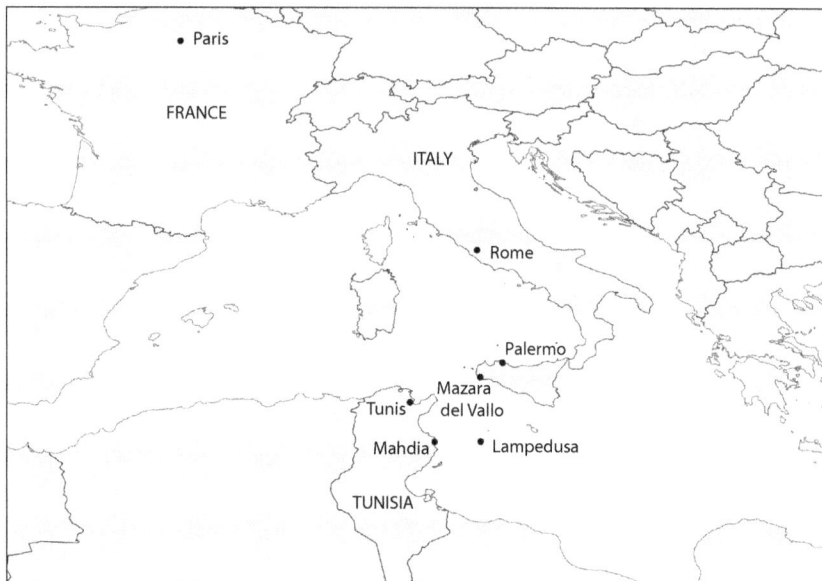

FIGURE 1.   Map of the central Mediterranean. Source: Author.

Mazara del Vallo thus represents an ideal laboratory in which to analyze the potential of Mediterranean borderlands as a model of copresence of people of different national and religious backgrounds; as an example of a "mixed" cultural space in which more inclusive understandings of belonging can emerge, compared with nationalist ones; and as an epicenter of Mediterraneanist politics that call into question the material and symbolic bordering of the Mediterranean. More specifically, the book explores three questions. First, to what extent are people of Tunisian descent able to build stable lives and achieve sustainable livelihoods in Mazara del Vallo? Second, to what extent does the "hybrid" Mediterranean culture that has emerged in the city challenge more general assumptions about the incompatibility between Sicilians and Tunisians, and the notion that North African and Muslim migrants may have difficulty integrating into Europe? Finally, what effect do different strands of Mediterraneanist politics have on the lives and livelihoods of the city's Tunisian population?

The book primarily addresses these questions through ethnographic research within the Tunisian community and with promoters of Mediterraneanist projects in Mazara. However, Mazara—as indeed any "place"—cannot be analyzed in isolation (Massey 1994). Its local dynamics are shaped by flows of people, capital, and ideas that connect the town to other sites in Europe and North Africa, as well as political and economic decisions taken at other scales. Thus, to understand the livelihood options and legal status of people of Tunisian descent in Mazara del

Vallo, their insertion into the city's social and economic fabric, and the Mediter-raneanist politics that emerged in the city, I begin by situating contemporary Mazara within a longer history of Italian and European colonial, immigration, and regional development policies that led to the transformation of the Mediter-ranean Sea into the material and symbolic border of Europe. Within this his-torical overview, I pay particular attention to the little-known history of Sicilian southward migration to colonial Tunisia in the late nineteenth century, with a focus on processes of symbolic boundary-drawing and debates about coexistence between Sicilians and Tunisians under the French Protectorate. Conceptually, this focus is motivated by postcolonial and decolonial scholarship on migration, which argues that current debates about migrant integration are not a response to a new challenge of societies attempting to grapple with difference, but instead reproduce tropes of racial difference that emerged in colonial debates about how to effectively manage colonial subjects (El-Tayeb 2011; Sayyid and Dabashi 2015). While there is no direct colonial link between Italy and Tunisia, the Ital-ian government maintained a strong diplomatic presence in colonial Tunisia and tried to wield influence over the territory, particularly by attempting to generate and maintain loyalty to Italy among the substantial number of Sicilians who had migrated to Tunisia in the early years of the French Protectorate. Thus, colonial Tunisia—like contemporary Sicily—was also a borderland context, marked by everyday interactions between Sicilians and Tunisians, as well as by vivid debates about how to manage coexistence between them. In contemporary Mazara, some proponents of Mediterranean multiculturalism invoke "coexistence" in colonial Tunisia both as a model for multicultural coexistence in contemporary Sicily, and as a legacy that has made Sicilians particularly open to living with difference. Identifying colonial Tunisia as a "starting point" for the analysis of contemporary borderland politics allows us to trace longer histories of celebrating Mediterra-nean coexistence in borderland sites characterized by profound inequalities, and thus to show how contemporary forms of Mediterraneanist politics may also par-adoxically help perpetuate material inequalities and symbolic hierarchies. This historical analysis also sheds light on the longer history of Sicilians affirming their own precarious Europeanness by emphasizing their differentiation from Tunisians, a dynamic that also emerges in contemporary Mazara.

Overall, I make three arguments in the course of this book. First, I argue that histories of marginalization within the nation-state do not automatically trans-late into alternative understandings of belonging, or indeed initiatives assert-ing cross-border solidarity. While Mediterranean borderlands such as Sicily may be sites of day-to-day familiarity and interaction between people of differ-ent backgrounds, they may also be sites of accentuation of difference, particu-larly in moments of scarcity. Sicilians' history of marginalization thus does not automatically translate into solidarity with migrants hailing from the southern Mediterranean. While solidarity initiatives have certainly emerged, Sicilians— as themselves precarious Europeans—have a long history of affirming their full "modernity," Italianness, and Europeanness through *differentiation* from an "even deeper South" represented by North Africans, both in a colonial context such as late nineteenth-century Tunisia, and following the fortification of the Mediterranean border in the early 1990s. Understanding the interplay of these different degrees of marginality—internally marginalized populations versus externally marginalized colonial subjects/migrants—is key to identifying the conditions under which solidarity movements can emerge and be effective.

Second, I argue that depoliticized celebrations of Mediterranean coexistence and cross-Mediterranean interconnection do not address material inequalities or symbolic hierarchies between people of European and North African descent in the Mediterranean region. For Mediterraneanist projects to serve as such an emancipatory and transformative politics of solidarity, it is necessary for them not only to idealize the copresence of people of different backgrounds in the same spaces, but also to recognize and seek to overcome long-standing inequalities between people of European and North African descent both across borders and in southern European borderlands.

Finally, at a more conceptual level, I suggest that in order to call into question the "naturalness" of the Mediterranean border, rather than idealize intermediate spaces of coexistence or binational and bicultural subjects that might call the border into question, it is more effective to reconstruct the processes of material and symbolic boundary-drawing through which this border was created and naturalized. Showing the historical construction of this boundary, in fact, allows us to contest its naturalness. But what, exactly, are borders?

Bordering, Uneven Development, and Racialization

In its everyday usage, the term *border* evokes a pencil-thin line separating colorful polygons on a political map. According to this image, borders are clear boundaries that demarcate the separation between distinct geopolitical entities. As many border scholars have shown, however, borders cannot simply be reduced to lines. Border work of surveillance, demarcation, and exclusion occurs at multiple sites within and beyond the physical borders of nation-states (Bialasiewicz 2012; Brown 2010; Casas-Cortes et al. 2016; Cobarrubias et al. 2023; Graham 2010; Petti 2007; Weizman 2007) and is carried out by a heterogenous group of state and nonstate actors, leading some to theorize borders as assemblages (Hess 2010; Mezzadra and Neilson 2013; Tsianos and Karakayali 2010). Theorists of borderlands also critique the notion of the border as a line, arguing that the physical line of the border is flanked by a broader "ribbon" characterized by cross-border exchange and hybrid cultural forms that call into question the notion of a homogeneous and bounded national identity (Brambilla 2015; Dear 2013). Taken together, these descriptions of borders allow us to avoid the "territorial trap" (Agnew 1994) of reifying borders and the territories they enclose, by showing that bordering is a process that occurs in multiple locations alongside the border line, that today's borders were historically produced through violent processes, and that nation-states are not as homogeneous as they claim to be.

These theories, however, all conceive of borders primarily in geopolitical terms. This book instead invites us to look at borders differently: not simply as lines of geopolitical separation but as one dividing line within broader relational geographies of sociospatial difference. In other words, the book situates borders alongside other forms of spatial differentiation within the geopolitical units they enclose. In more concrete terms, this implies that if we study the Mediterranean border alongside geographies of uneven development within Europe, it is possible to conceive of the Mediterranean as one line of demarcation of sociospatial difference that exists alongside informal lines of demarcation of difference between northern and southern Italy or between northern Europe and its southern states: Portugal, Italy, Greece, and Spain. Certainly, many scholars have taken into account questions of uneven development in their analyses of Mediterranean migration, as part of a broader line of scholarship on the relationship between border fortification and economic inequalities, including the precarization of migrant labor (Mezzadra and Neilson 2013; Tazzioli 2023). Studies on bordering and uneven development have focused particularly on the effects of economic marginalization in Europe's southern border regions on the lives, livelihoods, and politics of migrants (Dines 2022; Frazzetta and Piazza 2020; Perrotta 2014b; Piro 2014), as well as the specific nature of immigration debates that emerge in those contexts (Panebianco 2022). They have also highlighted how different actors in peripheral border regions respond to this economic marginality, from public officials' attempts to enhance regional development through cross-border collaboration initiatives (Galemba 2012; Kutz and Giglioli 2021) to migrants' decision-making about onward migration (Dimitriadis 2021; Mas Giralt 2017; Schapendonk 2021). However, this work focuses primarily on the consequences of the economic marginality of border regions, paying less attention to its origins or the impact of the fortification of external borders on these regions' position within the nation-state.

Analyzing the interplay between the demarcation of external borders and the management of internal geographies of uneven development allows us to frame borders as simply one line of division within broader geographies of uneven development. This implies, then, that bordering is a process of making some lines of demarcation more significant by accentuating and naturalizing them and making other ones less so by ignoring them or actively intervening to reduce their import. As I show in chapter 1, in the context of the Central Mediterranean Corridor, this occurred through a combination of Italian and European regional development projects that attempted to bridge developmental divides between northern and southern Italy (thus making this internal geography of uneven development less significant) and the fortification of the Mediterranean border (which made this dividing line more significant).

The interplay between external bordering and internal boundary-drawing also involves processes of racialization. The interplay of national development projects targeting southern Italy and the fortification of the Mediterranean border led to a shift in Italian depictions of Sicilians. As chapters 1 and 2 discuss, at the turn of the twentieth century Italian scholars and national public servants described Sicilians and Tunisians as similarly "backward" and "uncivilized," but by the second half of the twentieth century, the Italian press clearly cast the Mediterranean Sea as the main dividing line between development and underdevelopment—or between "modern" and "backward" subjects. The Italian public debate thus only came to identify the Mediterranean as the natural border of Europe as a consequence of the production of spatial and racialized difference between populations of the extreme periphery of Europe (Sicilians) and North Africa (Tunisians).

Analyzing bordering as a process of simultaneous minimization of internal and accentuation of cross-border difference, and highlighting the relationship between bordering and racialization, suggests that the creation of borders in a context such as Italy may actually show points of similarity with settler-colonial processes of bordering. Decolonial and critical border scholars focused on the United States have shown how the fortification of US borders is part of a long history of racial anxiety manifested in attempts to bound the nation against undesirable external others while pacifying internal ones (Hernández 2018; Nevins 2002). The current territorial unity of settler states such as the United States and Israel was produced through violent processes of territorial annexation and pacification of populations of annexed territories (Hispanos and Native Americans in the US Southwest, or Palestinian citizens of Israel), alongside the separation of organically connected territories and populations across new borders (Anzaldúa 1987; Barrera 1979; Hernández 2018; Pappé 2006; Simpson 2014). In non-settler-colonial states, however, these processes of assimilation/exclusion are less visible. Thus, there is a tendency to naturalize borders of nonsettler states, because they were not created through colonial conquest, settlement, and assimilation/elimination of native populations. However, if we take into account the history of incorporation of internal peripheries that was necessary for nation-building in Europe (Curtis

1968; Hechter 1975; Moe 2002; Schneider 1998; Weber 1976), we see that processes of violent incorporation of territory and the management of "less civilized" populations was also constitutive to the creation and consolidation of European nation-states. This internal process often occurred alongside the definition of the external symbolic boundaries of the nation by tracing the boundaries between "civilizable" poor European subjects and "noncivilizable" colonial subjects in European colonies. In essence, the current borders of European nation-states, like settler-colonial borders, were also produced through the violent incorporation of territory and the coercive assimilation of populations. Understanding this history is crucial, because it allows us to call into question the current fortification of borders by dispelling any notion of natural borders for Italy and Europe and by showing how notions "cultural difference" between Europeans and North Africans—currently at the core of many migration debates—were produced historically. Paying attention to internal inequalities also allows us to see the relationships between migration, coloniality, and nation-building in a new light.

Migration, Coloniality, and Nation-Building

Mainstream Italian and European discussions about immigration consider anti-migrant sentiment to be a normal response to the arrival of external migrants whose culture may be at odds with that of the receiving country. This framework characterizes both conservative and liberal commentary on immigration, albeit with some differences, and frames much scholarship on migration to Europe (Favell 2001). According to this interpretation, for their integration to be successful, migrants and their descendants must adapt to the society in which they are now embedded.

However, some scholars and migrant-rights activists, including a growing movement of descendants of immigrants, are increasingly questioning this framework, arguing that contemporary material and symbolic boundaries of the nation are the product of long histories of racialized exclusion (El-Tayeb 2011; Hawthorne 2022; Sayyid and Dabashi 2015). Thus, contemporary migrants are simply a new population being excluded by the racialized symbolic boundaries of the nation (El-Tayeb 2011; Khiari 2009; Kipfer 2011; Solomos et al. 1982). Drawing on the conceptual framework of the coloniality of power, which argues that the uneven power relations created in the context of European colonialism continue to have significant effects in the present, multiple studies have shown that the current racialization of migrants in Europe draws on and reproduces the racialization of colonial subjects in Asian and African colonies of European states (Grosfoguel 2003; Hall 2000; Khiari 2009; Kipfer 2011; Solomos et al. 1982). Thus, contemporary questions about Tunisians' ability to integrate into Italy and Europe draw on older tropes developed in colonial Tunisia about the incompatibility of Tunisians with Europeanness.

This framework, however, leaves some questions unanswered. Can we really speak of the racialized tracing of the external boundaries of Italy when southern Italians were historically also racialized? Shouldn't debates about immigration be very different in northern and in southern Italy, due to the South's own marginalized position within the nation-state? With a few exceptions (De Genova 2017; Hawthorne 2022), postcolonial and decolonial analyses of migration to Europe tend to treat Europe as an undifferentiated entity and thus consider internal territorial inequalities and internal processes of racialization to be of minor significance in comparison to broader processes of defining external boundaries. But we must understand the interplay of such internal and external processes of racialization if we are to fully understand debates about immigration and processes of racialization in southern Italy. Literature on internal colonialism (Blauner 1969; Hechter 1975; Quijano and Ennis 2000), colonialism within one country (Moe 2002; Schneider 1998), and territorial marginalization within Europe (Curtis 1968; Weber 1976) suggests that the contemporary racialization of migrants is inextricably connected to attempts to "modernize" and "civilize" populations of internal peripheries. By analyzing Sicilian debates about immigration, we can see that this connection is multifaceted. On the one hand, Sicilians (as an internally marginalized population) were historically racialized in very similar ways to Tunisian colonial subjects—indeed, scholarly accounts of colonial Tunisia describe poor Sicilian settlers in very similar terms to Tunisians, as having, for example, poor hygiene and little discipline (Carletti 1903; Loth 1907). More recently, in the 1960s and 1970s the Sicilian press described the poverty of Tunisian immigrants as reminiscent of that of Sicilian emigrants. On the other hand, however, internally marginalized subjects have often affirmed their full modernity through their differentiation from colonial subjects. Both in colonial Tunisia and in contemporary Italy, projects of "modernizing" Sicilians through education or regional development were a means of differentiating them from Tunisians and thus affirming their modernity. This was not only a state-sponsored project but was also embraced by Sicilians themselves, who—as I show in chapter 4 in the context of Mazara—were able to affirm in everyday life their own modernity through their differentiation from Tunisians. Symbolically delineating the external boundaries of Italy and of Europe was thus central to asserting the full Italianness and Europeanness of internally marginalized subjects. Certainly, Sicilian intellectual and political elites have sometimes celebrated their proximity to Tunisia and have indeed insisted on this as a Sicilian specificity that set it apart from northern Italy and northern Europe. However, in the majority of cases, this did not serve to question their own Italianness and Euro-peanness—and thus the symbolic boundaries of Italy and Europe—but rather to redefine Sicily's geographical and cultural proximity to North Africa as an asset for Italy and Europe.

What, then, of Mediterranean borderlands such as Sicily as hybrid or inter-connected spaces that call into question the bounded and homogeneous nation-state? Is this merely an intellectual fantasy of scholars or activists who are looking for an alternative model to the current status quo of material and symbolic border closure? Do Mediterraneanist politics that emerge out of spaces such as Mazara have anything to offer as a project of solidarity or an attempt to dismantle mate-rial and symbolic borders? To answer these questions, it is necessary to explore the politics of hybridity and "in-betweenness" in more detail.

The Politics of Mediterranean Mixing

The field of mixed race studies and some critical analyses of multiculturalism have grappled with the potentials and pitfalls of celebrating mixing in order to challenge racialized boundary-drawing. Overall, they have argued that these cel-ebrations do not necessarily translate into progressive politics. Spencer (2006), for instance, has shown that the idea of mixed race—which appears to tran-scend racial categories—actually reifies the category of race itself. In more gen-eral terms, this means that celebrating mixing necessarily assumes that there are separate entities that come together to mix. In the context of the Mediterranean, celebrating Mediterranean mixing assumes a long-standing innate cultural differ-ence between Europeans and North Africans. Similarly, celebrating hybrid Medi-terranean borderlands reifies the notion of separate coherent nation-states that are blended in the borderland.

Celebrations of mixing not only reify difference but also—as Glissant (1989) argues in *Caribbean Discourse*—obscure uneven power relations between the dif-ferent groups that are mixing, as well as the violent histories through which this mixing took place (Hawthorne and Piccolo 2016; Welch 2010). This is also the case with celebrations of Mediterranean coexistence in contemporary Italy and in colonial Tunisia, which ignore—and thus reproduce—material inequalities between the different populations that are coexisting in the same space.

Celebrations of mixing also create symbolic hierarchies between the differ-ent entities that are said to be mixing. Mixed race scholars have argued that mainstream celebrations of mixing usually refer to the partial incorporation of a subordinate group into a dominant one, not forms of mixing that challenge the dominant group (De la Cadena 2005; King-O'Rian et al. 2014). Critical scholars of multiculturalism have argued something similar, showing how contemporary neoliberal multiculturalism celebrates the partial aesthetic incorporation of "diversity" in a manner that can facilitate the circulation of capital but is hostile to forms of mixing that challenge dominant understandings of the national community (Ferguson 2007; Goonewardena and Kipfer 2005; Povinelli 2002). This is also the case in contemporary Sicily, as well as in colonial Tunisia, where forms of mixing that partially incorporate certain Arab/Muslim/Tunisian elements into a hegemonic French/Italian/European culture are celebrated, but forms of mixing that redefine the essence of Frenchness/Italianness/Europeanness are frowned upon. This model also implies a symbolic hierarchy between an assumed universalist European culture, capable of accepting and managing diversity, and an Arab/Muslim one, supposedly unable to accommodate diversity and peaceful coexistence.

Historically, scholarship on the Mediterranean has not dealt in detail with the politics of celebrating Mediterranean mixing, nor, indeed, questions of hierarchy and inequality in Mediterranean borderlands. Studies of the region in fact tend either to reconstruct long histories of population movement and economic and cultural exchange between North Africa and Europe (Clancy-Smith 2010; Davi 2000; Melfa 2008) or to celebrate the assumed Mediterranean multicultural conviviality produced by this exchange (Chambers 2008). Work that calls into question the multicultural Mediterranean tends either to dispute the significance of shared cultural traits between its northern and southern shores (Herzfeld 1984) or to investigate the conditions in which the Mediterranean becomes significant to participants in cross-Mediterranean economic, political, and cultural exchanges (Ben-Yehoyada 2018). In more conceptual terms, debates about the region tend to oscillate between theories of its unity and its fragmentation (Lombardi-Diop 2021), without a basis in a detailed analysis of uneven power relations and inequalities.

Some scholarship on the nineteenth-century Mediterranean represents an exception to this trend, however, by reconstructing uneven power relations in mixed Mediterranean spaces. Various urban historians have, for example, shown that the "cosmopolitan" cities of the southern and eastern Mediterranean under both Ottoman and European colonial rule were highly hierarchical spaces (Bromberger 2007; Haller 2004; Lafi 2013). Indeed, these cities were marked by strong economic hierarchies structuring the relations between more and less "cosmopolitan subjects," because cosmopolitan circles were often elite spaces, connected both economically and culturally to the European metropole (Haller 2004; Mills 2010). In addition, the copresence of different national, linguistic, and religious communities did not necessarily mean their fusion, because interaction between these communities occurred alongside careful guarding of their boundaries

(Bromberger 2007; Dakhlia 2005; Largueche et al. 2001). Within more contemporary scholarship, the Black Mediterranean collective has shown how the romanticization of the Mediterranean as a space of convivial exchange ignores violent histories of oppression and ongoing uneven power relations across this sea (Danewid et al. 2021; Lombardi-Diop 2021), highlighting in particular how certain celebrations of Mediterranean mixing perpetuate the symbolic exclusion of Blackness from Europe (Hawthorne 2022). In this book, I adopt a critique similar to that of the Black Mediterranean collective but extend the focus from anti-Black racism to Islamophobia, as people of Tunisian descent in Italy are primarily racialized as Arab and Muslim, through what Mayanthi Fernando (2014) defines as a racialized notion of difference that combines race, religion, and culture. As the book shows, particularly in chapter 5, celebrations of Mediterranean mixing may reproduce Islamophobic tropes by setting a Mediterranean "cosmopolitanism" against an alleged monolithic Islam. Analyzing this in detail is crucial to explaining both the racialized exclusion of Tunisians in Sicily and the ambiguous politics of Mediterraneanism in Tunisia, which may serve simultaneously as an anti-Islamist discourse and as a means to symbolically position the country as a "modern" interlocutor for Europe.

But does this mean that Mediterraneanist politics cannot be redeemed as an emancipatory project? Despite its critiques, scholarship on the Black Mediterranean has shown how racialized populations may indeed reappropriate notions of Mediterranean mixing as a claim to postcolonial belonging and as a means to center the experiences of Black subjects in southern Europe (Danewid et al. 2021; Hawthorne 2022). As I examine in chapters 3 and 4, this was also the case for some people of Tunisian descent in Mazara, who adopted Mediterraneanist politics to articulate claims of belonging and demands for public resources. Thus, we should not discount the emancipatory potential of celebrations of Mediterranean mixing, but we should guard against simply assuming it. Celebrating Mediterranean cosmopolitanism may indeed be disruptive of the status quo, because it represents a direct attack on the language of right-wing nationalists. In addition, many proponents of Mediterraneanist politics in Europe are cognizant of uneven power relations between people of European and North African descent and explicitly seek to address them. For instance, the "transgressive cosmopolitanism" embraced by some European migrant solidarity movements calls for Europeanness to be transformed through the arrival of migrants and refugees (Rygiel and Baban 2019). In other words, it explicitly critiques bounded understandings of national identity and uneven power relations between European citizens and migrants.

Celebrating Mediterranean cosmopolitanism should not, however, mean ignoring power relations between the northern and the southern shores of the Mediterranean. This is particularly pertinent in Italy, where a common assumption is that Italians (particularly in the South) cannot be racist due to their own subordinate position within Europe, or that they are not responsible for colonial violence because Italy was only a minor colonial power. However, as scholars who have studied the politics of solidarity in settler-colonial contexts and international solidarity campaigns suggest (Boudreau Morris 2017; Hill 2018), it is possible to both affirm a shared history of marginalization and to recognize contemporary differences in power and privilege. Thus, invoking a Mediterranean "sameness" and recognizing the history of discrimination faced by southern Italians can provide the basis for solidarity and collaboration, but this must be accompanied by an effort to eliminate material inequalities and symbolic hierarchies in the region, to question the naturalness of European borders, and to embrace a politics of collective emancipation.

Ambiguous Positioning in Mediterranean Borderlands

A few weeks after arriving in Mazara in February 2014, I was wandering through the narrow streets of the "Casbah" neighborhood in the town's historic center, trying out my new camera by documenting the decorative ceramic tiles that celebrate the town's Arab past and its ongoing connections with North Africa. About halfway down a deserted alleyway, just as I was taking a picture of tiles celebrating "tolerance," I noticed two young men of Tunisian descent—probably in their late teens—walking in my direction. Not wanting to appear like a tourist, and also conscious of the flashiness of my new equipment, I quickly slipped my camera into my bag. Despite my best intentions, however, the gesture had hardly been discreet. As they passed me, I overheard one man muttering to the other in Tunisian Arabic: "Shūf kīfēsh khabbeīt al-kāmīra mtā'hā?" (Look how she hid her camera). Turning toward me with an accusatory look, he switched to Italian: "Sei proprio un'ignorante!" (You are really ignorant). Mortified by this exchange, I tried desperately to repair the incident: "Ma non è per voi!" (It's not because of you) I exclaimed in Italian. As the two men walked away, clearly not persuaded, I blurted out in the wrong Arabic dialect, "'an jad, mish 'ashānkom!" (Really, it's not because of you). The two young men stopped, clearly startled, and walked back to me. "Are you Lebanese?" asked in Arabic the one who had admonished me earlier, adding, "What are you doing in Mazara?" I replied in the same language, "No, no, I am not, I am Italian, from Bologna." Skeptical, he retorted, "I have never met an Italian who speaks Arabic." When I explained I had studied it for a long time, and had lived in the West Bank, he concluded, "Ah, you must be here to study 'integration.'" We chatted briefly, mixing Italian and Arabic, and parted ways somewhat more amicably than we had met.

Despite its resolution, I could not stop thinking about this incident. It was difficult to admit both my lack of tact and the fact that—despite my research focus and broader political commitments—I was not able to undo years of implicit bias picked up by growing up in Italy, according to which I associated young Tunisian men with danger. This was a common complaint of many men of Tunisian descent I spoke to during my fieldwork, who mentioned daily instances of being perceived as a threat by their Italian cocitizens. Reflecting on the episode years later, I see another side of this incident—the ability to disassociate from an uncomfortable position of privilege by embracing an "ambiguous" or "intermediate" identity. But what is at stake, both intellectually and politically, by embracing this ambiguous or intermediate position? And how is it tied to my broader motivations to write this book?

When I came of age in the first decade of the twenty-first century, at the time of the "war on terror" and the US-led invasions of Iraq and Afghanistan, demonstrating the fallacy of Huntington's (1993) "clash of civilizations" theory and building activism and civil society bridges between Italy and the Middle East and North Africa (MENA) region were political projects shared by many young Italian activists. As the Mediterranean Sea became increasingly fortified both materially and symbolically as a "civilizational fault-line," this commitment quickly translated into pro-migrant activism. Celebrating the Mediterranean as a space of exchange and interconnection, and building cross-Mediterranean solidarity, appeared an obvious response. Throughout these and other activist spaces, however, there was little self-questioning of Italians' positionality. As a less-visible partner in US and European military endeavors in the Middle East, Italians' politics were rarely questioned when they participated in solidarity delegations to locations such as the Palestinian West Bank or 2011 postrevolutionary Tunisia. At the same time, activists themselves rarely questioned their own positionality—partially because of an assumed affinity and commonality between Italians and populations of the southern Mediterranean. In graduate school, as I began to dive into the small but growing field of scholarship on Italian colonial history, I realized that these observations were symptomatic of a broader national myth of "Italiani brava gente" (Italians, good people), which has permeated national consciousness since the end of World War II. With a few exceptions (Labanca 2002), a recognition of and reckoning with Italian colonial violence has generally been absent from Italian historiography. This absence was even more prevalent in Italian public debate, which assumed that Italians had been more benevolent than other colonial powers thanks to their status as a "minor power," that Italian Fascists had been more benign compared to German Nazis (Focardi 2016), and that Italians in the present (particularly in the South) were less racist than other Europeans because of their own history of racialization.

Seeking to better understand this positionality was a key motivation to write this book. I wanted to understand the process of boundary-drawing through which Italians, particularly in the South, became fully "European" and how this process was always partial and unfinished, allowing (southern) Italians themselves to claim an "intermediate" position. At the same time, I wanted to investigate how it might be possible to mobilize colonial history in a way that did not simply idealize Italians as "minor" colonizers or paint an idyllic portrait of Mediterranean coexistence but actually shed light on processes of boundary-drawing and differentiation that allowed Italians to claim Europeanness. It was precisely these questions that led me to identify Mazara del Vallo as the epicenter of this study and to include a brief field visit to Lampedusa: I wanted to study processes of boundary-drawing and coexistence in the southernmost peripheries of Italy, where the inhabitants' own Italianness had long been questioned, in order to address broader questions about Italians' positionality in the Mediterranean context.

In Mazara, I planned to focus on relations between Sicilians and Tunisians in various arenas of everyday life (occupation of urban space, school, and labor), as well as public discourse and political projects in the city that celebrated multicultural coexistence and cross-Mediterranean connections. As I carried out fieldwork, however, my plans changed. An obvious site of interaction between Sicilian and Tunisian workers, the fishing sector, was an almost exclusively male space, and—as an Italian woman in my late twenties—negotiating access to it was somewhat complicated. In addition, anthropologist Naor Ben-Yehoyada's work, conducted only a few years earlier, provided a comprehensive overview of daily relations on the fishing fleet as part of a broader process of everyday region-making in the Mediterranean (Ben-Yehoyada 2018). I therefore primarily addressed questions of labor relations by interviewing union staff and participating in union labor-rights clinics, as well as interviewing family members of Tunisian workers. These and other interviews revealed that, rather than the questions of identity and boundary-drawing I had initially planned to address, the main issues of concern among Mazara's Tunisian community were the increasingly precarious nature of their livelihoods in the aftermath of the 2008 economic crisis and the implication of this precarity on immigration status.

With this economic context in the background, the city was at that time also witnessing an unprecedented level of political organizing by the Tunisian community, in particular around municipality-sponsored events celebrating Mediterranean mixing and interconnection. Thus, I refocused my ethnographic research on specific instances of celebration of Mazara's Mediterranean identity that became the object of political contestation (such as the opening of Casa Tunisia in Mazara's old Casbah), interviewing Sicilian and Tunisian actors involved, and conducting background archival research on these projects in municipal records and in local media. This focus meant that a large portion of my research within Mazara's Tunisian community involved people who were particularly politically active and vocal, such as the founders of local Tunisian organizations, union employees, service providers, and teachers. Through these relationships, however, I was able to access broader family networks, including less publicly visible individuals, both in Mazara and in Mahdia (Tunisia) in order to conduct oral histories and interviews on histories of migration to Italy, changes of livelihood and immigration status, and experiences of everyday life in Sicily.

To understand the longer history of boundary-drawing between Sicilians and Tunisians, as well as colonial legacies in contemporary debates about Mediterranean coexistence, I combined ethnographic research in Mazara with archival research on late-nineteenth-century colonial Tunisia. Italian colonial school archives, housed at the Italian Ministry of Foreign Affairs, represented a crucial source of information about daily relations between Sicilians and Tunisians, debates among Italian elites about the effects of this proximity to Tunisians on the habits and character of Sicilians, and about attempts to "civilize" Sicilian settlers in Tunisia. Fieldwork in Mazara del Vallo, however, revealed another research path, as some Mazarese Catholic organizations were working directly with descendants of Sicilian settlers in Tunisia as part of a broader twinning program between the dioceses of Mazara del Vallo and of Tunis. These networks allowed me to conduct ethnographic research and oral histories with descendants of Sicilian settlers who had continued to live in Tunisia sixty years after decolonization. This research, combined with a reading against the grain of the existing historiography of Sicilian migration to Tunisia, allowed me to frame colonial Tunisia as a precedent example of how celebrations of Mediterranean coexistence can exist alongside persistent material inequalities and symbolic hierarchies, and as a key moment of boundary-drawing between Sicilians and Tunisians that allowed the former to assert their (precarious) Europeanness.

Despite efforts to understand the production of (southern) Italians as precarious European subjects, the book argues that it is important to transcend an excessive focus on positionality. Indeed, in a quest to undo long-standing "West/Rest" dichotomies symbolized by the Mediterranean border, it argues that searching for a perfect "intermediate" borderland, or an intermediate and "mixed" subject, is a futile pursuit. Instead, it is necessary to understand positionality, power, and privilege as a basis to build bridges of solidarity across difference. These questions have become particularly relevant since the 2010s—a period of heightened nationalisms throughout Europe and of the blossoming of solidarity initiatives in the Mediterranean region, both between post–Arab Spring social movements and southern European antiausterity ones (Solera 2013) and between citizens, migrant workers, and other racialized populations in southern European regions grappling with the social and economic fallout of post-2008 austerity measures (Arampatzi 2017; Carney 2021; Rozakou 2012). A central tenet of many of these movements was the need to build bridges across difference, with the understanding that neoliberalism and austerity were common conditions that affected both shores of the Mediterranean (Carney 2021; Solera 2013) or represented a "great equalizer" between racialized populations that had a long experience of precariousness and middle-class southern Europeans whose safety nets were eroded in the post-2008 period (Bassel and Akwugo 2017; Cabot 2016).

On the one hand, solidarity movements of this type rooted in Greece, southern Italy, or spanning the two shores of the Mediterranean do show how solidarity, as a form of costruggle that recognizes the other as equal but also understands the structural reasons behind inequalities, can represent a means to rework understandings of citizenship and belonging in more radical and inclusive ways (Cabot 2016; Carney 2021; Solera 2013). On the other hand, scholars of these social movements have recognized how some forms of solidarity—particularly when worded in the language of hospitality—can reproduce uneven power relations (Mitchell and Sparke 2018; Rozakou 2012). Others have shown the differential effects that austerity measures promote along lines of race, gender, and citizenship or on populations of the southern Mediterranean with limited rights to mobility (Carastathis 2015; Giglioli 2021). Thus, both scholars of Mediterranean social movements and participants in the movements themselves have highlighted the importance of recognizing the uneven ways in which neoliberalism and austerity are experienced in the region, and thus of centering the needs and demands of most marginalized subjects (Bassel and Akwugo 2017), including those located on the southern shore of the Mediterranean.[1] Carefully articulating the intersection of similarity (of condition, or of culture produced through long histories of interconnection) and of difference in power and privilege, and seeking to address it, is the key to building lasting movements of solidarity in the Mediterranean region.

Organization of the Book

The first part of the book reconstructs processes of boundary-drawing that allowed Sicilians to be produced as precarious Italian and European subjects and allowed Sicily to be transformed from a periphery of Italy and Europe to the fortified border of Europe in the Mediterranean. This history serves to situate Mazara del Vallo within broader geographies of bordering and uneven development in the Euro-Mediterranean region and within longer histories of boundary-drawing and celebrations of coexistence. Chapter 1 provides an overview of two-way labor migration between Sicily and Tunisia from the late nineteenth century to the present, on the backdrop of shifting Italian and European regional development, colonial, and immigration policies. It also traces the history of Italian and European Mediterraneanist thought. I note that Sicilians have historically defined their full Italianness and Europeanness not only through their differentiation from Tunisia/Tunisians but also through a strategic celebration of their Mediterranean cosmopolitanism. Celebrations of Mediterranean coexistence have thus long been accompanied by the creation of material and symbolic borders.

Chapter 2 further develops this argument through a focus on late nineteenth-century Sicilian migration to colonial Tunisia. It provides a detailed overview of historical debates about Sicilians' racial and cultural proximity to Tunisians and of attempts by French colonial authorities and Italian diplomatic ones to "modernize" poor Sicilian settlers, differentiating them from Tunisian colonial subjects. Here I also reconstruct how the French colonial notion of the *fusion of the races*—a vision of Mediterranean coexistence under the hegemony of French language and culture—represented a key strategy to build consensus around colonial rule. Celebrations of Mediterranean coexistence of this kind have a long history of maintaining uneven power relations between Europeans and North Africans. Following Tunisian decolonization, the majority of Sicilians left colonial Tunisia, and the history of their presence in the territory is little remembered. However, many themes from that historical moment—such as notions of the incompatibility of Tunisians with Europeanness or the ambiguous politics of celebrating Mediterranean coexistence—reappear in contemporary Sicily.

The second part of the book further develops these arguments by focusing on the contemporary Mediterranean borderland of Mazara del Vallo, addressing everyday processes of boundary-drawing and practices of coexistence between Sicilians and Tunisians in this southern European periphery, as well as Mediterranean politics that emerge in the city. Chapter 3 reconstructs how the broader processes of bordering and the regional development projects discussed in chapter 1 were lived and experienced in the context of Mazara del Vallo, examining the changing labor conditions, legal status, and economic stability of people of Tunisian descent in the city from the 1970s to the present. Based on ethnographic research on Tunisians' livelihood strategies, as well as their engagement with Mediterraneanist politics, the chapter explains how the precariousness of Tunisians' everyday life in Mazara leads them to have limited buy-in for politics celebrating Mediterranean coexistence in the city. Indeed, rather than an open and cosmopolitan Mediterranean borderland, they see Mazara as a "backward" periphery, not "European" enough for them to achieve the dreams for which they had crossed the Mediterranean.

The following two chapters turn to analyzing the potential and pitfalls of Mediterraneanist politics in more detail, with a particular focus on how they allow for simultaneous boundary-drawing and celebration of coexistence. Chapter 4 analyzes the rise of Mediterraneanism as a neoliberal regional development project in Mazara del Vallo in the first decade of the 2000s, when, in order to access national and EU cross-border cooperation funding and attract tourism, the city's municipal authorities began to market the town as a multicultural Mediterranean hub. Through examination of the tensions that emerged around the rebranding of Mazara's central immigrant neighborhood from a dangerous area to an exotic Casbah, I show that the municipality's Mediterraneanist projects, despite celebrating the town's Tunisian community, were not able to address its long-standing political and economic marginalization. Through the lens of the urban space of the Casbah, I also trace micro-processes of boundary-drawing between Sicilians and Tunisians in Mazara del Vallo, as well as a reclaiming of Mazarase identity as "mixed" with North Africa, that accompanied the town's shifting position within broader Italian and Mediterranean geographies of uneven development.

Chapter 5 further develops the book's analysis of borderland Mediterranean politics by focusing on Catholic initiatives of service provision to migrants and cross-Mediterranean cooperation. I first analyze how representatives of Catholic institutions frame the challenges of Tunisian migration to Italy and then set this against discussions about religious difference within Mazara's Tunisian community. This analysis views Catholic Mediterraneanist projects as engaging in a process of symbolic boundary-drawing by creating a hierarchy between (Catholic) Sicilians, assumed to be open to interreligious dialogue, and (Muslim) Tunisians, considered closed to these exchanges. These projects partially depend on an idealized depiction of colonial coexistence in Tunisia at the turn of the twentieth century (discussed in chap. 2), which some Catholic voices cast as a successful model for contemporary multicultural Europe.

Finally, in the conclusion I argue against idealizing "intermediate" subjects and spaces—such as Mediterranean borderlands and their inhabitants—as key subjects and loci of cross-border coexistence and solidarity. Indeed, celebrations of Mediterranean coexistence that emerge from these borderlands have long existed alongside material inequalities and symbolic hierarchies in these spaces, by either ignoring them or reinforcing them. Instead of assuming that spaces of Mediterranean mixing translate into solidarity, or that claiming a Mediterranean "sameness" is an effective means to question material and symbolic borders, I suggest that it is necessary to develop relationships of solidarity across the Mediterranean or between people of European and North African descent, relationships that recognize not only a similarity of conditions but also structural inequalities and thus work to center the voices of those who are excluded by borders. Through the analysis of activist Mediterraneanist projects that advocate for freedom of movement, postcolonial belonging, and an end to neoliberal austerity in the Mediterranean region, I argue that it is indeed possible to reclaim Mediterraneanism as a transformative political project if we recognize and challenge uneven power relations that traverse Mediterranean waters. By so doing, it is possible to build cross-Mediterranean bonds of solidarity that challenge the fortification of that sea and that work toward equity and justice in the region.

MEDITERRANEAN INTERCONNECTIONS
Migration, Colonialism, and
the Southern Question

The island of Lampedusa was little more than a military outpost for much of Italy's history after unification. A marginal island within a marginalized region of Europe, Italy's southernmost landmass offered few opportunities to its inhabitants, who relied mainly on fishing. Despite the tourism boom that began in the 1990s, its water supplies and educational and medical infrastructure remain precarious today. During the summer tourist season, several daily charter flights connect the island to major Italian and European cities. In winter, Lampedusa is served by only one daily flight from Palermo, Sicily's regional capital, or an eight-hour overnight ferry ride from Porto Empedocle on the southern Sicilian coast. During the winter months, the island becomes semi-deserted, with the majority of Lampedusa's six thousand official residents leaving for the Sicilian mainland until spring (Orsini 2015).

Despite its isolation, however, since the 1990s the island of Lampedusa has jumped to national and European prominence. As the European Union (EU) fortified its southern border, Lampedusa's proximity to North Africa placed it at the center of undocumented migrants' routes to Europe. Lampedusa's symbolism as a bastion of fortified Europe in the Mediterranean led more than three hundred Italian and European migrant-solidarity activists to converge on the island in January 2014 as cold winds swept its semi-deserted landscape, populated only by its few year-round inhabitants and some members of the Italian navy.[1] The activists had come together to produce the Charter of Lampedusa, a shared statement on migrants' rights spurred by a tragic shipwreck of migrants off the coast of the island in October 2013 in which more than 350 people lost their lives. This incident had occurred in the context of an intensification of cross-border migration since 2011, when political instability in North Africa, combined with reduced coastal surveillance, caused a spike in migration to the island from Tunisia and Libya. The activists thus converged on Lampedusa to express an alternative ethos to border fortification and to call for universal freedom of movement (*La carta di Lampedusa* 2014).

The mayor of Lampedusa, Giusi Nicolini, was a guest of honor at the event. As a longtime advocate for migrant rights, her inaugural speech was carefully crafted to cater both to the activists gathered on the island and to some more skeptical members of her constituency. In her opening words, she declared that Lampedusa represented a shared Mediterranean space that could bring together marginalized people from southern Europe and North Africa: "I want to welcome you and recognize the fantastic level of participation I see here today . . . a small demonstration that Lampedusa can draw on its role in the Mediterranean to become a meeting place for people to come together to discuss, testify, launch messages and work with the local community, in order to connect the rights of those who are obliged to flee from their countries, and the rights of populations obliged to the fate of a border, rights that are cut in half, denied and stepped on."

The island's inhabitants present at the meeting adopted a diversity of positions toward immigration. Members of an activist collective called Askavusa—which had co-organized the Charter of Lampedusa event—expressed solidarity with migrants and emphasized the conditions they shared with them, underlining how both Lampedusani and migrants were victims of a global economic system that wreaked havoc on their communities. Other speakers were more skeptical of these analogies, however, and expressed their unease with the amount of attention migrants were receiving in comparison to Lampedusani. In particular, they were concerned about the impact of migrants, and the media attention they attracted, on the island's tourist industry. Taking the floor after the mayor's speech, a representative of Lampedusa's chamber of commerce declared, "People only talk about the problem of migrants, whom we have always welcomed! But there is also another side of the story: the inhabitants of Lampedusa, and the weight that this has on our economy." A woman described as a "mother of Lampedusa" followed suit, combining these concerns with more general ones about the island's insufficient medical and educational infrastructure: "In Lampedusa we feel like foreigners! Geographically we are much closer to Africa. . . . For Italians we don't exist! They only notice us with the problem of the 'illegals.' 'Illegals' so to speak, because they are people like us . . . rights should be universal, and guaranteed to all, so we must put on the same level the rights of those who arrive, and the rights of those who are already here."[2]

Since the tightening of EU immigration legislation in the mid-1990s, Italian and European media and popular representations have defined the Mediterranean border as the key dividing line between migrants hailing from the Global South and a Global North that must figure out how to absorb them. The words of the mayor and of the other Lampedusani call into question the homogeneity of this Global North, and instead identify three distinct spaces: the North (Italy or Europe), the South (Lampedusa or southern Italy), and the Deep South (North Africa). On the basis of this definition, they make a series of claims about the relationship between different forms of social and spatial marginality. First, they claim that migrants' rights are connected to the rights of Lampedusani, whether by analogy (they share the same experiences of marginalization) or by opposition (migrants' rights come at the expense of Lampedusani's rights). Second, they claim that Lampedusani are closer to North Africa than to Italy, geographically and in terms of their social and economic rights, but that as Italian and European citizens, they should have more rights than North African migrants. Underlying these claims are different understandings of the Mediterranean Sea: a shared space in which populations from its northern and southern shores are both marginalized by the northwestern European heartland and thus should be in solidarity with each other because of the conditions they share, or a dividing line that clearly distinguishes European subjects deserving economic prosperity and a social safety net from non-Europeans whose access to these rights is not Europe's concern.

The statements by the representative of Lampedusa's chamber of commerce and of the "mother of Lampedusa" may appear to be classic examples of blaming migrants for the Global North's economic woes and of complaining about migrants' alleged preferential access to economic assistance over that of national citizens. However, these Lampedusani paint a more complex picture, one in which the rights of Italians are not simply juxtaposed to those of migrants. Instead, southern Italians feel doubly squeezed between a North that ignores their needs and a Deep South that impinges on their resources. Taking the claims of the Lampedusani seriously suggests that if we are to understand contemporary processes of bordering at Italy's and Europe's southern periphery, we must analyze the interplay of multiple forms of sociospatial marginality: the internal marginalization of southern Italy on the one hand, and on the other, the hardening of the Mediterranean border and the racialization of migrants from the southern Mediterranean. Analyzing the interplay of these two processes allows us both to understand how the Mediterranean came to represent the southern border of Europe and to explore conditions in which cross-Mediterranean solidarity can arise between differently marginalized populations on its northern and southern shores.

In this chapter, I provide a historical and conceptual analysis of the relationship between the "othering" of cross-Mediterranean migrants and the marginalization of Sicilians in the process of defining the civilizational boundaries of Europe. I analyze this process at three moments characterized by different territorial and political configurations within Italy and Europe and by different types of cross-Mediterranean relations: late nineteenth-century colonial Tunisia, Sicily in the 1970s and 1980s, and Sicily at the turn of the twenty-first century. At each of these moments, I explore how Italian national and local politicians, economic elites, and intellectuals addressed internal inequalities within the country alongside the relationship between Sicilians and Tunisians, reflected alternatively in colonial, immigration, and cross-border cooperation policy. In order to understand processes of boundary-drawing and the interplay of multiple marginalities in the central Mediterranean, however, some broader theoretical considerations are in order. Thus, the next section discusses how drawing the material and symbolic boundaries of the nation has always involved defining the ambiguous status of both populations of internal peripheries and "external" colonial subjects and migrants.

Nation-Building, Incorporation, and Exclusion

The question of who can be successfully incorporated into the body politic of the nation animates immigration debates throughout Europe, particularly in relation to Muslim immigrants from the Middle East and North Africa. Underlying this framing is the assumption that these immigrants embody a form of difference that is difficult to incorporate into a purportedly homogenous nation-state, be it on ethnic, linguistic, or religious terms.[3] The problem of incorporation and management of difference into the nation-state is not, however, a new issue provoked by the arrival of "external" migrants. It is instead an older problem that accompanied the creation and consolidation of most European nation-states, just as they were embarking on imperial endeavors. Nation-building efforts in the middle and late nineteenth century thus grappled with the question of incorporation of difference with regard to both their internal peripheries and their colonies. In many cases, the processes of nation-building and empire-building occurred synchronously (Bayly 2004; Rabinow 1989), and theories of difference and techniques of managing population traveled between metropole and colony.

Incorporating "culturally different" populations from internal peripheries—internal regions characterized by economic marginality, linguistic diversity, and in some cases a history of political autonomy—was a concern throughout Europe, from long-consolidated nation-states such as France and England (Curtis 1968; Weber 1976) to more recent ones such as Italy (Schneider 1998). In many cases, rural populations did not speak the national language and were incorporated into the nation through coercive assimilation practices, some of which were enacted in schools. National elites often viewed the populations of their internal peripheries and of their colonies in a similar manner. In France, for instance, urban middle classes considered peasants to be "savages" (Weber 1976), while British elites considered the populations both of the Celtic fringe and of their overseas colonies to be incapable of self-rule (Curtis 1968). These analogies have led scholars such as Hechter (1975) to describe the incorporation of internal peripheries and their populations as "internal colonialism"—a concept coined in the Americas to refer to the ongoing subordination and dispossession of people of non-European descent in settler-colonial contexts (Barrera 1979; Blauner 1969; Gonzales Casanova 1965; Quijano and Ennis 2000).

Internal peripheries and colonies not only shared a similar problematization of their inhabitants but also were structurally connected. In many cases, in fact, colonies could absorb the excess population of internal peripheries, thereby mitigating regional and class tensions within European nation-states. This meant that in the colonies there were two types of subordinate populations to be managed: colonial subjects and working-class European settlers (Stoler 2002). Interconnections between colony and metropole meant that techniques for managing and "civilizing" populations traveled widely between the two spaces. In French colonies, this occurred in multiple realms, ranging from attempts to modernize and regulate populations through architecture and urban planning (Rabinow 1989) to techniques for the teaching of French to students who were nonnative speakers (Sugiyama 2007; Weber 1976). In some cases, more repressive techniques also traveled between metropole and colony, such as the use of similar military tactics to quell revolts in the Italian South and in Italian colonies (Del Boca 2005).

If European governments used similar techniques to manage colonial subjects and the populations of their internal peripheries, they did so with very different aims. Populations of internal peripheries needed to be fully assimilated into the body politic of the nation. This was particularly important in the colonies, where the "civilizing" of poor whites was often in part a strategy used to clearly mark racial boundaries. In colonies with a large European working-class population, social and spatial separation were key means to distinguish colonial subjects and poor white populations, through techniques of urban planning (Abu-Lughod 1980; Rabinow 1989; Wright 1991) or the careful policing of gender and sexuality (Stoler 2002). Unlike poor whites, colonial subjects, it was thought, could only partially be modernized and civilized, often with the intention to create native intermediaries to serve the colonial administration and to create some level of buy-in for colonization (Fanon 1965). Regardless of their level of assimilation to Europeanness, however, colonial subjects were only rarely recognized as citizens of the colonizing country (Kipfer 2011; Lewis 2014).

Following decolonization, a number of European states in the second half of the twentieth century turned these colonial strategies for managing "uncivilized" populations inward. Their key challenge of the 1950s and 1960s, in fact, was to fully modernize and develop internal peripheries and their populations. In the case of Italy (Lombardi-Diop 2013), for instance, techniques to cleanse and modernize colonized populations were refocused inward to target rural populations of internally marginalized regions (such as Sicily). Colonial population-management techniques also targeted newly arrived migrant workers, who often hailed from former colonies (Khiari 2009; Ross 1995).

Similarities in the racialization of colonial subjects and migrants show continuities in the racial bounding of many European nation-states between the colonial period and following decolonization (El-Tayeb 2011; Grosfoguel 2003; Hesse and Sayyid 2008; Khiari 2009; Kipfer 2011; Solomos et al. 1982). Current questions about the ability of migrants to adapt to European culture are in fact remarkably similar to historic debates about colonial subjects' capacity to achieve European levels of "civilization" (Solomos et al. 1982). These continuities may be interpreted as an example of Quijano's concept of *coloniality* (Grosfoguel 2003; Hesse and Sayyid 2008; Quijano and Therborn 2007)—the persistence of uneven colonial power relations following decolonization. This does not mean that the racialization of migrants in the metropole is an exact copy of the racialization of colonial subjects in the colonies. The political climate and labor market of the metropole produce contextually specific understandings of difference between national subjects and migrants. However, these new understandings of difference are informed by the way in which national boundaries had historically been drawn in relation to colonial subjects (Kipfer 2011; Solomos et al. 1982). If we consider European colonialism beyond single colonial administrations, as the more general creation of a global color line (Du Bois 1989; Getachew 2019), it is also possible to interpret the racialization of migrants not hailing from former colonies as an example of coloniality (Grosfoguel 2003).

A common critique of postcolonial and decolonial analyses of migration is that this framework may fall into the trap of what Goswami calls methodological nationalism (Goswami 2004) by not taking into sufficient account social and spatial inequalities within the metropole and thus reifying European nation-states— and sometimes Europe as a whole—as a bounded and undifferentiated entity. Consequently, the incorporation of internal peripheries may be naturalized, while violence and coercion are only associated with external territorial expansion. Analyzing the incorporation of internal peripheries and their populations alongside the management of colonial subjects—and later migrants—instead, allows us to denaturalize the current borders of the nation-state by highlighting the interplay of processes of (often violent) incorporation, assimilation, and exclusion that led to the creation of the current material and symbolic boundaries of the nation. In the following sections, I will turn to analyzing this interplay in the context of Italy and Tunisia from the period of French colonial rule over Tunisia to the present.

Colonial Emigration and the Southern Question

In the late nineteenth and early twentieth centuries, the problem of incorporating poor southern Italians into the nation-state was linked to debates about colonial expansion, and the positionality of poor southern Italian settlers in European colonies in relation to colonial subjects was a key concern for Italian diplomats and state officials. Since its 1861 unification, Italy had been characterized by uneven development between its northern and southern regions. In Italian theoretical and political debates, this disparity is referred to as the *Southern Question* (Gramsci 1971), a term that refers to the problematization of the South as underdeveloped, backward, and ultimately different from northern and central Italy. The problem of the South's "backwardness" was of immediate concern to Italy's post-unification government, as both a political and economic problem, and as a threat to Italy's claims to modernity. Thus, northern Italian elites sought to prove their own full Europeanness by attributing Italy's backwardness entirely to its southern regions (Schneider 1998), a discourse that collapsed the considerable social and economic diversity in southern Italy—reflected in early statistical studies of Italy's population, economy, and society (Patriarca 1998)—into a monolithic "other" of the North (Moe 2002; Perrotta 2014a; Schneider 1998). They did so in part by drawing on a much longer northern European tradition of depicting southern Italy as a liminal zone at the edge of Europe (Moe 2002).

    In this context, two main explanations for the "underdevelopment" of the South emerged. The post-unification Italian government attributed the South's underdevelopment to its social and economic structure, drawing on an 1877 parliamentary report on Sicily by two Tuscan senators: Leopoldo Franchetti, later a colonial advisor to the Italian government in Eritrea, and Sydney Sonnino (Moe 2002). Italian positivist criminologists, instead, invoked ideas of racial difference to explain southern Italians' alleged propensity to criminality (Gibson 1998). More specifically, they theorized a hereditary transmission of physical and psychological characteristics that they interpreted as tied to criminal behavior.

This explanation emerged in the context of the "war on brigandage"—a conflict between the central government and groups of organized resistance in the Sicilian countryside (Del Boca 2005). However, not all Italian scholars of the time considered northern and southern Italians to be racially different; there was a conceptual split between Aryanists and Mediterraneanists (Gibson 1998). The former considered northern Italians to be Aryans and thus more civilized than southern Italians, who were purportedly mixed with a Semitic element. Cesare Lombroso, founder of the Italian school of positivist criminology, was a supporter of this theory and pointed to the "Arabness" of Sicily as an explanation for the prevalence of violent crimes on the island (Gibson 1998). Mediterraneanists did not draw a dividing line between North and South, but they considered the Italian population as a whole to be characterized by centuries of Mediterranean mixing. Italy's Mediterranean heritage was precisely what rendered the country the cradle of Western civilization (De Donno 2006; Gibson 1998; Giuliani and Lombardi-Diop 2013).

Sicily played a central role in national theorization about the Southern Question. While it was one of the richest regions in the South, with some sectors of its agricultural production well inserted into global markets (Lupo 1990) and a middle class that was highly represented in national bureaucracy (Gramsci 1971), the region was heavily pathologized in national intellectual discussions that paid little attention to these nuances. While Franchetti and Sonnino's parliamentary report had focused on Sicily as a unique case (Lupo 2015), the content of this analysis was reproduced in subsequent scholarship as emblematic of the South as a whole, set against a "normative" North (Moe 1998). By the 1890s and early 1900s—partly under the influence of racial theories that interpreted economic difference in racial terms (Patriarca 1998)—dualistic interpretations that pitted southern "archaism" against northern "modernity" had become commonplace in Italy (Lupo 2015).

The Southern Question translated into Italian foreign and colonial policy through emigration. In the years following unification in 1861, 13 million Italians left the peninsula, primarily from the South, and headed to the Americas, northern Europe, and to some extent North Africa (Choate 2008). The sheer number of people leaving the country placed emigration at the center of public debate, often in conjuncture with the question of colonialism. On the one hand, advocates of colonial expansion argued that Italy needed to acquire colonies to settle Italian emigrants and thus avoid their mistreatment elsewhere. On the other hand, advocates for "emigrant colonialism" believed that Italy could best support its interests abroad not through military conquest but by nurturing feelings of national belonging in its emigrants worldwide (Choate 2008). These two theories would compete from the late 1800s until the rise of Fascism, which discarded the emigrant colonialism theory to focus instead on colonial expansion as a strategy to keep emigration within Italian territory (Giuliani and Lombardi-Diop 2013). The Fascist regime also embraced Mediterraneanism as an ideology that could both justify colonialism and embrace southern Italians as part of the nation. Claims of Italy's ancient Mediterranean lineage served to legitimize Italian colonization of North Africa as a return to the lands of the Roman Empire—a rhetorical strategy that had also been embraced by Italian liberal governments in the late nineteenth century (Fuller 2007). Within Italy, until the 1937 *Manifesto della Razza* (Race Manifesto), the Fascist regime cast "Latin Mediterraneity" as the essence of Italianness—a discourse that included and centered southern Italians as an integral part of the nation (Giuliani and Lombardi-Diop 2013).[4]

Tunisia lay at the heart of late nineteenth-century Italian colonial aspirations and Mediterraneanist visions. In 1881, approximately 11,200 Italians lived in the territory (Davi 2000), divided into two main groups: a small bourgeois elite, largely made up of Jewish families of Tuscan origin with a strong sense of identification with Italy, and a large group of working-class migrants, primarily from Sicily (Clancy-Smith 2010).[5] The establishment of the French Protectorate over Tunisia in 1881 produced political shock waves in Italy, costing the prime minister of the time—a staunch opponent of Italian colonial expansion—his premiership (Choate 2010). The assumption in Italy had been that Tunisia would come under Italian influence due to its geographical proximity to Italy and its substantial Italian population. However, at the 1882 Berlin conference, the German and the English delegations supported French control of Tunisia; fear of Italian control over both sides of the Strait of Sicily had proved stronger than their interimperial rivalry with France for control of North Africa (Choate 2010; Shorrock 1983). French control did not mean the demise of Italian settlement in Tunisia nor of Italy's attempts to exercise political influence in the territory. Unlike its plans for Algeria, France mainly conceived of Tunisia as a colony of exploitation. Thus, French settlers remained few and were mainly limited to diplomatic functionaries and large investors. The number of Italians, however, soared by over 60,000 people between 1881 and 1911 (Choate 2007) as jobs provided by the protectorate's large-scale public works programs, and possibilities of agricultural land ownership thanks to French land reforms, attracted large numbers of Italian working-class migrants, many of whom were from Sicily (Melfa 2008).

The Italian commercial and professional elite in Tunisia had a strong national affiliation with Italy, but working-class Sicilian migrants had little sense of their Italianness and bonded more strongly through their regional or even local areas of origin (Choate 2007). Italian diplomatic authorities therefore embraced the project of emigrant colonialism, attempting to nationalize working-class Sicilians through schooling, as well as cultural and recreational activities. In brief, emigration to Tunisia simultaneously provided an escape valve for the social and economic tensions of Sicily, and southern Italy more broadly, and a way for the Italian government to promote its interests abroad through its diasporic population. French authorities strongly opposed these efforts and sought to Francophonize the working-class Sicilian population to strengthen French control of the territory.

French scholars and colonial authorities in Tunisia did not see working-class Sicilians much differently from their Tunisian colonial subjects. Sicilians and Tunisians lived in the same neighborhoods, or in close proximity, and shared many living habits and customs. This proximity was reflected in descriptions of Sicilians written by French scholars in Tunisia, who often drew on theories of difference produced by Italian scholars. For example, in 1901 the quarterly magazine of the Institut de Carthage, a French cultural association in Tunisia, published a translation of Franchetti and Sonnino's report on the causes of Sicily's "backwardness" in an article titled "Our Sicilian Migrants in Their Own Land." In the introduction to the article, however, the translator argued that these characteristics were quite similar to those of Tunisians: "In Sicily one finds the same organization . . . as in the societies of North Africa: narrow group spirit, formation of clans, challenges to the central government by these clans. . . . The laws of the Berbers of the Tunisian south . . . are not without analogies with the primitive organizations of Sicily. The many comparisons that can emerge from these parallels . . . are of the highest sociological and ethnographic interest" (Germain 1901, 61).

Other French accounts of Sicilian migrants adopted language quite similar to that of Italian positivist criminologists, describing Sicilians as both passive and impulsive, thanks in part to their history of racial mixing with Arabs. For example, Gaston Loth, director of the Alaoui teacher training college in Tunis, observed, "Coming from a mix of different races . . . the main trait of the man of the Italian south is the fatalistic resignation of his ancient Arab masters. . . . Generally enduring the difficulties of his fate without complaints, he sometimes—like the Arabs—has sudden awakenings, instant rages, only to fall back to his usual resignation" (Loth 1905, 17). Interestingly enough, the Algiers school of psychiatry would eventually cast these characteristics as typical North African psychological traits, only to be contested by Frantz Fanon, who considered them instead as examples of the psychological effects of colonization (Fanon 1965; Garnaoui 2021).

If French scholars in Tunisia identified cultural and racial similarities between Sicilians and Tunisians, they also advocated for the assimilation of Sicilians into Francophone modernity, with the objective of making them full French citizens and thus consolidating French control over the territory. Loth, for instance, advocated for mixed marriages between French and Italians (who were primarily Sicilian) in order to assimilate the latter (Loth 1905). Saurin, an advocate for the

French settler lobby, expressed the stakes of Italian assimilation in both political and religious terms: "We cannot . . . send back our Latin brothers, nor create a Great Wall of China between Sicily and Tunisia. Even if we were able to, we have no interest. They [Sicilians] are a precious aid that will help us make this country a Christian land, where Muslims will no longer be able to get rid of us" (Saurin 1899, 10).

Despite perceiving Sicilians and Tunisians to be similar, French scholars argued that Sicilians, unlike Tunisians, could be modernized and civilized, and thus made fully French. Certainly, there were efforts to modernize and Franco-phonize Tunisians, particularly the elites (Sugiyama 2007). This, however, was aimed at creating consensus in favor of French rule, since Tunisians could only in rare cases become French citizens. Sicilians, for example, were tried through the French justice system (Lewis 2014), and French protectorate authorities pushed to educate them in French schools (Sugiyama 2007) and to naturalize them as French citizens (Bonurra 1922). As chapter 2 will discuss in more detail, this differentiation between Sicilians and Tunisians occurred despite French protec-torate authorities officially embracing policies of Mediterranean coexistence, according to which all populations of the territory could live together peacefully under the banner of French language and culture (Sugiyama 2007).

In essence, in the first few decades of the French Protectorate over Tunisia (between 1881 and 1911), emigration, colonialism, and the Southern Question were strongly connected. Both French and Italian authorities considered Sicil-ians to be closer in their customs to Tunisians than to the French and Italian bourgeoisie, yet both considered the "civilization" of these migrants and their incorporation into French or Italian modernity important to furthering their political and economic interests in the territory. Thus, French Protectorate Tuni-sia may be considered a first moment in the tracing of sociospatial boundaries between Sicilians and Tunisians. In this period, invocations of the Mediterranean served multiple purposes. On the one hand, they functioned as a racial discourse, alternatively theorizing differences between northern and southern Italians or celebrating Italy's distinct and unifying mixed Mediterranean racial heritage. On the other hand, Mediterraneanism also served as a justification of Italian rule in North Africa and as a French technique of colonial rule.

Strategic Mediterraneanism and the Internal Southern Question

Between the 1950s and the early 1990s, with the exception of energy policy, Ita-ly's relationship with the southern Mediterranean disappeared from the national public debate, and the main developmental divide of public concern became that between the North and the South of the country. In the context of Tunisia, following the country's decolonization in 1955 and land nationalization a decade later, most Italians left for France and, to a lesser extent, Italy (Kazdaghli 1999). Within Italy, references to colonialism became proscribed following the end of Fascism and the loss of the country's colonies due to its capitulation in World War II (Labanca 2002). References to race also disappeared, as part of a more general disavowal of biological racism in Europe in the aftermath of the Holocaust. In this context, the Italian state recast the Southern Question as an entirely internal problem and as a high priority. Law 646/1950 established the Intervento Straordinario (Extraordinary Intervention) for the development of the South and created an independent agency to manage its funds and oversee its implementation: the Cassa per il Mezzogiorno (Fund for the South; Gualini 2004). Initially funded through the Marshall Plan and focusing on developing agriculture and key infrastructure such as roads, piped water, and electricity, from the early 1960s the focus shifted to industrial development, concentrated around regional development poles (Ginsborg 1990). The Cassa also funded the development of the fishing sector on Sicily's southwestern coast, which would eventually attract the first northward Tunisian migrants to Italy.

These years saw a proliferation of new inquiries into the Southern Question by both Italian and foreign scholars. They generally followed one of two trends, reflecting a broader dichotomy between modernization and dependency theory in global underdevelopment debates of the time (Cassano 2009; Perrotta 2014b). The first trend explained the South's poverty in terms of its deficiencies, no longer defined in racial terms but in cultural ones (Banfield 1958). The second saw the underdevelopment of the South as the direct counterpart of the development of the North, as a result of late nineteenth- and early twentieth-century policies favoring the industrial North over the agricultural South (Davis 1998). In essence, between the 1950s and the 1980s, the Southern Question was highly debated as an internal national question. Public neglect of Italy's colonial history (Labanca 2002), and the relative numerical insignificance of immigration at the national level, meant that the country's relationship with North Africa was seldom a subject of discussion.

The lack of public attention to migration did not mean, however, that none was occurring. The first groups of Tunisian migrants began to travel to Sicily in the late 1960s and early 1970s, and this migration intensified in the mid-1970s as a response to immigration restrictions in traditional migration destinations such as France and Germany (Daly 2001; Hibou et al. 2011). Tunisians were attracted by employment possibilities in the Sicilian fishing and agricultural sectors, expanding thanks to the development boost provided by the Cassa per il

Mezzogiorno. The lack of visa requirements for Tunisians also meant that going to work in Italy was relatively easy, and this migration corridor was largely characterized by seasonal migration, with Tunisian men going to work in Italy for a few months a year while supporting their families in Tunisia.[6] One of the rare newspaper articles on the topic, published in the Sicilian left-wing newspaper *L'Ora*, described Tunisian migrants simultaneously as a paradox and an ethnographic curiosity:

> There are thousands of them throughout Sicily . . . loaded with suitcases so similar to those of Sicilian emigrants. . . . They return . . . to a Tunisian South that is much deeper than our own. Who are these people, who . . . have given so many Sicilian towns, which suffer from emigration, the grotesque dimension of a "host country"? From what reality have they been catapulted here, to a place from which people have always fled? . . . On the road to Kairouan [Tunisia] . . . you find mud houses, Bedouins desperately searching for water . . . kilometers and kilometers under a ruthless sun. Women . . . looking for water . . . children surrounding cars . . . asking for "argent" [money]. (Giaramidaro 1975, 11)

Most news articles on immigration adopted a similar tone, focusing on similarities between Tunisian immigrants and Sicilian emigrants, or commenting on the paradox of Sicily becoming a "promised land" for migrants from a much deeper South. A couple of articles in a center-right Sicilian newspaper in the 1980s mentioned labor competition between Sicilians and Tunisians, describing the latter as "people who agree to the hardest jobs for absolutely humiliating sums of money" thus "coming to take places that could be left to our unemployed" (Conti 1980, 1; Mignosi 1980, 8). However, this type of rhetoric was quite rare.

Although migration was not then a highly politicized topic, some Sicilian politicians did address the question in the context of their more general interest in the island's relationship with the southern Mediterranean. As the post–World War II Extraordinary Intervention to develop the South was drawing to a close in the 1980s and the single European market was on the horizon, Sicilian politicians across the political spectrum became interested in strengthening the island's relationship with the southern Mediterranean as a way to boost its economic and political position within a unified Europe. For the Communist member of parliament Agostino Spataro, who was part of the National Parliamentary Association of Italo-Arab Friendship, advocating for North African migrants' rights was connected to his political activity with the Arabic-speaking world, centered on contrasting Cold War militarization of the Mediterranean and the North Atlantic Treaty Organization (NATO) presence in Sicily (Spataro 1986). His activities had involved proposing Italy's first immigration law in 1980 and advocating the construction of a trans-Mediterranean gas line between Algeria, Tunisia, and Italy that connected to the Italian mainland via the Sicilian town of Mazara del Vallo (Ben-Yehoyada 2014). The Christian Democrat mayor of Mazara del Vallo, Nicolò Vella, instead, had advocated for Tunisian migrants' rights, as part of negotiations with Tunisian authorities to safeguard the interests of his town's fishing fleet, and saw cross-Mediterranean cooperation as central to bringing newly independent North African countries toward the capitalist West instead of the Soviet Union.[7]

These Sicilian initiatives were consistent with Italian diplomatic efforts to carve out a foreign policy that would facilitate the country's access to North African oil and gas reserves, on which it was highly dependent (Ben-Yehoyada 2014; Mourlane 2012). Following World War II, the Italian government's objective was to develop a diplomatic position that would simultaneously promote the country's economic interests in the region while also situating Italy as a mediator between the United States and the Soviet Union in the Mediterranean (Mourlane 2012). The Christian Democratic Party was the main promoter of this position, but it was shared by politicians across the political spectrum, leading to the founding of multiple national and regional cultural institutes aimed at strengthening Italy's relationship with North Africa in the 1950s and the 1960s. During the same period, the European Economic Community signed its first economic agreements with recently decolonized North African countries (Ben Hamouda 2012).

Despite its similar ambitions in the southern Mediterranean, the Italian government was highly concerned that Sicily, with its long-standing "orientalist" tradition, a strong independentist movement, and special political autonomy enshrined in Italy's 1946 constitution, would forge its own independent relations with the Arabic-speaking world (Frusciante 2012). This fear materialized in 1977, when the Sicilian Regional Assembly signed economic cooperation accords with the Libyan government, leading to the opening of a Libyan consulate and cultural center in the regional capital, Palermo (Spataro 1986). Despite the opposition of the Italian government, this cooperation continued until the mid-1980s (Spataro 1986). More generally, in the late 1970s and early 1980s, interest in political, economic, and cultural cooperation with North Africa blossomed among the island's intellectual and political elites. Cultural interest in Sicily's ninth- and tenth-century Arab history and in the contemporary Arab world translated into Arabic language classes, cultural initiatives bringing together the "peoples of the Mediterranean," and publications. The Sicilian left-wing newspaper L'Ora, for instance, began to publish a biweekly insert on political, economic, and cultural affairs of the Arab world, and it also published job offers for Italians in the Middle East together with information for companies wanting to invest there. Its first edition, published on November 20, 1979, explained these aims, drawing a clear connection between the island's history of Arab rule and its contemporary economic aspirations: "We are convinced that . . . for Italy, and particularly Sicily, the time has come to address its development challenges by getting to know well . . . our most natural counterpart: Arab countries. . . . How could a newspaper like *L'Ora*, so quintessentially Sicilian, forget the profound influence that Arab culture has had on its [Sicilian] customs, on its language, on its architecture" (*L'Ora* 1979, 1).

In the late 1970s and early 1980s, immigration from the southern Mediterranean was thus mainly an ethnographic curiosity in Sicily, hardly a subject of public debate. It was only addressed politically in the context of broader political and economic cooperation initiatives with North Africa. Even at the height of the Fishing War with Tunisia, when the Tunisian coast guard was firing at Sicilian vessels entering their territorial waters (Ben-Yehoyada 2014), Sicilian media and politicians did not depict the southern Mediterranean as a threat to the island but as a possible—though troublesome—business partner. Mediterraneanism remained essentially a geopolitical and development discourse. All this would change by the mid-1990s as the "immigration problem" exploded into public debate within Sicily and throughout Italy.

Reframing the Southern Question in the Epoch of Border Fortification

Between the late 1980s and early 1990s, preparations for the creation of the EU led to a reconceptualization of Italy's internal geographies of uneven development and its relationship with the southern Mediterranean. Starting in those years, and continuing into the 1990s and early 2000s, Italian national political and policy interest in the Southern Question waned as the national public debate came to focus on growing migration from the southern Mediterranean, thus casting the Mediterranean Sea as the key dividing line between development and underdevelopment.

By the mid-1980s, the rationale and effectiveness of the Intervento Straordinario was under question, particularly in the North. After some reform in 1984, the program was abolished in 1992, a year before the implementation of the single European market. The program's termination was spurred by budgetary constraints required for Italy's entrance into the single market and to bring Italy's regional development assistance in line with European Commission guidelines (Davis 1998; Gualini 2004). This change did not mark the end of government assistance to southern Italy but did redefine it within a broader framework of state and EU aid to "depressed regions" and made access to funds contingent on competitive bidding by local governments.

Some such funds were available through the EU, which had expanded its cooperation efforts with the southern and eastern Mediterranean through the 1995 Euro-Mediterranean partnership. This agreement, signed in Barcelona between the EU and ten partner countries, sought to foster cooperation in political, economic, and sociocultural affairs (Paoli 2012). From an economic perspective, the main priority was to create a Mediterranean free-trade area. Tunisia was the first southern Mediterranean country to sign such a free-trade agreement with the EU under this framework. From a political and sociocultural perspective, the EU's main concerns were the management of "regional tensions," the rise of Islamism (generally framed as a threat by the EU), and—most importantly—the prevention of undocumented migration to Europe (Paoli 2012). Overall, EU cooperation with the southern Mediterranean was posited on the need to stabilize the region to limit northward migration (Bialasiewicz et al. 2013; Jones 2006). In this context, funding for programs for cross-Mediterranean economic and cultural cooperation became available, particularly for local governments in regions on the Mediterranean Sea. This funding program pushed various Sicilian local governments, such as the city of Mazara del Vallo, to embrace Mediterraneanist language and to engage in projects of cross-Mediterranean cooperation to capture EU funds.

Cross-Mediterranean accords received little public attention in Italy and in Sicily, however, unless they were concerned with the management of migration. By the early 1990s, this issue was at the center of Italian public debate, with Italian migration legislation changing substantially as a consequence of the redrawing of Europe's internal and external borders. The creation of the EU in 1993 had harmonized immigration policy among EU countries. The implementation of the Schengen agreement in 1995 eliminated internal EU border controls but at the same time led to the strengthening of external border controls (Casas-Cortes et al. 2013; Rinelli 2016). In 1990, in preparation for these changes, the Italian government passed the country's first comprehensive immigration law (Law 39/1990), known as the Legge Martelli. Among other things, this law introduced a visa requirement for Tunisians. Tunisian migrants who had previously traveled to Sicily to work seasonally in fishing and agriculture were no longer able to do so, and in the first years of the law's implementation they were regularly denied entry at Sicilian ports (Giornale di Sicilia 1990a, 1990b, 1990c). The principles of the Legge Martelli that regularized the situation of migrants present in Italy and regulated new migration more stringently were further specified in Law 40/1998 (Legge Turco-Napolitano), which introduced migrant detention centers such as the one in Lampedusa, and Law 189/2002 (Legge Bossi-Fini).

These stricter border controls made undocumented migration by boat increasingly common and spurred international cooperation within the European Union and between EU and southern Mediterranean countries to monitor and fortify the Mediterranean border (Bialasiewicz 2012; Casas-Cortes et al. 2013, 2016). In 1998, following lengthy negotiations, Italy signed accords with Morocco and Tunisia involving them in the surveillance of their coasts and the acceleration of procedures for repatriating their citizens—a highly contentious issue (Zaiotti 2016). A few years later, in 2007, Italy signed agreements with Libya (Bialasiewicz 2012). These bilateral agreements between Italy and North African countries were part of a broader process of EU border externalization through a range of bilateral and multilateral initiatives, a policy that was made explicit by the EU's 2005 Global Approach to Migration (Casas-Cortes et al. 2015). Coordination between different EU countries was facilitated by the creation of Frontex in 2005, a joint migration management program designed both to aid governments at moments of large arrivals of undocumented migrants and to facilitate collaboration with countries bordering the EU in monitoring the EU's borders (Casas-Cortes et al. 2014).

The intensification of border control as a result of Italian migration legislation, intra-EU cooperation in border monitoring, and externalization of border controls to North Africa was matched by an unprecedented attention to immigration in the Italian and Sicilian media. From less than ten articles a year in the 1970s and 1980s to approximately fifty in 1990, both of Sicily's major newspapers—*Giornale di Sicilia* and *La Repubblica*—featured more than two hundred articles on immigration each year by the end of the decade.[8]

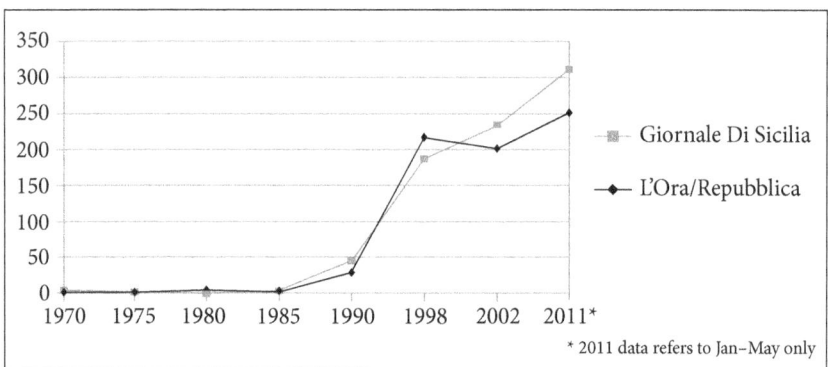

FIGURE 2. Sicilian media coverage of migration. Number of migration-related articles published by year in *L'Ora* and *Giornale di Sicilia*. Source: Author.

TABLE 1.   Sample of Sicilian media headlines on immigration

	MILITARY METAPHORS	EMERGENCY	HEALTH
Giornale di Sicilia	Continuous **assault** on Lampedusa. In only 24 hours, more than 250 arrivals (July 28, 1998) Sicily, migrant **assault** (February 13, 2011)	Illegal [immigrant] **emergency**, first detention center opened (July 3, 1998) **Emergency** again in Lampedusa (May 15, 2011)	Pantelleria and the invasion of illegal [immigrants]. The mayor: "There is a **risk of disease**" (June 30, 1998) Flurry of arrivals of illegal [immigrants]. **Health alarm** (August 18, 2002)
La Repubblica	Pantelleria **assaulted** by illegal [immigrants]. In two days, 100 disembarked (February 14, 1998) **Fear of invasion**: Sicily cannot absorb a maxi-wave of migrants (February 24, 2011)	Illegal [immigrant] **emergency**, mass arrivals in the south (July 2, 1998) Arrivals **emergency**, Berlusconi allocates 1 million euros (February 19, 2011)	More migrants than inhabitants. Lampedusa at the brink of collapse and there is a **risk of epidemics** (March 22, 2011)

While some articles covered new migration legislation and amnesties granting work permits to migrants already in Italy, the majority focused on the arrival of undocumented migrants by sea. Despite the different political orientation of the two papers, their headlines were remarkably similar, invoking military metaphors, emergencies, and, to a lesser extent, health threats. According to this framing, the Mediterranean Sea emerges clearly as a fundamental dividing line between development and underdevelopment.

Sicilian media coverage of the 1998 spike in Tunisian migration to Italy, and the subsequent migration readmissions accords signed between Italy and Tunisia, provides a good example of this framing. Commenting on these events, journalists primarily described working-class Tunisian migrants as desperate people fleeing poverty. A July 19, 1998, article published in the center-left newspaper *La Repubblica*, for instance, described a migrant detention center in Agrigento, on the Sicilian mainland, in the following way: "Behind barbed wire, surveilled by the police, are the men who arrive to Lampedusa thinking that it is . . . the new America. Tunisians, Moroccans, desperate people . . . Europe, the dream of the illegal migrants, remains outside [the detention center] . . . inside there is only despair, faces marked by poverty and misery" (Filetto 1998, i).

A few days earlier, on July 26, another article on the situation on the Tunisian coast had recounted this story:

> The police are everywhere except for the coasts. . . . Those who can . . . board the boats . . . try the adventure of disembarking on Italian shores. . . . Tunisia at the end of the millennium remains a country of great contradictions. . . . The landscape is still largely despairing: large swaths of uncultivated land, dry bushes and cactuses where the hand of man has not been seen for centuries. . . . We travel on taxis that feel the weight of the years . . . but they come with sophisticated stereo systems. Privileges of the sub-proletariat that cannot give up the superfluous. (Sergi 1998, 13)

To some extent, these descriptions of Tunisian poverty are not that different from those of the 1970s, which marveled about the existence of an "even deeper South" than Sicily. However, by 1998 the existence of this "even deeper South" was neither a paradox nor a curiosity: the simultaneous demise of the Southern Question as an object of public debate and the rising focus on immigration had cast the Mediterranean as the obvious dividing line between wealth and poverty. This trend is clear in the July 19 article, which offers a stark opposition between "faces marked by poverty and misery" inside the detention camp and outside in Sicily, which had come to be a stand-in for Europe as a whole. The July 26 article in turn described the extreme poverty of rural Tunisia in apocalyptic terms but did so with a hint of sarcasm and class prejudice, commenting on wasteful spending of a "sub-proletariat that cannot give up the superfluous"—a classic "culture of poverty" trope (see, for example, Lewis 1966) that explains the persistence of poverty as a consequence of poor spending habits.

The Sicilian press also attributed classic tropes of so-called underdevelopment, historically attributed to the Sicilian public sector, to Tunisian authorities, accusing them of lack of goodwill and of incompetence—for example, in the quote that "police are everywhere except the coasts," as well as coverage of negotiations between Italian and Tunisian authorities on migration management accords. *La Repubblica*, for example, quoted a member of the Italian negotiating team complaining about his Tunisian counterparts: "In their way of negotiating they are Levantine . . . if they were Swiss, we would either agree on everything or we wouldn't. But these ones add more items every time, and we have to start negotiating from scratch!" (Ansaldo 1998, 3). These depictions of the southern Mediterranean contrast starkly with those of the 1970s and 1980s in the Sicilian press, which had focused on the potentials of cross-Mediterranean cooperation as a development engine for Sicily. Despite the presence of numerous cross-border cooperation initiatives at the local level, as well as twinning programs between Sicilian and Tunisian cultural and educational institutions, in the public debate North Africa had gone from a potential business partner to a source of undesirable migrants.

The emergence of the Mediterranean Sea as the primary dividing line between North and South did not mean, however, that internal territorial divisions entirely disappeared—nor did national tropes about Sicilian deficiency (Carney 2021). Indeed, questions about how different regions would share responsibility for managing large numbers of migrants disembarking on Italy's southern shores brought back to life older struggles between Sicily and the Italian government, and between Italy and elsewhere in the EU more broadly. These tensions initially exploded in 2011, in the context of post–Arab Spring migration to Europe. Following the ousting of Tunisian president Ben Ali on January 15, 2011, some six thousand Tunisians took advantage of the decreased surveillance of the Tunisian coasts and attempted to cross the Mediterranean, landing on the island of Lampedusa (Garelli and Tazzioli 2013). The management of this migration flow sparked considerable tensions between Sicily and northern Italy, and between Italy and the EU. Within Italy, the mayor of Lampedusa and other Sicilian elected officials complained about being left alone by the central government to manage migrant resettlement (Lauria 2011a, 2011b; Pecoraro 2011), while richer and more resourceful northern Italian regions refused to resettle migrants on their own territory (Lorello 2011)—complaints similar to those raised by Lampedusani at the 2014 *Carta di Lampedusa* meeting. At the same time, at the national level Sicily's alleged incapacity to effectively manage migrant flows led to the reemergence of tropes about the inefficiency of Sicilian public administration (Carney 2021). Within the European Union, similar dynamics emerged, with other European countries reluctant to aid Italy financially or to resettle migrants and asylum seekers, pointing out that Italy accepted asylum seekers at one of the lowest rates in the EU. In early April, the Italian government granted temporary protection permits to the six thousand Tunisian migrants who had arrived on Lampedusa, as part of an agreement with the Tunisian government, which in turn promised to intensify its own coastal surveillance (Nesticò 2011a, 2011b; Perini 2011), but France and Germany refused to allow these permit holders to enter their countries (Caldanu 2011; Coppola and Polchi 2011; Pisa 2011).

Eventually tensions within the EU subsided, and many Tunisian migrants were able to make their way to France. Similar tensions would arise a few years later, however, in the context of the 2015 EU refugee crisis, when—following the arrival of large numbers of refugees in Italy and Greece from Syria, Central Asia, and sub-Saharan Africa—other EU countries intensified border controls to prevent asylum seekers from claiming asylum in their territories (Guiraudon 2018).[9] While this burden was somewhat lightened by the agreement to transfer candidates whose claims were most likely to be successful to other EU countries, this involved only a small number of asylum seekers. Italy and Greece continued to manage the bulk of cases (Trauner 2020), creating territorial tensions within the EU that still persist.[10]

Within Italy, these tensions contributed to the victory of the right-wing Lega party in the 2018 political elections—an event that simultaneously reflected the demise of the Southern Question in relation to immigration and brought to the forefront territorial tensions around the management of migration. The Lega was founded in Italy's northern regions in 1991 as the Lega Nord, running on a platform of regional autonomy that depicted southern Italy as an economic burden on the country. In the 2010s, however, the party rebranded and changed its name to Lega, dropping any references to the North/South divide while adopting an anti-immigrant stance. As part of its broader Euroskepticism, it also accused the European Union of providing insufficient assistance to Italy in migration management and resettlement, particularly in the context of the 2015 refugee crisis. This messaging allowed the party not only to win the 2018 national elections but also to garner some support in Italy's southern regions, an ultimate marker of the extent to which the demise of the Southern Question and the fortification

FIGURE 3. Car in Lampedusa supporting the Lega, 2014. The signs on the car read: "No to the abolishment of the Bossi-Fini [immigration law]" and "Shame! The left and the smugglers are accomplices in the destruction of Lampedusa. Only the Lega can stop this massacre." Source: Author.

of the Mediterranean border had rhetorically transformed southern Italy from a periphery of Europe to its bastion in the Mediterranean.

Relational Geographies of Sociospatial Difference

The historical overview laid out in this chapter shows that there is nothing "natural" about the Mediterranean Sea's current role as a dividing line between "the West and the Rest." Indeed, the public debate in Italy and Sicily only started to refer to the Mediterranean as the most important dividing line between development and underdevelopment in the mid-1990s, thanks to the accentuation of socio-territorial differences across the Mediterranean and attempts to homogenize geographies of uneven development within Italy and Europe. Over the century and a half discussed in this chapter, the modernization of southern Italians in colonial Tunisia, the development of southern Italy between the 1950s and 1980s, and the process of European integration in the 1990s represented attempts to diminish social and territorial differences internal to Italy and Europe, with the consequence of accentuating differences between southern Italy and North Africa. Through this process, internal peripheries of Italy and Europe such as Sicily and Lampedusa became outposts of Europe in the Mediterranean—despite remaining some of the poorest regions of the EU.

If, following Nicolas De Genova, we consider Europeanness as a racial formation of whiteness, and the EU's borders as a new color line, the process of making southern peripheries such as Sicily fully part of Europe can be understood as a process of the whitening of "off-white" or "not-quite white" marginal areas (De Genova 2017). But this chapter has shown that the process of tracing and retracing racialized boundaries of Europeanness has also been framed, interpreted, and addressed as a problem of uneven development. This was visible in Sicilian media coverage of migration, in particular in the way their coverage of Sicilian versus Tunisian poverty changed over time to squarely identify "underdevelopment" with the southern Mediterranean following the tightening of Italian immigration legislation and fortification of the Mediterranean border. It was also visible, however, in post–World War II Italian state policies intended to make southern Italy fully "modern" through national development programs that sought to bring it "up to speed" with the rest of Italy. This analysis suggests that borders should be understood as part of a relational geography of sociospatial difference: one of many possible developmental and racial/cultural dividing lines that acquire significance in a given moment. Bordering, then, occurs by accentuating certain forms of social and territorial difference, and mitigating others.

Throughout the history of social and spatial differentiation between Sicily and Tunisia, Italian and Sicilian actors repeatedly invoked notions of Mediterranean cooperation and interconnection. This paradox can be explained by the fact that Mediterraneanist politics did not call into question the symbolic role of the Mediterranean as a "civilizational" boundary but instead served to affirm (southern) Italy's cultural and geopolitical centrality to Europe, as well as to legitimize Italian influence over North Africa. As we have seen, in the late nineteenth and early twentieth centuries, Italian celebrations of Mediterranean mixing constituted both an attempt to define an Italian racial identity and a justification for the country's colonial aspirations in the southern Mediterranean. Between the 1950s and the 1980s, strengthening cross-Mediterranean ties represented a means for Italy, and for Sicily specifically, to strengthen its economic position vis-à-vis both northern Italy and northern Europe. In the first decade of the twenty-first century, Italian and EU celebrations of the Mediterranean served to pave the way for cross-Mediterranean economic cooperation, while also enlisting North African governments to support the EU's migration and security agenda—a vision that cast North Africa as a source of undocumented migration and possible terror attacks, and therefore a threat to Italy and Europe. Thus, throughout this period, celebrating Italy's or Sicily's Mediterranean identity did not mean questioning Italy's or Sicily's Europeanness.

This chapter has reconstructed processes of boundary-drawing that allowed Sicilians to be produced as precarious Italian and European subjects, and Sicily to be transformed from a periphery of Italy and Europe into a fortified border of Europe in the Mediterranean, focusing primarily on the intersection of Italian and European regional development, colonial and immigration policies. However, to fully understand how these processes of differentiation operate, and how they coexist with the celebration of Mediterranean interconnection, it is necessary to focus on the scale of everyday life in borderland contexts. The next chapter will do so by focusing on late-nineteenth-century colonial Tunisia: a moment of vivid debates about Sicilians' racial and cultural proximity to Tunisians, attempts by French colonial authorities and Italian diplomatic ones to "modernize" poor Sicilian settlers, and also the celebration of Mediterranean mixing through the French colonial policy of the "fusion of the races." The following chapters will turn to examine similar questions in the context of the contemporary Mediterranean borderland of Mazara del Vallo.

FUSING THE RACES OR TRACING THEIR BOUNDARIES?

The Paradoxes of Colonial Mediterraneanism

"When I was young, I used to live in the medina . . . our Arab neighbors were very nice . . . but the Arabs were oppressed by the Europeans . . . they didn't have any rights! . . . The first time I went to Palermo, when the ship entered port, I started crying. When my father asked me why, I answered: "Why are Italians sweeping the streets?" You see, in Tunisia I was only used to seeing Arabs do this type of work, never Europeans!"[1]

Recounting these memories, ninety-three-year-old Giuseppina described her childhood growing up in colonial Tunisia during the 1930s and 1940s. Giuseppina, who now lives in a comfortable apartment on the outskirts of Florence, was born in Tunis in the 1910s. Her family had a history similar to that of other Italians of Tunisia in the years before World War II; originally from the Sicilian countryside, they had emigrated south to French Protectorate Tunisia at the turn of the twentieth century, fleeing from the poverty that characterized the island in the decades following Italian unification. Unlike the majority of this community, however, Giuseppina had remained in Tunisia following decolonization, only moving to Italy in the late 1980s for her children's higher education.

Giuseppina's description of her childhood provides an intriguing window into social relations in colonial Tunisia. On the one hand, she describes Sicilians and Tunisians living in proximity and familiarity. Her family, similarly to many other Sicilians, lived in the old Arab neighborhood (the medina) and had frequent and friendly daily relations with Tunisians. On the other hand, her words clearly describe a society marked by hierarchies between these two groups—a hierarchy that was clearly visible to her eyes as a small girl who associated menial tasks such as street cleaning with work done only by Arabs.

In this chapter, taking inspiration from Giuseppina's words, I use the lens of colonial schools to investigate simultaneous processes of boundary-drawing and relationships of coexistence between Sicilians and Tunisians in French Protectorate Tunisia. Colonial schools, as well as other sites of socialization, played a key role in "modernizing" and "civilizing" poor Sicilians and thus differentiating them from Tunisians. However, Sicilians and Tunisians generally lived in the same neighborhoods and frequently interacted in multiple arenas of everyday life for the duration of French rule over the country. In addition, French colonial authorities explicitly embraced a vision of Mediterranean coexistence in Tunisia, reflected clearly in their educational policies. How was it possible to draw the material and symbolic boundaries of Europeanness, all while celebrating mixing and coexistence?

This chapter addresses this question by focusing primarily on the first three decades of French colonial rule in Tunisia, between 1881 and 1911. Certainly, over the seven decades of French rule between 1881 and 1954, colonial institutions and policies changed considerably.[2] In addition, shifting geopolitical configurations in Europe had repercussions on intercommunal relations in Tunisia and on French colonial policy (Jerfal 2001). However, the first three decades of the protectorate period are particularly significant, since they witnessed the creation of institutions, such as the legal system (Lewis 2014) and the educational system (Sugiyama 2007), that would shape subsequent intercommunal relations in the territory. In addition, the establishment of the French Protectorate reorganized long-standing relations between different national and linguistic communities, and this period therefore witnessed an extensive debate between French colonial authorities, European diplomatic missions, and the Tunisian Husainid ruling family about the status of different populations in Tunisia (Largueche et al. 2001), particularly as they concerned the "nature" and status of poor Sicilian settlers.

"An Undeniable Racial Affinity with the Tunisian People"

Shortly after taking control of Tunisia in 1881, French authorities carried out a complete reform of the legal system that simultaneously limited the influence of other European nations in the territory and created a unified group of "Europeans" out of the Italian, Maltese, Spanish, and French populations that inhabited Tunisia. Previously, European nationals in Tunisia were subject to the *capitu-*

lations regime—a system according to which all of their affairs, including the administration of civil and criminal justice, were regulated by their respective consulates (Clancy-Smith 2010; Jerfal 2001a).[3] In 1883, in an attempt to limit the influence of other European governments (Lewis 2014), French authorities abolished this regime. In its place, they established a dual legal system, according to which all European nationals would be tried by French courts, while the affairs of Tunisians would be regulated by "native" courts.[4] This legal reform transformed the mosaic of communities that had characterized Tunisia into two clear camps: Europeans (regardless of their nationality) and Tunisians (Jerfal 2001; Lewis 2014; Noureddine 2001). In practice, this demarcation of identity was more fluid than its legal structure would suggest. In her detailed study on the evolution of the legal system in colonial Tunisia, Lewis (2014) shows how both Europeans and Tunisian colonial subjects would often claim different identities in different moments in order to better protect their interests, just as they had done under the capitulation system (Clancy-Smith 2010). However, at a conceptual level, the division of Tunisia's population between Europeans and Tunisians was clear.

The establishment of the French Protectorate over Tunisia set off political shock waves in Italy, which had its own colonial ambitions for the territory. Tunisia had a long-established Italian community (Clancy-Smith 2010), and by 1881 Italian nationals outnumbered the French by ten to one (Davi 2000). The repercussions of the French takeover were significant enough to cost Prime Minister Benedetto Cairoli, an opponent of Italian colonial expansion, his premiership (Choate 2010). Within Tunisia, a small but well-established group of Italian professionals had also supported Italian control over the territory. These were largely Jewish families, established in Tunisia since the turn of the nineteenth century, and very well connected to the Husainid ruling family that had governed the territory prior to French takeover (Clancy-Smith 2010). Under pressure from this local Italian bourgeoisie, in 1896 the Italian government negotiated accords with French authorities to maintain a series of legal and commercial privileges for Italian nationals originally guaranteed in an 1861 convention between the newly unified Italian state and the bey of Tunis (Lewis 2014).[5] This accord included the authorization to continue to operate—but not expand—Italian institutions in the territory, such as hospitals and schools (Lewis 2014; Sugiyama 2007). Thus, despite the establishment of the French Protectorate, Tunisia remained a site of the ongoing production of Italianness.

Creating Italians was necessary, because at the turn of the twentieth century the majority of Tunisia's Italian population was Italian in name only. According to the 1906 census, approximately 80 percent of Italian nationals were of Sicilian origin (Direction Générale de l'Agriculture 1915), coming mainly from the areas of Trapani, Marsala, and Mazara del Vallo (Loth 1905; Melfa 2008), as well as the island of Pantelleria. They were primarily working-class, largely illiterate or with very limited formal education, and had little sense of being citizens of a recently unified Italy.[6] A small part of this population was rural, but the majority had settled in cities, primarily in the capital, Tunis (Direction Générale de l'Agriculture 1915; Loth 1905; Melfa 2007).

In rural areas, Sicilians settled on small farms or in ethnically homogeneous villages (Melfa 2008). In urban centers, they generally lived in proximity to Tunisians, either in the same neighborhoods or in adjacent ones. In Tunis and other major cities, poor Sicilians initially settled within or near the old Arab medinas (Sebag 1998). As Sicilian migration increased following the establishment of the French Protectorate, Sicilian informal neighborhoods sprang up in the European quarters of various Tunisian cities, often on less desirable—and thus cheaper—land (Giudice 2006; Melfa 2007).[7] In central Tunis, Sicilian migrants settled in the Petite Sicile—a swampy area owned by the Gnecco family, members of the established Italian bourgeoisie in the territory, who allowed Sicilians to build small houses on their property in exchange for a modest rent (Giudice 2006).

Following a common trope that associates neighborhoods' unsanitary and cramped living conditions with the "lack of civilization" of their inhabitants (Fanon 1965; Gandy 2008; Kooy and Bakker 2008; Ross 1995), middle-class French and Italian commentators identified Sicilians' precarious living conditions as proof of their backwardness and dangerousness.[8] In Tunis, for instance, the Petite Sicile neighborhood was known for its "bad odors during the summer, activities of little nobility, and a Sicilian population of modest condition . . . difficult to associate with and dangerous" (Giudice 2006, 185). Proximity and similarity in dwellings between Sicilians and Tunisians also led middle-class commentators to describe these two populations in very similar terms. Gaston Loth, for instance, French director of the Alaoui teacher training college in Tunis, described Sicilian settlements, arguing, "Coming from . . . slums or the frightful little houses of the Sicilian countryside, how could the poor immigrants not accept, at the beginning, to settle in the fundouk of Arab towns, all jumbled together people and animals" (Loth 1905, 335). Similarly, a 1903 report by the Italian consul in Tunis noted: "In the urban centers (and also in rural agglomerations) the Italian colony represents the connecting link between the indigenous and the European element, partially because . . . Sicilians . . . have an undeniable racial affinity with the Tunisian people. And one may say that, even topographically, the working-class strata of our colony play the role of bringing together and fusing the different sections of Tunisia's population" (Carletti 1903, 56).

Some French and Italian commentators also described Sicilians as impulsive, violent, and predisposed to criminal activity. In the last decade of the nineteenth century, the Francophone press in Tunisia waged a vicious campaign against

Sicilian immigration, warning its readers of the "Italian peril" (Noureddine 2001). This campaign mainly reflected labor competition (Melfa 2008) and land ownership (Saurin 1900) concerns of a small French settler lobby. However, members of the Italian bourgeoisie made similar references to Sicilians' nature (Montalbano 2018), often using the language of positivist criminology discussed in chapter 1.[9] In his end-of-year report of July 28, 1899, for instance, the director of the Italian elementary school Principe di Napoli, located in proximity to the medina of Tunis, described his students' background by noting: "This colony is primarily made up of co-nationals coming from Sicily. . . . They would be happy people, if atavistic tendencies, favored by the ignorance in which people of those lands have lain for the longest time, did not make them . . . waste their salary on parties and clothes, and . . . consider it cowardly not to make justice with their own hands.[10] . . . Bloody crimes are committed frequently, almost daily . . . as acts of bravery and revenge."[11]

Sicilians' alleged predisposition to criminality and similarity of their customs to Arab customs did not prevent the Italian bourgeoisie of Tunis or French colonial authorities from considering them an essential tool in developing European control over the territory (Melfa 2008). The same writers who described Sicilians as primitive and uncivilized also characterized them as good workers, resistant to the heat, and thus valuable to the French colonization project. Gaston Loth, for instance, described Sicilian peasants as similar to Arabs but also as hard workers: "In all the regions in which they are implanted, Sicilian farmers show the same endurance, the same qualities of sobriety and of economy. They are happy to simply be a little less poor than in their homeland. . . . As soon as they have built . . . a sort of hut, similar to the humble cottage of the Arab, they get to work" (Loth 1905, 219–220).

For Sicilians to fully support Italian or French ambitions in Tunisia, however, they had to be "modernized," civilized, and made into national (French or Italian) subjects. More specifically, it was necessary to correct flaws in Sicilians' language, cleanliness, and demeanor acquired through daily life in poor neighborhoods within or near the medinas and through daily interactions with Tunisians. An essential instrument for this transformation was colonial schools.

Making Europeans: Colonial Schools

At the turn of the twentieth century, a broad network of European educational institutions covered Tunisian territory. French institutions were dominant numerically over Italian ones, with 175 and 21 schools, respectively. In Tunis, proportions were more equal, as French schools outnumbered Italian ones by only three to one—thirty-three French schools operated alongside eleven Italian ones (Machuel 1906).[12] Both French and Italian schools had a long history in Tunisia. French religious orders founded the first French schools in the 1830s and 1840s (Machuel 1906). Following the establishment of the protectorate, French authorities created the directorate general of public education in Tunisia in 1883. This brought all existing French schools under direct control of the state and expanded their network by founding public elementary and secondary schools throughout Tunisian territory (Sugiyama 2007).

The first schools that taught in Italian were also founded in the 1830s, under the initiative of the local Italian bourgeoisie (Montalbano 2018). Following the country's unification in 1861, the Italian government began to provide financial and logistical support to these schools as part of a broader vision of *emigrant colonialism*—the attempt to expand Italian influence abroad by cultivating the loyalty of Italian emigrants (Choate 2008). Italian schools in Tunisia thus were part of a broader network of Italian government schools in the Mediterranean basin, central to Italian foreign policy in the region (Choate 2008). Italian schools continued operating despite the French takeover of Tunisia. An 1896 treaty between France and Italy allowed existing institutions to continue to operate but did not allow the creation of new schools (Choate 2010). Because of immigration, the number of Italian students greatly exceeded the capacity of Italian schools. In addition, some educated Italian families began to send their children to French schools out of class prejudice against the working-class students in Italian schools and to better position their children in new political reality of the French Protectorate (Montalbano 2018). This meant that French and Italian schools had roughly equivalent numbers of Italian students.[13] It also meant that the majority of students in French schools were Italian nationals (Montalbano 2018).

Competition between these two school systems to attract Italian nationals was fierce, since contests over education were central to broader power struggles over influence in Tunisia (Choate 2007, 2008; Montalbano 2018; Sugiyama 2007). Despite their competition, however, both school systems had similar aims of "civilizing" Sicilian students, while also demarcating difference and establishing a hierarchy between Europeans and non-Europeans.

Producing National Subjects: Italian Schools

Following the establishment of the French Protectorate, Italian schools in Tunisia primarily attracted a working-class student body, as mastery of the French language and access to French diplomas became important for professional success.[14] In Tunis, the majority of Italian schools were located near the Arab

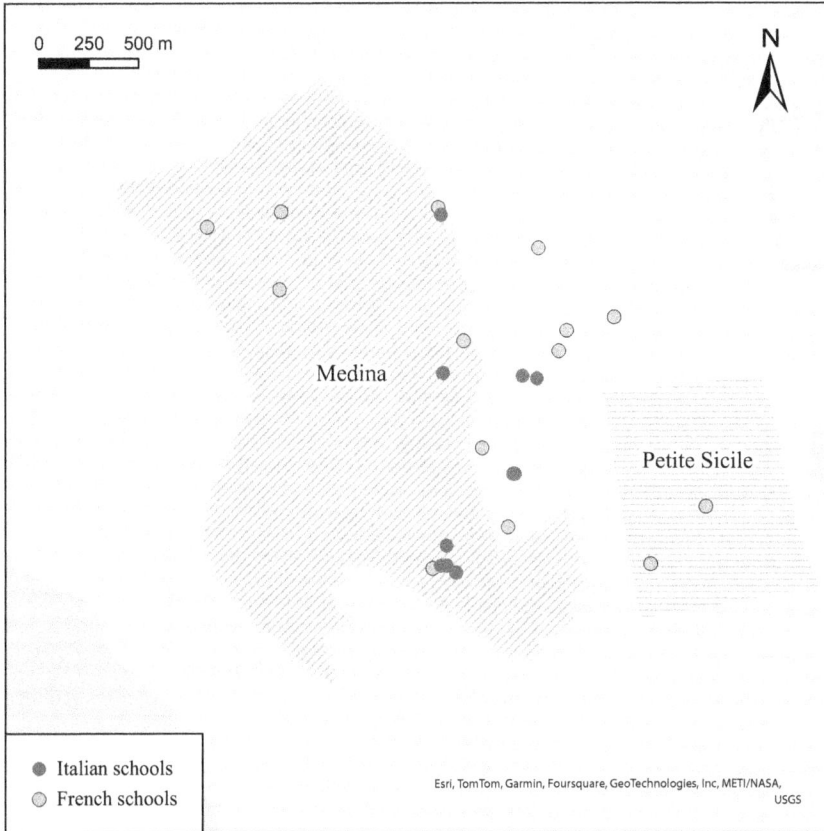

FIGURE 4. Map of Italian and French schools in Tunis, 1906. Source: Author, based on data in Machuel 1906.

medina, in neighborhoods inhabited by poor Sicilians, Maltese, and Tunisians.[15] This meant that Sicilian students shared urban space, customs, and language with Tunisians. This environment contrasted starkly with that of the teachers, who were generally middle class and often new to Tunisia. Many came from Italy, or from other Italian schools abroad, and considered their time in Tunisia a temporary career move (Montalbano 2018). They often held strong class and regional prejudices against their Sicilian students. While some of their school reports painted a compassionate portrait of the children, many explained students' meager academic success as a consequence of their alleged mediocre intelligence. In her 1906 final report, for instance, one of the first-grade teachers of the Margherita di Savoia girls' elementary school explained why, in her view, half of her students had failed the school year: "I faced a large, loud and rebellious group of students . . . intellectually I faced a mediocre element . . . lively girls, and generally truthful, but . . . raised in misery and . . . in the streets. I found in them the ills of an uncivilized environment."[16]

Similarly, in his 1895 final report, the director of the Umberto I boys' elementary school explained students' lack of interest in history by referring to their class and regional origin:

> The southern worker . . . only goes to . . . school to learn how to write a letter and to learn elementary arithmetic . . . his indifference for all other aspects of civic life is deplorable. . . . Last year, the Società Operaia attempted to organize conferences on themes such as history, geography, hygiene . . . with a recreational aim . . . one evening, Captain Pierotti's lecture on the Italian Risorgimento began with twenty people in the audience and finished with only six, half asleep from boredom! We can conclude that the southern worker remains unprepared to receive the benefits of education.[17]

The social and political value of school was, however, equally if not more important than students' intellectual progress (Montalbano 2018).[18] In their reports, various teachers underlined how school was essential in cultivating poor Italian workers' loyalty to Italy. For instance, writing in 1896, the director of the Italian commercial school observed: "Most of the students come from families lacking education: their home is detrimental to school, not helpful. . . . There was little or no [academic] success. . . . One of the causes . . . is the need to admit all those who request it. . . . Italian school abroad . . . has primarily an attractive aim . . . not only scientific and literary propaganda, but more importantly national propaganda, Italian propaganda."[19]

To "make" Italians, schools in Tunisia followed the same curriculum as those in Italy, where compulsory education was limited to the first three years of elementary school (Floriani 1974).[20] During these years, three subjects were central to the modernization and nationalization of Sicilian students: hygiene, history, and Italian. Hygiene—a classic medium through which to civilize poor whites in a colonial context (Stoler 2002)—was both a subject of instruction and a more general habit to be instilled among Sicilian students.[21] In an 1896 trimestral report, for instance, the director of the Umberto I boys' elementary school underlined the importance of hygiene for students living in Arab neighborhoods: "Here, in the Arab neighborhood, the poorest Europeans come to live. . . . Our students are in miserable conditions . . . they are poorly dressed, yet they keep themselves fairly clean and pay attention to hygiene, because we do not stop threatening them, scolding them . . . persuading them" (Cybeo 1896a).

A similar report, written in the same year by the director of the Principe di Napoli boys' elementary school situated in the old medina, framed students as a conduit to educate their families about hygiene: "We diligently watched over the personal cleanliness of students. . . . If they showed up without . . . clean clothes, we would send them home to ask their mothers to wash and mend them. . . . We never missed an occasion to teach students principles of hygiene, in order for these notions to arrive to families through their children" (Sironi 1896).

History was, in turn, central to nationalizing poor Italian students. It was taught starting in first grade, and in the first three years of elementary school it focused entirely on the Risorgimento (Italian unification). References to the Risorgimento and to the Italian royal family were also prevalent in Italian composition and memorization classes.[22] "All compositions, dictations, readings, stories, poems . . . ," explained the director of the Margherita di Savoia girl's elementary school in 1898, "are inspired by the great Italian homeland, and no holiday . . . is unobserved in this temple dedicated to keeping alive our love for Italy" (Mascia Merolli 1898). After the first three years of elementary school, the history curriculum broadened. However, it retained a focus on sparking students' patriotic sentiment. "The teaching of history," explained a fourth-grade teacher in the Margherita di Savoia girls' elementary school in her final report, "should not consist in a cold presentation of facts and dates, but should be lively, in order to speak to the imagination of the girls, and to fill their heart with love for our homeland."[23]

Italian language was the most difficult vehicle through which to nationalize Tunisia's Sicilian population, due to the distance between the formal Italian taught at school and the daily languages of colonial Tunis (Sicilian dialect, Tunisian Arabic, and French). Italian students used to speaking, as the director of the Italian commercial school noted in 1896, "a real mix of the most barbarous elements of the different languages and dialects spoken in this cosmopolitan city" struggled to master Italian grammar.[24] Elementary school teachers' reports were peppered with accounts of their pedagogical challenges: "We took the greatest care in teaching Italian language, because it is . . . difficult, as a consequence of the [students'] mixing of languages, and because it forms the strongest connection between the colonies and the mother country.[25] . . . We carry out frequent . . . exercises of conversion from singular to plural, from masculine to feminine, and vice-versa. . . . These exercises could seem excessive or premature elsewhere, but they are extremely useful for [Sicilian] students used to speaking Arabic."[26]

Pedagogical difficulties in elementary schools were exacerbated by their chronic overcrowding, particularly in the lower grades, since the French authorities did not authorize the opening of new schools and often denied requests from existing schools to add new classes or to move them to larger buildings.[27] Overcrowded classrooms, which sometimes held up to a hundred students per class, often resulted in students repeating grades multiple times and led many to

eventually leave school. This meant that despite the best efforts of Italian authorities, illiteracy rates of Italian nationals remained high. In addition, mediocre
learning conditions in Italian schools convinced some families to send their children to French schools, where the number of Italian students continued to rise
(Sironi 1896).

Producing Cosmopolitan Subjects: French Schools

Large numbers of Italian students attended French schools throughout Tunisia.
However, their strongest influence on Italian communities was in rural areas,
where no Italian schools were present historically and where French authorities
promptly shut down attempts to create clandestine ones (Montalbano 2018). In
this context, French teachers, directors, and school inspectors described the challenges of "modernizing and civilizing" Sicilian students in a similar manner to
their Italian counterparts. For instance, in a 1901 speech during an end-of-year
school prize ceremony, the French director general of education Louis Machuel
reflected on the progress that had occurred in a rural elementary school for girls,
attended almost entirely by Sicilian students:

> Four years ago, I went to inaugurate a girls' school . . . in the country-
> side, in the midst of a population of simple workers, mainly of foreign
> nationality. . . . The teacher had the difficult and delicate task, of teach-
> ing not only . . . French to the girls . . . but also of polishing their primi-
> tive nature, of giving them . . . habits of politeness, good manners, clean-
> liness and morality that often they did not have in their families. . . .
> Eight months later I returned to see this school . . . I saw . . . our young
> students . . . clean, their hair carefully combed . . . their clothes in a per-
> fect state. . . . Once the cleanliness inspection was finished, they went
> into the classroom singing a simple verse, correctly pronounced, but
> with a slight foreign accent.[28]

Despite French and Italian educators' similar mission to "modernize and civilize" Sicilians, their pedagogy was different. Italian schools had the explicit aim
of transforming "backward" Sicilians, negatively influenced by their proximity
to Tunisians in dwellings, customs, and language, into national subjects. French
schools instead explicitly sought to create "coexistence" between the different
national, linguistic, and religious communities of the protectorate. Both their
educational structure and their model of coexistence, however, created material

and symbolic hierarchies between the French (a category into which protectorate authorities sought to assimilate Italians) and the Tunisians.

French educational policy in Tunisia, spearheaded by its first director general of education, Louis Machuel, was inspired by the notion of the *fusion des races* (fusion of the races; Sugiyama 2007). This was a polysemic term that appeared in texts by French authorities, intellectuals, and political activists in various French North African colonies, with a range of different meanings. Some proponents of the fusion des races understood this as biological mixing between Italians and French (Bonurra 1922; Loth 1905) or between French men and Arab women (Abbassi 2009; Gastaut 2001; Streiff-Fénart 1990), to create a population suited to living and working in the North African heat.[29] Other proponents understood it as a form of acculturation (Sugiyama 2007), according to which French language and culture should form the basis for the coming together of different populations. Both visions shared the assumption that French control over North Africa would be strengthened by the mixing of people from different backgrounds through the universalism of French language and culture.

Machuel embraced the cultural version of the fusion des races as a means to create support for French rule among both Europeans and the Tunisian elite, with the objective of creating a "softer" form of colonial rule than in neighboring Algeria (Sugiyama 2007; Tselikas and Hayoun 2004). The founders of the Alliance Française of Tunis also espoused this assimilationist vision as part of their broader objective of "moral conquest" (Sugiyama 2007). In his 1907 book on French colonization of Tunisia, Gaston Loth, director of the Alaoui teaching college in Tunis, explained the value of mixed education to create Francophiles out of the varied population that inhabited Tunisia at the turn of the twentieth century: "Side by side, on the same desks, little girls of different races and nationalities become neighbors . . . it is thanks to our work that foreign girls—Italian, Maltese, Jewish Tunisian—will become and will remain friends of the French school, in other words friends of France" (Loth 1907, 92).

According to Machuel's vision, embracing the fusion des races also meant developing a model of bilingual education. Born and raised in Algeria, he himself was bilingual in French and Arabic (Sugiyama 2007). His educational policy had the simultaneous objective of making European residents of Tunisia French, exposing Tunisians to French language and culture, and teaching Arabic to Tunisia's French population.[30] To do so, he oversaw the creation of a large-scale program of bilingual French and Arabic education, both for indigenous Tunisians and for Europeans—a policy questioned by some members of the French settler lobby, who were opposed to public expenditures to educate the "natives," fearing that this might spark anticolonial movements (Soumille 1975; Sugiyama 2007).

European and Tunisian students, however, did not generally study in the same establishments. Certainly, colonial schools such as those described by Loth were open to all students. However, Tunisians who studied in these schools were mainly members of the elite (Bachrouch 1985; Sugiyama 2012), and—particularly in secondary schools—they represented a small proportion of the students in comparison to Europeans (Tselikas and Hayoun 2004). The bulk of Tunisian children were instead educated in modernized religious schools, or in Franco-Arab elementary schools designed specifically for Tunisian children (Bachrouch 1985; Sugiyama 2012). The latter were unevenly distributed across Tunisia, leaving swaths of the interior of the country underserved.[31]

In addition, the inclusion of Arabic in the curriculum of French schools did not mean that the two languages were accorded the same status. French educators considered French the language of science, knowledge, and progress (Boughedir 2004), in contrast to Arabic (specifically its colloquial Tunisian variety), which was a necessary and practical tool to governing the territory and to limiting the influence of the Italian elite, who were often fluent in this language (Sugiyama 2007). Loth clearly expressed this vision, arguing for the benefits of including Arabic in the curriculum of French schools:

> It is indispensable . . . that French students . . . learn the language of the natives. So . . . in almost every school in Tunisia . . . we have organized . . . Arabic courses . . . only spoken Arabic . . . of which knowledge is fundamental in . . . daily relations with Muslims . . . most Maltese, Italian and Greek children speak Arabic. We would have left our compatriots in a disadvantaged situation if we had not given them the means to . . . acquire this language. (Loth 1907, 87)

Embracing multilingual education also did not mean embracing hybridization of language or code-switching. French intellectual elites—who were favorable to multilingual education—were extremely critical of the creolization of languages that occurred in the streets of Tunis. For instance, writing in 1922, fifteen years after Louis Machuel had left his position as director general of public education, Albert Canal, representative of the Society of North African Writers at the 1922 colonial exposition in Marseilles, complained: "In North Africa, French is poorly spoken. . . . People who, as children, played in the streets with little Arabs . . . little Italians, little Maltese, acquired . . . defects of expression that are really hard to eliminate" (Canal et al., n.d., cited in Sugiyama 2007, 189).

In sum, while French education policy embraced ideas of mixing and coexistence between the different populations, languages, and cultures present in colonial Tunisia, this vision of coexistence produced symbolic and material hierarchies. At a symbolic level, designating French language and culture as the universalist arena of coexistence for people from different backgrounds cast this language and culture as superior to others that could not play this role. On the material level, French educational policies perpetuated structural inequalities between different populations in Tunisia, despite being addressed to all residents of the territory. French schools educated Sicilians with the objective of modernizing this "assimilable" population, who could eventually become French citizens. Educating Tunisians was instead intended to create a bilingual educated elite that could act as an intermediary for French colonial authorities but had limited possibilities of becoming French citizens.[32]

In essence, despite their differences, both French and Italian schools were sites of European subject formation, in which poor, "backward" Sicilians could be modernized into French and Italian subjects. This process, however, occurred through the drawing of boundaries between Sicilians and Tunisians. In Italian schools, aimed at creating Italian citizens, this differentiating aim was clear— particularly because these schools almost exclusively educated Italian nationals. French schools appeared more open on the surface, since their educational philosophy was inspired by ideas of mixing and coexistence. Since this vision of coexistence produced both material and symbolic hierarchies, however, it contributed to processes of tracing the boundaries of Europeanness to include Sicilians but exclude Tunisians.

Coexistence and Inequality in Colonial Tunisia

Colonial schools were one of many sites of socialization of Sicilian settlers, and— as school reports themselves suggest—Sicilians and Tunisians regularly interacted in many social spaces. At the turn of twentieth century, their interactions were relatively peaceful. Sicilians and Tunisians lived in the same neighborhoods, cooperated in the workplace, and eventually even joined the same trade unions (Jerfal 2001). Absence of overt conflict between communities and daily relations of familiarity, cordiality, and even friendship did not, however, mean that these two communities were equal, nor that Sicilians did not have prejudice toward Tunisians (Jerfal 2001).

According to some studies, relations deteriorated during the first few decades following the establishment of the protectorate. In the city of Sousse, for instance, site of the third-largest Italian community in Tunisia, this occurred as Italian commercial elites grew closer to French authorities to safeguard their economic interests (Jerfal 2001). The turn of the twentieth century witnessed a surge in violent Italian crimes toward Tunisians and in Tunisian robberies from Italians, as

a "reaction against poverty and exploitation, especially because they were committed against sections of society that had benefited from the colonial system"
(Jerfal 2001, 338).

Differentiation between the two communities, and Sicilians' inclusion in the
category of Europeans, became particularly clear in two episodes of overt conflict
between Sicilians and Tunisians in the city of Tunis in 1911 and 1912. In November 1911, multiple days of skirmishes between Sicilians and Tunisians erupted
after an Italian national allegedly killed a Tunisian by firing into a crowd at a
protest against the surveying of the Djellaz cemetery in Tunis. The following year,
Tunisian protestors boycotted the Italian-owned and -operated tramway system
in Tunis after a streetcar struck and killed a Muslim Tunisian child (Sghaier 1999).
To some extent, these events can be interpreted as a consequence of heightened
tensions between Italians and Tunisians following the Italian conquest of Libya
in 1911. This received widespread support from Tunis's Italian community but
was strongly opposed in the Tunisian Arabic press, which described it as an
attack on Islam (Sghaier 1999).[33] These tensions also testify, however, to Italians'
privileged position vis-à-vis Tunisians. By the second decade of the twentieth
century, Tunisian workers had seen their economic condition deteriorate (Ayadi
1986), leading to resentment focused on unequal treatment in the workplace.
Indeed, one of the central demands of the tramway boycott movement, alongside
reduced speeds in Arab neighborhoods, was salary equality between Tunisian
and Italian employees (Khairallah 1934). In addition, the 1911 and 1912 episodes demonstrate the extent to which Sicilians were clearly incorporated into
the category of Europeans. The 1911 and 1912 events in fact represented the first
moment in which the elite Tunisian nationalist movement collaborated with the
masses in an anticolonial revolt, one that was addressed not against the French,
but against the Italians (Ayadi 1986). Certainly, Italians may have represented
an easier target than the French, or French authorities themselves may have
encouraged—or at least not attempted to quell—these hostilities as a means of
strengthening their own rule (Ayadi 1986). However, the fact that Sicilians could
represent a target for the growing frustrations of poor and dispossessed Tunisians testifies to their privileged position within the social hierarchy of colonial
Tunisia.

The de facto differentiation between Sicilians and Tunisians would become
clear at Tunisian decolonization in 1956, when the bulk of Tunisia's Italian population lost the privileges they previously had, such as access to land and preferential access to certain professions, and as a result left the country (Kazdaghli 1999).
Former settlers often explain their departure as a consequence of the overturning
of social relations in the wake of decolonization. Giuseppina, whose memories of

mid-century colonial Tunisia opened the chapter, recounted how her husband, Vito, had closed his tailoring business because "he could not accept making clothes for Arab clients. Before, he used to work only for the French or for the Italians." Similar sentiments emerge in the words of other settlers, referring to the social changes after decolonization.[34] In fact, Europeans who remained in Tunisia after decolonization were allowed to retain their nationality and to receive work and residency permits in Tunisia. Sicilians' memories of decolonization, however, testify the extent to which they divided the population of Tunisia between Arabs and Europeans, clearly placing themselves in the latter camp.

Traces of an Invisible Past

"Tunisia used to be a Mediterranean country, but now it has become an Arab one!" exclaimed Sarah, summarizing the six decades of social, cultural, and political transformation that the country had undergone since decolonization. On the afternoon of our interview, the coastal suburb of Tunis of Halq-al-wad was buzzing with life.[35] Families who could afford it had left the sweltering heat of central Tunis to pass the summer by the seaside, where they were joined by Tunisians of the diaspora visiting for the holidays. The hum of Vespas along the main road, and the teenage boys crowding the cheap food stalls, gave Halq-al-Wad the ambience of a popular seaside resort. Crossing the doorway of Sarah's house, however, the hustle-and-bustle of the street gave way to a quiet Mediterranean garden, reminiscent of southern France.

Sarah was born and raised in Tunis, as were her parents and grandparents, yet little Arabic was spoken in her house. Her Tunisian housekeeper, cook, and gardener spoke to her in French, as did the group of upper-middle-class professional Tunisian women who gathered in her house every week. Her children, who were going to university in France, had little interest in returning to Tunisia after their studies. Nevertheless, Sarah insisted, her family belonged in Tunisia; they had been there for four generations. As one of the few remaining Italians of Tunis, she made it her mission to preserve the historic memory of the community and assert their belonging in contemporary Tunisia, even as she bemoaned the manner in which—in her eyes—the country had become much more "Arab" and "Muslim," and thus less cosmopolitan, over the course of her life.

About forty-five minutes away, in a suburb on the opposite side of the city, lies another remnant of the Italian community of Tunis. In a beautiful unmarked villa up on a hill, two dozen elderly men and women pass the last days of their lives in a comfortable yet solitary retirement home. French is the dominant language, peppered with a few Italian words, although the Tunisian medical and care staff exchange the occasional word in Arabic with each other.

"Are you from the RAI TV?" ask two elderly gentlemen whom I sit down to interview, referring to when Italian national television interviewed them a few years previously for a feature on this "little-known" community.[36] Reconstructing their life trajectories through our chat proves to be more difficult than I had thought; piecing together dates, turning points, or linear trajectories out of eighty years of memories that superimpose events, places, and people is nearly impossible. Yet out of my conversations with the elderly residents of the retirement home, a common feeling emerges—a profound sense of solitude shared across class and educational background. It is a solitude created by being the only one of the family who did not leave for Europe after decolonization, a disorientation created by the disappearance of the Italian world of central Tunis they grew up with.

Margherita, the director of the center, has also seen her world disappear. Of relatively humble origins, she grew up in the medina of Tunis in a very socially conservative family. Currently, however, she and her husband—also an Italian of Tunis—divide their time between a spacious apartment in an upscale suburb of Tunis and white stone villa in the seaside resort of Hammamet—the same town where Italian socialist politician Bettino Craxi self-exiled in the 1990s to escape corruption charges. Margherita is a social butterfly and speaks fluent Tunisian Arabic, yet her life revolves around the Italian and French consulates. She clearly identifies the invisible barriers between her immediate social circle and the broader Tunisian society, as she comments on the 2011 revolution: "I was happy about the uprisings," she tells me, despite having considered evacuating the country at the time, "but I didn't participate. You see, it was *their* uprising. We are not Muslims." To her children, these divisions could not be clearer—after their university studies in France they have no intention of returning. *Out of place* is the first term that comes to mind when describing the latest generation of Italians of Tunis, currently in their twenties, educated and raised to live in the remnants of a Francophone world of a colonial Tunisia that no longer exists.

On the northern shore of the Mediterranean, the descendants of the Italians of Tunis are similarly invisible. Following decolonization, most Sicilians of Tunisia left for France or for large Italian cities. Some, however, returned to their parents' region of origin, and a small number of Sicilians from Tunisia currently live in the Sicilian town of Mazara del Vallo on the southwestern coast of the island. Whether scattered throughout the Italian peninsula, or concentrated in smaller cities such as Mazara, most descendants of Italians of Tunisia have little time for, or interest in, keeping this history alive. Tunisia is a nice memory, a quirky piece of family history, or—perhaps—a sporadic destination for a summer vacation. Occasionally, however, journalists, migration activists, or academics return to this history, with the more or less explicit aim of intervening in contemporary migration debates.

Mobilizing the Colonial Mediterranean

Since the early years of the twenty-first century, Italy, France, and Tunisia have all witnessed a growing interest in the history of Italian settlers in Tunisia. In Italy, descendants of this community have published autobiographical novels (Pendola 2000) and collaborated with filmmakers and nongovernmental organization (NGO) workers to document their history.[37] Italian scholars have published monographs on the everyday lives of working-class members of this community, as well as on its political life (Blandi 2012; El Houssi 2014; Melfa 2008; Rainero 2002). With different degrees of explicitness, many of these accounts were motivated by the desire to intervene in contemporary immigration debates. As chapter 5 will discuss, some of the Catholic figures who mobilize this history in the Sicilian town of Mazara del Vallo cast colonial Tunisia as a model of coexistence in the present. Other Italian NGO workers, artists, and academics recount Italians' history of poverty and emigration as an effort to inspire empathy among Italians toward contemporary migrants (Blandi 2012).[38] An unspoken assumption behind this analogy is that Italians who migrated south were in a structurally similar position to Tunisian migrants in contemporary Italy, a notion that disregards the colonial nature of Tunisia in the late nineteenth and early twentieth centuries.

Most scholarly research on the Italian community of Tunisia is, however, written in French and produced by scholars based in French and Tunisian universities, often in collaboration with each other. In France, this scholarship is part of a broader rising interest in so-called *pied-noir* history, as descendants of French settlers in North Africa began to challenge the institutional amnesia that surrounded their existence after decolonization. In Tunisia, scholars at the Higher Institute of the History of the National Movement spearheaded the research as part of a broader effort to frame Tunisia as a cosmopolitan mosaic created through the contribution of European minorities to the country's economic, cultural, and artistic patrimony (Alexandropoulos and Cabanel 2000; Bessis 2006; Kazdaghli 2006). While scholars do not explicitly state this, highlighting Tunisia's Mediterranean cosmopolitan heritage represents a challenge to Islamist understandings of the country's culture and geopolitical positioning.

Some Italian, French, and Tunisian scholars do mention invisible barriers that ran through the space of colonial Tunisia, focusing for instance on the lack of cooperation between Italian antifascist activists and the Tunisian decolonization movement (El Houssi 2014; Rainero 2002), tensions between hierarchy and coexistence (Alexandropoulos and Cabanel 2000), the positioning of Italians within colonial social hierarchies (Davi 2000), or the progressive deterioration of relationships between Italians and Tunisians (Jerfal 2001). However, the bulk of research on this period focuses on peaceful coexistence. Where it does address conflict, it mainly focuses on interimperial rivalries between France and Italy. Tunisians appear either as a backdrop to these tensions or as a population with whom Italians had peaceful and cordial relationships (Valenzi 2008). These accounts thus clash with the analysis by Tunisian theorist of decolonization Albert Memmi of the positionality of Italians in Tunisia in the latter years of the protectorate in his well-known book *The Colonizer and the Colonized*. Describing the paradoxes of familiarity and friendship coexisting with hierarchy and inequality, he wrote: "Almost all the Italians speak the language of the colonized, make long-lasting friendships with them . . . but they are in a better situation than the colonized. . . . [They have] advantages which the colonized certainly does not have: better job opportunities, less insecurity against total misery and illness, less precarious schooling. . . . As much as they may be outcasts in the absolute sense, their behavior vis-à-vis the colonized has much in common with the colonizer" (Memmi 1965, 14).

Drawing on Memmi's analysis, I have focused in this chapter on French Protectorate Tunisia as a site of material and symbolic drawing of the boundaries of Europeanness, in which French policies of coexistence created symbolic hierarchies between different populations in the territory and were thus integral to colonial rule. Certainly, Tunisia at the turn of the twentieth century was a multireligious, multilingual, and multinational space as well as a site of differentiation, uneven power relations, and privilege for Europeans. To some extent, which narrative to privilege could appear to be a debate primarily of interest to historians. However, in a moment of vivid debate over the future of multicultural Europe, the search for historical models of coexistence takes on a renewed significance, as readings of the past inform our analysis of contemporary migration issues and our imagination of possible futures.

The next three chapters focus on the contemporary moment, from the location of Mazara del Vallo, in the borderland context of southwestern Sicily. Much like colonial Tunis, contemporary Mazara is also a space of daily copresence of Sicilians and Tunisians in multiple spaces of everyday life, of celebration of the city's mixed Mediterranean nature, and of debate on the possibilities of coexistence between people of different national, linguistic, and religious backgrounds. Certainly, French Protectorate Tunisia and contemporary Sicily lack the direct connection between colony and metropole described by early postcolonial theorists of migration who, in contexts such as France or the United Kingdom, trace the direct transfer of colonial policies into the metropole to manage new immigrants (Khiari 2009; Ross 1995), as well as the reappearance of similar understandings of the racialized boundaries of the nation (Solomos et al. 1982). While contemporary Italian debates about migration and citizenship draw on a longer repertoire of debates about the management of colonial subjects in Italian colonies (Giuliani and Lombardi-Diop 2013; Hawthorne 2022), such a connection is tenuous in the case of Tunisia, because it was an "indirect" site of Italian colonization (Lombardi-Diop 2021). These connections are also not immediately visible in Mazara's socioeconomic fabric and political life, despite the fact that the province of Trapani was one of the main sources of Sicilian migration to Tunisia. Speculations about the colonial origin of Mazara's successful fishing sector, for instance through the return migration of Sicilians of Tunisia who had worked in fisheries in colonial Tunisia, turned out to be unfounded, as these return migrants were not major players in the 1960s boom of the sector (Ben-Yehoyada 2018). In terms of political discourse, Mazarese families with a history of migration to colonial Tunisia do not identify as a distinct community. While at least a dozen such families exist in the city, they are not significant actors in Mazara's vivid debate about the city's Mediterranean nature, nor about multicultural coexistence. They hail from different areas of Tunisia, and their experience of relationships with Tunisians in Tunisia is quite varied, as indeed are their opinions on contemporary Tunisian migration to Sicily (D'Arrigo 2006).

Direct references to colonial Tunisia do, however, appear in debates about multicultural coexistence in Mazara. As chapter 5 discusses in more detail, various Catholic actors in Mazara invoke the experience of coexistence in colonial Tunisia as an explanation for what they consider a unique Sicilian openness to diversity and as a model for coexistence in contemporary Europe. This mobilization of the past glosses over structural inequalities in colonial Tunisia and thus contributes to a broader depiction of Sicilians as intermediate borderland people, whose past or present position of relative privilege vis-à-vis Tunisians is left unexplored. Rather than seeking to prove these Catholic figures wrong, the analysis of colonial Tunisia articulated in this chapter suggests that deploying the model of colonial Tunisia in contemporary Sicily—or indeed elsewhere in Europe—risks reproducing the inequalities that characterized this space.

The depiction of colonial Tunisia presented in this chapter also provides a historically informed lens through which to analyze both everyday relations between Sicilians and Tunisians in Mazara and the debates about their coexistence. Understanding colonial Tunisia as a place of simultaneous proximity and familiarity between Sicilians and Tunisians, and of boundary-drawing between these populations, allows us to see similar processes at play in Mazara del Vallo. In other words, it alerts us to how sites of borderland coexistence may also be highly hierarchical and unequal spaces, and—on some occasions—sites in which precarious European subjects assert their own modernity through differentiation from "an even deeper South." In addition, understanding how the language of Mediterranean mixing was mobilized historically as part of a project to draw the different populations of colonial Tunisia together under the hegemony of French language and culture alerts us to how contemporary celebrations of Mediterranean interconnection and coexistence might create new symbolic hierarchies between Sicilians and Tunisians. The next three chapters explore these questions in more detail.

MEDITERRANEAN OR "NOT EUROPEAN ENOUGH"?

Drawing the Boundaries of Europe in Mazara del Vallo

A mere ninety nautical miles from the Tunisian coast, closer to Tunis than to Rome, Mazara del Vallo is known for being "the most Arab city in Italy." Between the ninth and eleventh centuries AD, under Arab rule over the island, this small town on the southwestern coast of Sicily was an important economic and political center. Today, Mazara's name is well known among commentators on migration as a unique example of successful integration. Differently from northern Italy, the story goes, in Mazara, Sicilians and Tunisians have long lived peacefully side by side, representing a model of borderland coexistence that could and should be replicated elsewhere in the country. Mazara has thus been featured in countless news articles, TV features, and academic studies aimed at uncovering the "secret" of this Mediterranean coexistence.

In reality, Mazara del Vallo's Tunisian community is not particularly sizable. Only about 10 percent of Mazara's 55,000 residents are Tunisian nationals—a proportion similar to the national average of resident foreign nationals and slightly lower than in industrial cities in the Italian North.[1] However, in a country that only began to experience large-scale labor immigration in the early 1990s, the city stands out for having one of the oldest resident migrant communities in Italy. Mazara's fishing fleet, the city's economic backbone, began to attract Tunisian labor migrants in the 1960s and soon grew to depend on their labor. Thus, over the past fifty years Mazara has been home to a small but stable community of working-class Tunisians.

Mazara's connections to Tunisia, however, go beyond its dependency on migrant labor. At the turn of the twentieth century, Trapani province, where

FIGURE 5.   Location of Mazara del Vallo. Source: Author.

Mazara is located, was a significant source of southward labor migrants to colonial Tunisia, some of whom returned to Mazara following decolonization. In addition, over the past fifty years Mazara has been embedded in a thick web of political and economic relationships with North Africa. Between the 1970s and the 1990s, the city's fishing fleet was engaged in a continuing low-intensity conflict with the Tunisian government over fishing rights, because some of the richest fishing grounds in the Mediterranean lie within Tunisian territorial waters. In addition, Mazara del Vallo is the landing site of the Algeria–Tunisia–Italy gas line, crucial to Italy's energy supplies (Ben-Yehoyada 2014). These connections engendered a long-standing cultural politics of Mediterraneanism in Mazara: the strategic celebration of the city's Arab heritage and cross-Mediterranean connections to create favorable geopolitical conditions for its economy.

Mazara's reputation led me to the city in early 2014, as the Mediterranean winter winds howled through its narrow streets, with a double mission in mind. First, I wanted to find out to what extent interactions between Sicilians and Tunisians in Mazara represented an example of what Michael Dear (2013) calls the "third nation" of the border—a space of mixing, hybridity, and cross-border interconnection that questions bounded notions of national identity. Could "coexistence" between Sicilians and Tunisians in this cosmopolitan Mediterranean borderland represent a successful model to contrast rising Islamophobia and racism elsewhere in Europe? Second, could Mazara's Mediterraneanist politics represent an effective political model to argue against nationalisms, to affirm commonalities with North Africa, and to call into question the fortification of the Mediterranean border? I found, however, that in the second decade of the twenty-first century, Mazara was living through a profound crisis.

Precarious Mediterraneanism

On the afternoon of March 6, 2014, Tunisians and Italians of Tunisian descent occupied more than half the seats of the conference hall of the municipality of Mazara del Vallo, and a buzz of excited conversations in Arabic and Italian filled the air. I had showed up to the event "Tunisia, Mare Nostrum: Face-to-Face," one of a series of public meetings with "migrant communities" organized throughout Italy by the Ministry of Labor and Social Policy and sponsored by the city—a typical example of local Mediterraneanist politics. The high Tunisian turnout at the meeting was unusual but not a coincidence. Activists of the Tunisian immigrant organization The Voice of the Tunisian Migrant/La Voce del Migrante Tunisino had spent weeks organizing the community. Citing the presence of representatives of the local and national government, the police, and the International Organization for Migration, they had pushed their compatriots to attend the event to voice their difficulties in accessing work, residency papers, and citizenship.

The event was, however, highly scripted. Following a series of short speeches by Italian authorities focused on Sicily's culture of hospitality, commonalities between the northern and southern shores of the Mediterranean, and the importance of the integration of migrants into Italian society, it was time for the voices from the Tunisian community. Ons, a woman of Tunisian descent in her mid-twenties who worked for the Italian union CGIL, took the floor: "I certainly appreciate that you created a program for integration. However, today I would like to start from article one of the Italian constitution: 'Italy is a republic founded on work.' . . . Now, to have work means to have a life, to have a salary—something that 80 percent of my community does not have! Of course, the crisis also affects Italians, but if an Italian cannot find work, he does not risk being displaced. We risk being deported!"

As the crowd murmured in approval, she continued, "In Mazara, all the seamen who arrived in the '70s and '80s are unemployed, or cannot access their pensions! Why? Because their employers never contributed to social security, or because they cannot become permanent residents. To become permanent residents, what do they need? A basic income that goes up every year! Does the minister ever put himself in our shoes?"

The facilitator smiled nervously, pushing Ons to wrap up. She finished, "To work on boats, immigrants need a residence permit, but to get a residence permit, they need a job. I don't know what they are supposed to do. We want the minister to tell us what we have to do, and to give us our rights!"

As Ons concluded her remarks, the audience became more animated, almost drowning out the musical interlude that followed her words. By the time a representative of the Ministry of Labor closed the meeting, many Tunisians had already left the room, disappointed at the lack of opportunities to intervene and frustrated by the lack of any—even evasive—answers to Ons's questions. Indeed, one of the representatives of the Ministry of Labor, a middle-aged man from northern Italy, pulled Ons aside right after the event to lecture her about the need for immigrants to integrate culturally before they made any sort of social or political demands.[2]

The tensions that exploded at the Tunisia, Mare Nostrum meeting were a common occurrence that year. Multiple events organized or sponsored by the municipality showcasing Mazara's Arab character and its model of integration were interrupted and contested by people of Tunisian descent. In the context of a widespread economic crisis that had given the fatal blow to the city's struggling fishing sector, livelihoods were precarious, and tensions were high. The 2008 Great Recession had resulted in regional unemployment rates soaring to more than 20 percent, and significant swaths of the population had been plunged into poverty. As Ons noted in her speech, Tunisian migrants were particularly vulnerable, because unemployment risked jeopardizing their immigration status. People of Tunisian descent who had acquired citizenship were also suffering; while they did not risk deportation, their stable legal status did not translate into the ability to find a job, receive fair compensation, or have their labor rights respected. In this context of widespread economic instability, Mazara's reputation as a Mediterranean cosmopolitan borderland had little meaning for Mazara's Tunisian community. To understand the causes of this limited buy-in to Mediterraneanist politics, we must explore in more depth how people of Tunisian descent experienced and explained their economic insecurity and political alienation.

Living the Crisis

Farah. The first time I entered Farah's house, a two-story building in Mazara's Casbah neighborhood, she struck me as relatively well-off. The entry hall, decorated with geometric ceramic tiles and potted plants, led up to a large, three-bedroom apartment. As I sat down to dinner one evening in her kitchen, together with her extended family, I noticed a postcard, written in Arabic, sent from a small town in the Italian Alps. It was from Farah's husband, temporarily working in northern Italy, where salaries and working conditions were considerably better than in Sicily. I would soon realize that my first impression of Farah's economic stability was inaccurate. Certainly, they did own their home—a difficult feat for people of Tunisian descent in Mazara. However, by early 2014 neither Farah nor her husband Ahmad were working full-time. Ahmad was only able to find work a few nights a week as a cook, while Farah employed a range of livelihood strategies, ranging from renting out rooms in her house, to caring for older Italians, to informally selling off-brand "made in Italy" clothing (bought in open-air markets, or in local sales) in Tunisia—a common backup livelihood strategy for people of Tunisian descent in Mazara. Farah's family's economic precariousness was reflected in daily household management choices, such as her reluctance to use any kind of heating despite outdoor temperatures dropping to 10 degrees Celsius. Adding to Farah's worries was her need to support two of her nephews, who had recently arrived in Italy while they waited for residency and work permits, which would allow them to move beyond Mazara to look for jobs. Both Farah and Ahmad nostalgically remembered their early years of immigration to Mazara, between the late 1980s and early 1990s, when work was abundant and their disposable income allowed them to visit the shopping center in nearby Castelvetrano, a habit they had been forced to abandon.

Despite their economic difficulties, Farah's and Ahmad's family was relatively privileged. Thanks to his lengthy residence in Italy and to his regular salary at the time of his application, Ahmad had been able to acquire Italian citizenship and to pass it to his underage children and, eventually, to his wife. Thus, Farah's family did not risk losing residency papers—a very real threat faced by many migrants in Italy as a consequence of their unemployment. Farah and Ahmed were also unusually politically active. Following the political opening created by the Tunisian revolution of early 2011, Farah had become engaged in both Sicilian and Tunisian electoral politics. During that same period, Farah and Ahmed had cofounded The Voice of the Tunisian Migrant. Despite their visibility and political leadership in Mazara, however, Farah and Ahmad would decide in early 2015 that there was no future for them and their family in Mazara, and leave the town for good to settle in France.

Hiba. Hiba had not attended the Tunisia, Mare Nostrum meeting. Her extended family shared many of the difficulties that had led members of the Tunisian community to fill the municipal conference room, but hardly anyone from her family showed up. To some extent, they had more immediate concerns on their minds. When I first walked into Hiba's ground-floor apartment, where she lived with her parents and the youngest of her four siblings, I was struck by its difference from Farah's home. While in Farah's house her preteen daughters would constantly shift the TV from Arabic to Italian and English channels, in Hiba's house the

TV and the majority of conversations were in Tunisian Arabic. Hiba's family, however, had longer roots in Mazara del Vallo. Her father was among the first generation of Tunisians to work in the town's fishing fleet, and he and Hiba's uncle had moved to Sicily in the late 1970s, when, as they would repeatedly point out, people could come and go easily, without visas. Hiba's father had emigrated to Mazara alone and shared accommodation with other men, as was the case for the majority of Tunisian migrants. Through his savings, he had been able to build a house in his hometown of Mahdia, on the central Tunisian coast, where one of his daughters currently lives with her family.

Hiba, her mother, and her siblings had initially remained in Mahdia, traveling back and forth to visit her father, but eventually they settled in Mazara, where they could access medical services unavailable in Tunisia. Since the 1990 immigration reform, resident foreign nationals had the same rights as Italian citizens in accessing medical care. This had allowed Hiba, who was born with a disability, to receive free medical care and a pension. By the time I met Hiba in 2014, however, she was not the only member of her family with a disability. Years of work at sea had rendered her father housebound, where he could breathe only with the aid of a cumbersome oxygen machine. Disability was a fate shared by many other Tunisian men who had worked on Mazara's fishing fleet.

Despite the modesty of their income, with the family of four depending entirely on two disability pensions, Hiba and her parents had managed to purchase their house with the assistance of the Catholic organization Caritas, which served as mediator with a local bank. The reliability of government-issued pensions had allowed the bank to approve their mortgage. Hiba's sister, who also lived in Mazara and who had a higher disposable income, had been unable to secure a similar mortgage because her husband was employed in the dwindling fishing sector, which left banks skeptical about the regularity and stability of their income. As I got to know Hiba's broader social circle, I realized that Tunisian families in Mazara were divided into two main groups. While all of them were struggling economically, those who had family members with some level of economic stability through disability pensions were content, like Hiba, to remain in Mazara. The others were looking for possibilities to move elsewhere in Europe—an endeavor that needed both economic and social capital to be successful.

Ons. Ons was well acquainted with stories such as those of Farah and Hiba. This was not only due to her professional work advocating for Tunisian migrants' labor rights within the Italian union CGIL, but also to her lived experience. Despite her father having worked in the Mazarese fishing fleet since the early 1970s, Ons's parents had never managed to buy a house in Mazara. For a long time, they were convinced they would return to Tunisia, where, thanks to her father's savings, they had bought a house in Mahdia in the early 1990s. The whole family rarely returned to Tunisia together, however, even for vacations, because the cost of tickets was too high. Meanwhile, the house served as a depot for used goods that Ons's father would bring from Italy to sell in Tunisian markets—an informal livelihood practice that the family used to supplement their income; the family of six otherwise relied on Ons's salary and her father's disability pension.

Ons's professional and personal experience had made her particularly skeptical of the city's Mediterraneanist politics and of attempts by the city government to market Mazara as a cosmopolitan borderland. She laughed when I asked her opinion on Mazara's reputation as an oasis of peaceful cross-cultural coexistence: "How can we talk about integration, if the basic situation is one of exploitation? Employers still see Tunisians as foreigners, as hungry Africans. A similar situation happens to me here in the union. Sometimes an Italian will come ask for help, and will ask me if I am Tunisian. Then they will ask to speak to someone else, because they think that an Italian will know the system better. One out of ten people reacts this way."

Ons's skepticism was also tied to her negative experience with local politics. As one of the more prominent people of Tunisian descent in Mazara, she had been invited a few years earlier by one of the left-wing parties to run in the local elections. However, neither she, nor other candidates of Tunisian descent who had run on the lists of other parties, had ended up winning a seat on the city council—in the list-based electoral system, their names were too far down to ever receive sufficient votes to be elected (Ben-Yehoyada 2011). Ons was resentful of the experience, because she suspected that she had been used to attract the Italo-Tunisian vote to a party that would then do little to address the material situation of the town's Tunisian population. Overall, the combination of these personal, professional, and political experiences had led Ons to be disillusioned with formal celebrations of Mazara as a haven of Mediterranean coexistence.[3]

The stories of Farah, Hiba, and Ons give us a window into the lived experiences of precariousness of people of Tunisian descent in Mazara in the early twenty-first century. Their class background, immigration trajectories, and economic precarity were typical of those of the rest of Mazara's largely working-class Tunisian community. In some respects, however, they were relatively privileged, since they had all managed to acquire citizenship or permanent residence and thus were able to access some level of state welfare, and—most importantly—they were protected against the threat of deportation. The situation of these three families—and of the community at large—had become particularly difficult following the 2008 recession. The seeds of their precariousness, however, were much older, the product of the combination of immigration legislation, the structural incorporation of migrants at the bottom of the labor market since the 1970s, and Sicily's own subordinate incorporation within the Italian and European economy. Let us explore this history in more detail.

Sicily, Land of Work: 1970s–1990s

In the 1960s, just as southern Italians were migrating in large numbers to search for industrial work in northern Italy and in the northwestern European heartland, the first Tunisian migrant workers began to arrive in Sicily to work seasonally in fishing and agriculture. This northward migration grew in the mid-1970s, when France and Germany—countries that had traditionally absorbed Tunisian migration (Hibou et al. 2011)—suspended the worker-recruitment programs that had attracted large numbers of labor migrants after World War II (Daly 2001). This change in policy rerouted Tunisian migration through Italy, which at the time did not require visas from Tunisian nationals. In this context, entering Italy as a tourist and saving money by working informally in the Sicilian agricultural sector represented a stepping stone for migrants to eventually move north to another European country (Cole and Booth 2007; Daly 2001). Many of the older generation of Tunisian labor migrants in Mazara nostalgically remembered a time in which they could easily travel to Italy with no hassle and regularly visit their families in Tunisia. Tunisians worked in agriculture throughout Sicily, particularly in the town of Vittoria in Ragusa province. In Mazara, Tunisian migrants instead were primarily employed in the fishing sector, which was booming thanks, in part, to the government's regional development funds for the South (Ben-Yehoyada 2018).

If a lack of immigration legislation made entrance into Italy easy, it also placed migrants in a vulnerable condition with regard to labor rights and medical care. These aspects became the object of a campaign by Agostino Spataro, a Sicilian Communist deputy to the Italian national parliament, who also pointed out how under-the-table employment of migrant labor was undermining hard-fought wage gains in southern Italian agriculture (Spataro 1980). In general terms, however, labor competition between migrant workers and Italians was not a highly politicized theme, because the commonsense understanding was that migrant workers were doing jobs that the children of Italy's postwar economic boom were no longer willing to do (Cole 1997). This analysis emerges clearly in a 1980 article published by the regional center-right-wing newspaper *Giornale di Sicilia*: "Sicily, land of work. It sounds like a fairy-tale. . . . Instead, it is the reality of thousands of 'refugees' coming from Third World countries . . . thirty-three thousand workers in a land that has . . .180,000 unemployed. . . . Will Sicily also see a 'war between the poor'? . . . In fact, immigrants take up positions left vacant by the 'intellectual unemployment' of youth who do not intend to suppress years of study and aspirations by going to work in the fields" (Mignosi 1980, 8).

In the early 1980s, the Italian government began to introduce immigration legislation. In 1981, Italy ratified the International Labor Organization convention 143/1975, which established the principle of equal treatment between citizens and noncitizens in the workplace (Mingione and Quassoli 2000). This ratification was codified in Law 943/1986, Italy's first legislation on migrant labor. This law, combined with a series of immigration amnesties in the 1980s, allowed many undocumented migrants who had been working in Sicily to obtain residency papers and thus to search for more regular employment in northern Italian industry (Mingione and Quassoli 2000).

By 1990, when Italy introduced its first comprehensive immigration legislation and a visa requirement for Tunisian nationals entering Italy, a clear regional pattern of employment for Tunisian migrants had emerged. With the exception of Mazara del Vallo's fishing fleet, in southern Italy Tunisian migrants were primarily employed in the agricultural sector, largely off the books (Cole and Booth 2007; Daly 2001). Northern Italy, however, offered employment in the small industries of the "Third Italy"—better-paying work on an official contract, which consequently tended to employ migrants with legal residency status. A common immigration trajectory was thus to arrive in southern Italy, work in agriculture to save money and wait for an immigration amnesty, and then head north (Daly 2001). These internal trajectories would, however, be significantly affected by the 2008 economic crisis and its aftershocks, which had dramatic effects on employment conditions for both migrant workers and citizens in Italy and across the southern Mediterranean (Cabot 2016; Carney 2021; Knight and Stewart 2016).

Migrant labor in Italy was largely employed in the informal economy. However, this type of labor arrangement applied not only to migrant workers. Some estimates consider informal labor to have constituted up to 50 percent of employment in southern Italy in the early 1990s, particularly in agriculture, care services, and small-scale family industries (Meldolesi 1998). In northern Italy, in turn, the success of small-scale family industries of the Third Italy was also based on the exploitation of low-cost, flexible and—in some cases—informal labor (Mingione and Quassoli 2000). Thus, the case of Italy resonates with Castles's (2011) analysis of how, throughout the Global North, the increasing employment of migrant labor was a response to a post-Fordist restructuring of labor markets that increased the demand for flexible labor. Throughout different contexts, the threat of deportation (Casas-Cortes et al. 2015), as well as differential access to labor protection and citizenship rights (Mezzadra and Neilson 2013; Papadopoulos and Tsianos 2013), produced migrant workers as a particularly vulnerable and easily exploitable category. More generally, the 1990s also corresponded to a general moment of increased precariousness of working conditions throughout Italy and the start of a gradual trend of impoverishment of the country that continues to the present (Carney 2021).

If migrant workers shared informal employment conditions with Italian nationals, the implications of this type of work on their long-term livelihood prospects were substantially different. The Bossi-Fini immigration law of 2002 connected grant of residency papers to a stable labor contract—a requirement that was at odds with the precarious, flexible, and short-term nature of migrant labor (Mingione and Quassoli 2000; Triandafyllidou and Ambrosini 2011) and consequently resulted in a constant threat of becoming undocumented. At the same time, decades of informal work, as well as undocumented status, would substantially affect Tunisian migrants' livelihood options in the early twenty-first century.

On (Not) Getting by on the Margins of Europe: The Early 2000s

By the early years of the twenty-first century, both sectors of traditional employment of people of Tunisian descent in Mazara—fishing and agriculture—were undergoing structural changes that would substantially affect their employment and earning prospects. Starting in the mid-1990s, national subsidies that supported the fishing sector had been cut as part of a broader reorganization of Italian regional development programs to prepare for the country's entrance into the European Community (Gualini 2004; Schneider 1998). The consequent rise in operating costs had led to the crisis of smaller businesses, the consolidation of the sector, and a drop in employment. This trend would intensify a few years later as a consequence of the European Union's 2002 Common Fishing Policy, which provided financial incentives for the scrapping of fishing vessels (Ben-Yehoyada et al. 2016). The agricultural sector was also transforming. Since the early 2000s, the European Common Agricultural Policy had pushed for specialization, leading some areas of Sicily to focus on providing produce in the offseason for northern markets. The small-scale family businesses that characterized large sectors of southern Italian agriculture had been increasingly incorporated into large distribution networks through production contracts. By pitting small farmers against each other, this type of distribution network created a downward pressure on prices, which resulted throughout the Italian South in the informal employment of migrant workers at wages well under the nationally regulated agricultural pay scale (Colloca and Corrado 2013; Mingione and Quassoli 2000; Triandafyllidou and Ambrosini 2011)—a classic strategy of dominating labor through the border and visa regime (Castles 2011; Meldolesi 1998; Papadopoulos and Tsianos 2013).

The combination of these structural transformations on the one hand, and histories of informal labor and undocumented migration on the other hand, made the situation of people of Tunisian descent particularly vulnerable by the 2010s. In particular, Mazara's Tunisian community had three main concerns: precarious labor conditions, difficulties acquiring immigration papers and Italian citizenship, and obstacles to accessing pensions. With regard to employment, finding a "good job" beyond fishing and agriculture had always been difficult for people of Tunisian descent. However, by the 2010s, finding any type of employment had become a challenge. One of Hiba's close friends, Imen—a twenty-eight-year-old woman of Tunisian descent who had been born and raised in Mazara—explained this dynamic clearly: "Before, when a new Tunisian arrived to Mazara, employers would go to his house to look for him to offer him a job . . . but now, if you go to the entrance of the old city at eight in the morning you will see a crowd of people looking for work . . . maybe they will get hired for the day, or maybe they will meet someone who will help them find a job, but at the end of the day all the men who hang out there are unemployed."[4]

In a context of reduced employment opportunities, Tunisian workers often found themselves in competition with both Italian workers and newer migrants. The former was mainly the case in the fishing sector, where some Tunisian workers would even pay Italian seamen to give up their precedence and allow Tunisians to embark in their place. Working at sea not only guaranteed a meager income but was also one of the few ways to obtain the regular work contract necessary for a residence permit. Competition with other migrants was particularly acute in agriculture, where both sub-Saharan African and Eastern European workers were regularly employed to reduce the cost of labor (Piro 2014).[5] In addition, the ranks of Tunisian workers had increased following the 2008 recession, as migrant workers who had lost jobs in the North had moved to southern Italy, where the cost of living was lower, to look for informal work in agriculture (Colloca and Corrado 2013; De Luca 2014; Foderà and Pipitone 2016; Piro 2014).

The extent of competition for jobs, and their informal nature, meant that demanding any type of labor rights—from an adequate salary to the full payment of social security benefits—was extremely difficult. Imen's husband, Rami, who was born and raised in Tunisia and had obtained his Italian residency papers through marriage, explained this dynamic, complaining about his ill treatment in Mazara's labor market:

> When you have a problem . . . you can go to the union . . . but when you go to your employer to demand your rights, you become someone

who is "not good." . . . I injured my back for six months. In theory, the Italian state should give you compensation. But when I went to submit the paperwork, I found out that my employer had never paid into the national insurance program. I could have complained, but I didn't because . . . you never know. You see, if you go ask for a job with your seamen's booklet, they can see who you worked for before. So they will call the person and ask, "Why did he only work with you for a year," for example. "What is his character like?" and your old boss might answer, "He is a hard worker, but he will make complaints." So then the new guy will say, "I am sorry, I don't have work for you."[6]

When I recounted this story to Ons, the employee of the CGIL union whom we previously met, she was not surprised, as this dynamic was quite common in Mazara's fishing fleet.

Unemployment, underemployment, and employment in the informal sector made it difficult for Tunisian migrants to acquire immigration papers, permanent residency, and citizenship. In a country that privileges citizenship by descent over birth and residency on national soil, naturalization is an arduous process. At present, one is not a citizen by virtue of being born in Italy. Instead, children of foreign nationals are allowed to apply for citizenship when they turn eighteen, provided they were born in Italy, had resided there continuously, and at least one of their parents had legal residency papers and was officially registered in an Italian municipality at the time of their birth. These legal requirements created considerable barriers for Tunisian Mazarese youth in accessing citizenship, because some had undocumented parents at the time of their birth and it was common for them to have lived in both Italy and Tunisia as children. Alternatively, one can apply for citizenship after ten years of residency in Italy, regardless of place of birth. This, however, is contingent on a personal annual income of approximately 8,500 euros—a number that increases according to family members (Prefettura di Verona and CIR Rifugiati 2023). Access to permanent residency is also income-dependent, although the minimum income is slightly lower, at approximately 5,800 euros.[7] These income levels, and the requirement that they must be formally documented in regular contracts, continued to represent a serious obstacle for Tunisian families in Mazara, particularly the larger ones. Many long-term Tunisian migrants in Mazara, who often had resided there since the 1970s, were still reliant on annual or biannual residency permits in the early years of the twenty-first century. These residency permits were in turn contingent on employment status. In this context, the specter of unemployment loomed large, because it endangered not only Tunisian migrants' livelihoods but their legal status as well.

This situation created a flourishing black market for labor contracts—yet another burden on Tunisian migrants' precarious incomes. Sometimes migrant workers would reach an agreement with their existing employers, with whom they worked informally, to write them a contract in line with regulations so that they could acquire or renew residency permits. The worker would then also pay the arrears of social security payments that the employer owed the state. In other cases, both the job itself and the employer were fictitious. In rural areas, Tunisian *caporali* (illicit recruiters of day laborers who served as middlemen between employers and workers) often sold these contracts. In the city, these counterfeit contracts were generally crafted by the official "voices" of the Tunisian community—individuals who were well connected to the municipality and inserted into local political relations of patronage. This type of illicit contract market was not unique to Mazara. The contradiction between the Bossi-Fini law's requirement of formal and regular employment to get a work permit, and the flexible and informal nature of migrant employment, created a similar black market throughout Italy (Avallone 2017; De Luca 2014; Perrotta 2014b; Triandafyllidou and Ambrosini 2011).

Histories of informal labor and difficulty in acquiring citizenship and permanent residency had substantial repercussions on the third area of concern for people of Tunisian descent in Sicily: access to pensions. As Hiba's and Ons's stories showed, in a precarious labor market, access to state-backed pensions represented a highly coveted source of regular income that made possible long-term saving strategies, such as buying a house. Accessing these pensions was not simple, however. Regardless of their contribution to social security, Italian citizens and permanent residents over the age of sixty-five have ensured access to a basic old-age pension. In a national context characterized by high levels of informal labor, this allows broad sectors of the population, regardless of their history of contribution to social security, to have access to a "social check" of approximately 450 euros per month. For nonnationals who are not permanent residents, access to retirement benefits depends on having at least twenty years of social security payments.[8] The informal nature of much migrant labor has meant that many of Mazara's Tunisian workers, despite having lived and worked in Italy since the 1970s, did not have sufficient years of contribution to Italy's INPS social security system to get a pension.

Access to retirement benefits presented additional problems if the retiree, or his family, had returned to Tunisia. Thanks to a 1987 bilateral accord, Tunisian nationals who had worked in Italy and had paid into Italian social security should have been able to access retirement benefits through the Tunisian Institute for Social Security. In practice, however, accessing these benefits without professional support was arduous, creating a need for mediators between Tunisian migrant workers and Italian state bureaucracy. Unions and Catholic service organizations provided this service for free, but for-profit agencies and individuals charged a fee—yet another burden for people of Tunisian descent.[9]

Overall, the difficulties experienced by people of Tunisian descent in employment, labor rights, and welfare are not surprising, but are a typical consequence of their *differential inclusion* into Italy. This concept, coined by Sandro Mezzadra and Brett Neilson (2013), refers to how migrants are fully incorporated and indeed essential to some areas of national life—such as the labor market—while being excluded from others, such as political, social, and economic rights. Thus, their immigration status does not exclude them from the nation-state, even if they are undocumented, but incorporates them in a subordinate manner. This was clearly visible in the experience of Tunisian migrants in Mazara, caught in a vicious cycle in which their immigration status made them highly vulnerable to exploitation and limited their access to welfare, while their meager wages and informal employment made access to citizenship or permanent residency difficult.

Differential inclusion into Italy, however, does not fully explain Tunisians' economic precariousness in Mazara. They were suffering not only from their own marginality but also from the economic marginalization of Sicily itself—a region with widespread informal employment (Meldolesi 1998) and high unemployment rates (18.6 percent in 2012)—within Italy.[10] This meant that even people of Tunisian descent who had acquired Italian citizenship or permanent residency—people like Farah, Hiba, and Ons—had highly precarious livelihoods. Italian youth of Tunisian descent saw limited prospects in Mazara, where getting an education was hardly a ticket to social mobility, but simply placed them in the same situation of "intellectual unemployment" of Sicilian youth that had been decried by *Giornale di Sicilia* in the 1980s (Mignosi 1980, 8). This was exacerbated by the fact that youth of Tunisian descent could not rely on financial support from extended family or on the informal networks that could help them find employment, which Italian Sicilian youth used. Permanent residents had even more limited opportunities because they were formally excluded from applying for public-sector jobs—a coveted source of employment in Sicily for its regular employment and full benefits (Farinella 2013). In essence, rather than a guarantee of a "good life," citizenship and permanent residence simply protected them from deportation and allowed them access to the livelihood strategies that Sicilians had long depended on: state welfare and emigration.

Both these strategies had their pitfalls. Certainly, old-age and disability pensions did represent a stable form of income, underpinning long-term saving strategies such as buying a house. However, access to this source of income was contingent on the destruction of Tunisian bodies. Recipients of disability pensions were generally middle-aged men who had developed chronic health problems due to their strenuous work on fishing boats. Their mobility was generally reduced, and some were housebound and dependent on an oxygen tank to survive. In the ten years since I carried out this research, both Hiba's and Ons's fathers, who had received these pensions, passed away in their late fifties and early sixties.

Emigration was highly desirable and the preferred livelihood strategy for youth of Tunisian descent who had the means to do so, as indeed it was for their Sicilian counterparts. Aziz, a prominent spokesperson for Mazara's Tunisian community in his late twenties who had also served on the municipal council, spelled out this dynamic clearly:

> Whenever I see people who have citizenship, I tell them: go on, leave! What the hell are you going to do here? Over the last five years "second generations" have all been going to Germany and France. There is work over there. I always tell them, you guys, you have Italian citizenship, take advantage of it! No constraints, no residency permits, nothing! Just go! Staying here makes no sense, there are no opportunities, not even for the children of Italians. So what future are you, the child of a fisherman, who don't have any connections, going to have?[11]

It was not, however, a guaranteed strategy for economic success, because it depended on having sufficient savings and connections elsewhere in Europe to be able to move there and look for a job. Many Mazarese youth failed in their attempt to find work in Germany and France; they ran out of money before finding a job and were obliged to return to Mazara's informal and highly exploitative labor market—a reality far from the aspirations for a better life for which people of Tunisian descent had originally migrated to Sicily.

Faced with a situation of economic precariousness coupled with relative immobility, one might imagine that people of Tunisian descent would mobilize to demand better working conditions, changes to immigration law, or indeed increased services from the municipality to buffer their economic precariousness. Indeed, in many parts of southern Europe, the fallout of post-2008 austerity policies engendered new forms of solidarity between migrant workers and increasingly precarious European subjects (Arampatzi 2017; Cabot 2016; Mitchell and Sparke 2018). However, with the exception of a small group of middle-class people of Tunisian descent that will be discussed in more detail in chapter 4, there was little mass mobilization in Mazara. To understand why that was the case, it is necessary to examine in more detail how people of Tunisian descent made sense of their economic precariousness.

Mediterranean or Not Italian Enough?

In the evening after the Tunisia, Mare Nostrum event that opened this chapter, I sat around the dinner table with Farah, her husband, Ahmad, and their eldest daughter. Their dissatisfaction was palpable, for they sensed that they had been used to create an audience for the event by Italian public officials who were not in fact sympathetic to their needs. "The ministry and the municipality are happy," exclaimed Ahmad. "A lot of people showed up. They made their video. For them it was a success! But what about all the people who came? No one listened to them."

"Yes," agreed Farah. "All this organizing work, and nothing came of it. We won't be able to convince people to show up again."[12] As Farah's words suggest, it was quite rare for people of Tunisian descent in Mazara to participate in the city's Mediterraneanist politics. They hardly ever showed up at public events and almost never articulated a collective voice. To a large extent, this working-class community was dealing with more pressing needs, such as ensuring their livelihood, obtaining and maintaining housing, and caring for their children. They saw little benefit in participating in public and political events that they thought would do little to address their daily material needs, and they had limited investment in a vision of a Mediterranean borderland that had little in reality to offer them in terms of a secure life and livelihood.

Indeed, beyond their disillusion with Mediterraneanist politics, people of Tunisian descent in Mazara also had little appreciation for Mazara's nature as an "in-between" space between North Africa and Europe. Certainly, they did appreciate the relative lack of racial microaggressions in Mazara, and—with the exception of a few more politicized members of the community—it was quite rare for people of Tunisian descent to attribute their difficult lives and livelihoods to racism. Some even asserted that their difficulties in accessing employment or welfare in comparison with Italians were normal, feeling that Italy had to take care of "its own" people before taking care of foreigners. At the same time, however, they decried their constant struggle in obtaining decent working conditions and in their difficult interactions with bureaucracy. Farah's husband, Ahmad, commented on this paradox when recounting his experience in living and working in northern and in southern Italy:

> In Sicily there is no real racism. In the North there are some cafés where the baristas won't even look at you in the face while they serve you coffee. When I was living there, I started to avoid a lot of places for that reason—I would only spend time in places where other immigrants hung out. But at the end of the day, up there they give you your rights. At the municipality, if you have the right to something they will give it to you. In Sicily everyone takes advantage of you![13]

Rather than a consequence of racism, many people of Tunisian descent attributed their precarious lives and livelihoods precisely to Sicily's "in-between" positioning between North Africa and Europe. In other words, if they associated Italy or Europe with access to good jobs, regular salaries, and full labor rights, then Sicily—which could not guarantee economic well-being—was "backward" and not fully Italian and European. In this sense, they inadvertently rearticulated tropes circulating at the national and EU level that blamed both Sicily's economic crisis and the limits of the island's migrant reception system on its alleged backwardness and inefficiency—a framework of analysis that willfully ignores broader structural factors, such as limited national funding for public administration (Carney 2021). Indeed, tropes of Sicily's deficient Italianness emerged quite often among people of Tunisian descent beyond Mazara as well. In interviews I carried out in Tunisia, men with a wide range of experiences of migration to Italy almost always mentioned Sicily's "backwardness." For instance, Mehdi, a Tunisian employee of the CGIL union who had returned to his homeland after twenty years in Italy to run the union's Tunis office, reflected on his experience:

> I arrived to Agrigento [Sicily], where I found work in the countryside with a farmer. The work in the fields was tough . . . I realized it was time to move on. . . . The farmer asked me where I wanted to go, and I answered "to the North." Very surprised, he warned me: "Be careful, they are racist there, not like us Sicilians!" . . . My journey ended in Modena [Emilia Romagna]. . . . I called my mother and told her that I had arrived in Italy. She was alarmed. "Where were you before? Weren't you already in Italy?" I reassured her immediately: "I was . . . but this is a very different Italy from where I was before!"[14]

Khaled and Majd, two middle-aged Tunisian men who had returned to their native Mahdia after multiple decades of work in different parts of Italy, had a similar analysis of their different experiences in the Italian North and South, and on the causes of their high levels of exploitation in Sicily:

> KHALED: To find work in Sicily, you used to wait around in a specific area until someone would come tell you that there was a job. In the North you just go put your name in the labor office, but in Sicily that doesn't exist! There are a lot of differences between northern and southern Italy in the way they treat you. Sicily is harder. In the North you get your rights, in Sicily, no!
>
> MAJD: In Sicily they are like Arabs. Marocchini! [Laughs] They don't care![15]

Marocchini (literally, *Moroccans*) is widely used in northern Italy as a deprecatory term to refer to southern Italians. In this context, Majd was making a further play on the use of the word by using it to argue that Sicily's informal labor market and lack of labor rights made it similar to an Arab country, and thus definitely not Italy or Europe.[16]

As these interviews show, disillusion with Sicily's "Mediterranean" nature among people of Tunisian descent can largely be explained by the limited benefits it provides them. Receiving no tangible perks from Sicilian politicians gesturing to the island's Arab past or to a multicultural Mediterranean present, most people of Tunisian descent have simply experienced Sicily as a land of exploitative labor conditions and Byzantine bureaucracy. However, the fact that they interpreted this as proof of the island's "backwardness" points to the broader hegemony of long-standing tropes about the lack of Europeanness of the Italian South (Davis 1998; Moe 2002). These tropes, discussed in chapter 1, date back to the decades following Italian unification, when national scholarly debates about developmental differences between North and South put forward theories of uneven development based on theories of racial difference (Gibson 1998) or social structure (Moe 2002). These theories ignored both broader national economic policies that had historically disadvantaged the country's export-oriented southern regions (Gramsci 1971) and the great diversity in social and economic structure between different areas of the South, hardly reducible to a common condition of "backwardness" (Lupo 2015). Persisting in both scholarship and popular culture well into the twenty-first century, this framework reacquired visibility at the national level in the aftermath of the 2008 financial crisis and the surge in undocumented cross-Mediterranean migration, as the national government accused Sicilian regional and local authorities of ineptness in managing this double crisis (Carney 2021). Generally, these narratives were circulated by intellectuals and politicians external to Sicily, or of Sicilian descent but long settled elsewhere. However, the hegemony of these tropes was strong enough that subjects such as Tunisian migrant workers, whose own belonging in Italy was being questioned through a tightening of immigration legislation, still reified the notion that the island was imperfectly Italian and European—and thus in need of "modernization and civilization" (Davis 1998; Moe 2002). Far from singling out Sicily, this was part of their broader framework of analysis of difference between "Europe" and Tunisia, which did not generally invoke historical or structural factors to explain differences in opportunity between the two contexts. Although in Tunisia after the 2011 revolution various social movements were beginning to invoke these questions to talk about internal developmental divides (Salman 2017), this framework had not made its way into commonsense understandings of uneven development in Mazara's Tunisian community.

In Mazara, however, some people of Tunisian descent were ready to mobilize politically through the language of Mediterraneanism. Since the early years of the twenty-first century, a small group of educated Tunisians had become visible in the town's political sphere. Some were middle-class figures who had arrived in Mazara from Tunis to provide services to the community. They were teachers at Mazara del Vallo's Tunisian school, employees in migrant-service organizations, or personnel of the Tunisian consulate. Others emerged out of the ranks of Mazara's working-class immigrant community. Often referred to in Italy as the "second generation," these were children of immigrants, born or reared in Mazara. They were invested in Mazara not as an abstract Mediterranean borderland but as their home. This group of visible and educated people of Tunisian descent engaged with the municipality's Mediterraneanist politics and adopted it to pursue their interests: to enter into relations of patronage with prominent political figures in Mazara or to take advantage of it as a political opening to demand rights and respect. The next chapter will address these dynamics in more detail.

MEDITERRANEAN REDEVELOPMENTS
"Ethnic Packaging" and Contested Urban Space

On December 13, 2013, via Bagno, a sleepy old street at the heart of Mazara del Vallo's "Casbah," saw an unusual bustle of activity. On an ordinary day, the street would mainly be populated by Tunisian men who congregated around a dimly lit coffeehouse, its only operating business. The majority of via Bagno's buildings were boarded up, and the street was generally avoided by local passersby, who preferred taking the parallel via Porta Palermo, considered less dangerous, or avoiding the historic core of the city altogether. That day, however, was different. A well-dressed delegation of a dozen government authorities, headed by the mayor, the Tunisian ambassador to Italy, and the Tunisian consul in Palermo, marched through the streets of the town's old center, surrounded by a thick array of policemen. About halfway up via Bagno, the delegation came to a halt in front of a recently renovated building. Near the cut-stone decorations of its doorframe, and in front of the bilingual Arabic and Italian sign that read "Daar Tunis–Casa Tunisia," the mayor turned to face the journalists:

> Casa Tunisia is a source of great pride for our administration! We have given a space to the Tunisian community, here not only to work but also to participate in our community's social life. We have the ambition to see Tunisians organize conferences, creating the conditions for dialogue not only on cultural, but also economic topics. Casa Tunisia will also be a place in which Sicilians will be able to participate in the daily life of the Medina and of the Casbah. My hope is that this new artifact

will be a starting point to relaunch our historic center, and the city of Mazara.

The Tunisian ambassador to Rome followed:

> Mazara del Vallo is well known for being a city that welcomes the Tunisian community, and we are grateful to the mayor for this beautiful and generous initiative. This is not a surprise in a region like Sicily, where there was a historic Arab presence, so let us work together to promote economic and commercial initiatives, and give more visibility to this region of the Mediterranean, contributing to peace and solidarity.

As the mayor reached for the scissors to cut through the inaugural blue ribbon strung across the building's door, Farah, one of the founding members of Voice of the Tunisian Migrant, pushed through the police cordon surrounding the Italian and Tunisian authorities. "Why are you pushing me back?" she challenged an officer, moving him to the side. "You are inaugurating this center without letting Tunisians know!" As the head of the local police and a couple of employees of the municipality attempted to quiet her, Farah continued, "We are in a democratic country; we have the right to speak!" The mayor turned toward her with a look of rage in his eyes. "No! You cannot speak now," he yelled. "You can speak when I say so!" Turning his back on her, he cut through the ribbon as the other members of the delegation clapped nervously, attempting to ignore the interruption. But Farah would not desist. Following the delegation into the building, she continued, switching to Tunisian Arabic: "No Tunisians were invited! And the Tunisian community in Mazara del Vallo has 3,000 Tunisians. This is an insult to all of us!" As the mayor and the Tunisian ambassador shuttled over to a corner to talk to the press, Farah turned to the Tunisian consul in Palermo: "You told us, 'I will let you participate, I will give you space.' We spoke to you in Trapani and you said, 'Since you have an association, I will let you participate.' What happened to your promises?"[1]

The Paradoxes of Mediterraneanist Recognition

The disruption of the opening of Mazara's Casa Tunisia raised a similar paradox to the contested Tunisia, Mare Nostrum event described in the previous chapter. It was yet another public event that formally recognized the presence and contributions of people of Tunisian descent to Mazara's economic and cultural life, while being contested by members of the Tunisian community. When Tunisian activists interrupted the events, they regularly invoked what they saw as the hypocrisy of local and national authorities, who celebrated the town's Mediterranean multiculturalism and its connections to North Africa while ignoring the pressing material needs of its Tunisian community, suffering from the double pressure of economic and legal precariousness. These problems were not new to the early part of the century. While the post-2008 economic recession had certainly exacerbated poverty within Mazara's Tunisian community, people of Tunisian descent had long lived in a situation of social and economic marginality within the town, as the previous chapter has shown. At the same time, Mazara del Vallo's local authorities had a long history of embracing Mediterraneanist rhetoric to protect the city's fishing sector, which was highly dependent on friendly relations with Tunisian authorities. These past celebrations of cross-Mediterranean connections had also paid little attention to Mazara's Tunisian community. If the paradox of simultaneously celebrating Mazara's Mediterranean nature and sidelining its Tunisian community was long-standing, why did people of Tunisian descent only begin to protest in the first decade of the century?

To answer this question, this chapter uses the lens of the built environment of the Casbah neighborhood, where Casa Tunisia was located, to analyze the effect of Mediterraneanist rebranding on the visibility, racialization, and political voice of the city's Tunisian community. This central neighborhood in the old city of Mazara del Vallo is highly emblematic of the city's Arab past, its current cross-Mediterranean connections, and its Tunisian community. With an urban structure that dates back to the ninth-century Arab conquest of Sicily, in the 1980s the Casbah was transformed from a working-class Sicilian neighborhood to a home for the majority of the city's Tunisian community. In this period, the neighborhood was in a state of physical disrepair and had the reputation of being a dangerous area. Between 2000 and 2015, however, the neighborhood became the target of an urban rebranding operation, with the municipality renovating the Casbah to showcase the city's Arab past and its current pan-Mediterranean diversity. The neighborhood was also the stage for a series of public events celebrating the city's Tunisian community and its long history of cross-Mediterranean relations—part of a broader effort to market Mazara del Vallo as a cosmopolitan Mediterranean borderland. Thus, the Casbah neighborhood represents an ideal lens through which to analyze the relationship between the municipality's changing rhetoric of Mediterraneanism and the racialization of the town's Tunisian community in the context of the changing economic fortunes of the town. The next sections trace the neighborhood's transformations from the 1960s to the mid-2020s, as a lens both into the changing political economy of the city and into shifts in the Mazarese public debate on Tunisian migration and cross-Mediterranean relations.

Everyday Conviviality in a Sicilian "Islamic Neighborhood"

Most mornings and late afternoons, if the weather is not too hot, groups of men congregate around Porta Palermo, a gate in the ancient Norman wall surrounding the city center that marks the northern entrance to the Casbah. Elderly Sicilian men sit on benches under the old gateway, while younger Tunisian men lean against the wall across the street, at the convergence of the two main roads that lead to the interior of the Casbah.[2] If you follow via Porta Palermo to the left, past the halal butcher and the Tunisian vegetable shop, two or three clothing and antique shops, and a Tunisian restaurant, you reach the well-off part of the old city center, via Garibaldi with its lively pub scene, the old Jesuit convent, the city hall, and the Mediterranean seafront. The other main artery, via Bagno, has no shops, only boarded-up residential buildings interrupted by a few well-restored houses. A series of alleyways, too narrow for a car to pass through, branch off these main arteries. Some of them are in a decrepit state, and their buildings have signs warning of their potential collapse. Others are well lighted and decorated with ceramic tiles and ornamental plants. In the early hours of the afternoon and on winter nights, these alleyways are semi-deserted, with the exception of the occasional passerby. On summer nights, they transform into a lively outdoor living room. While these evening social circles are separated by language and by background, many of the Sicilian and Tunisian families know each other well. Some are coworkers in the city's fishing fleet. Others have well-consolidated neighborly relations and exchange favors, such as taking care of each other's houses when they are out of town. However, these daily relations between Sicilians and Tunisians exist alongside the invisible barriers traced through different use of urban space and are absent from public discussions about the Casbah, which represent it as a coherent whole: a stand-in for Tunisianness that can either be accepted as an integral part of the city—or completely rejected.

According to a study by the University of Palermo, the neighborhood's Arab origins are still visible in its "Islamic structure": narrow alleyways that turn off into closed courtyards (Buscarino et al. 1980). In the 1960s and 1970s, these courtyards were hubs of everyday neighborhood life of working-class Sicilians who inhabited the neighborhood: communal areas used both as a social space and for domestic tasks, such as collective clothes washing. Calogero, a sixty-year-old lifelong Italian resident of the area who sells fish in the marina, remembers these days well. Over a cup of coffee in the living room of his restored family house in the Casbah, he recounted this history to me: "Only in this courtyard there were seven families . . . too many people. Each family had four, five, six

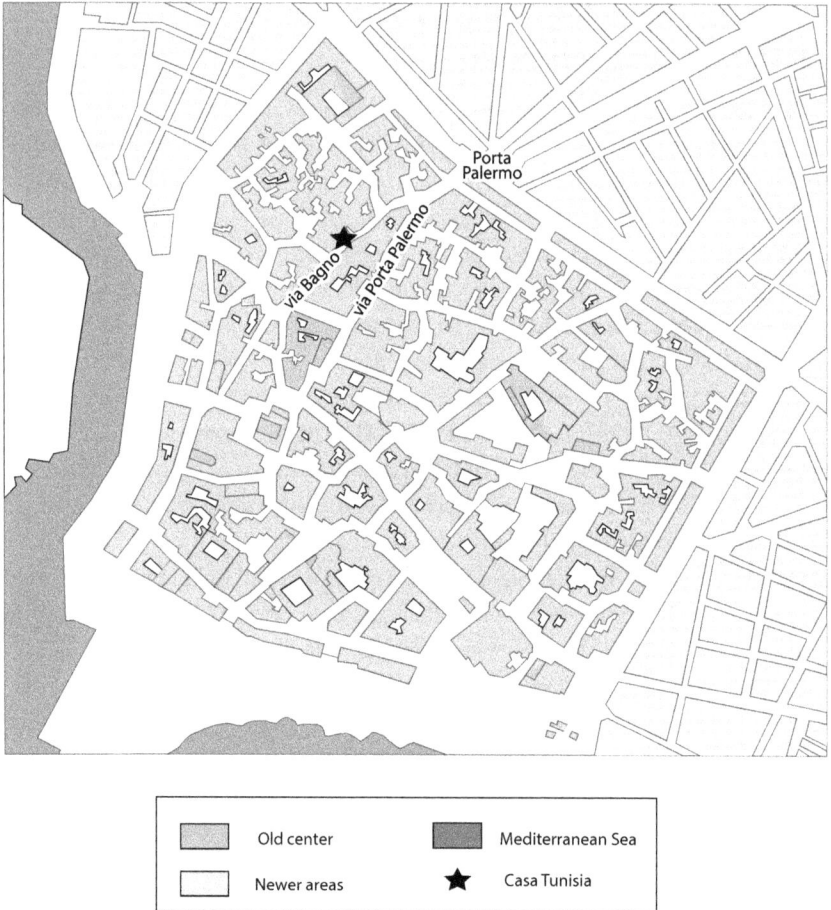

FIGURE 6.   Map of Mazara del Vallo's Casbah. Source: Author.

children . . . everyone here was a fisherman or a farmer. In the center of the courtyard there were stone basins to wash clothes, back then no one had running water at home. Some people had donkeys . . . old people used to tell stories, so in the evening we used to all get together."[3]

Business owners have similar memories of familiarity and safety in the old center. In informal conversations about the area's past, shopkeepers along Porta Palermo would often evoke tropes of small-town safety and sociability: "Life was good, we did well commercially! Children used to go to school without their parents! Via Porta Palermo was active, bustling, awake by eight in the morning. There was a pharmacy, clothing shops. Children basically lived in the street, they would only go home to sleep."[4]

Despite the centrality of the area's "Islamic structure" to everyday life in the neighborhood, the term *Casbah* was almost never used to refer to the area. Most long-term inhabitants of the area do not remember the term from their childhood. Calogero, for instance, has no memories of this term. "I don't know if it was called the Casbah in the old days," he pondered, when I asked him about the origin of the name. "I can tell you that I don't remember it. I never heard my mom say it either. I am sure they put this name later."[5] While the term *Casbah* does occasionally appear in newspaper articles of the mid-1970s, its use was only occasional and alternated with the name *Cortigliazzo* (see as an example Tartamella 1975). Some Tunisian migrant workers did live in the neighborhood, and one of the courtyards was informally referred to as *curtile de li Tunisini* (Sicilian dialect for *Tunisians' courtyard*). A series of newspapers from the mid- to late 1970s also referred to Tunisians living in Mazara's historic center (Betti 1979; Tartamella 1975; Vasile 1979). However, their presence was not considered a problem, and old-time residents and business owners never mention Tunisians in their memories, nor do they define the center as an "Arab space." Instead, they describe it as a space of nostalgic Sicilian small-town familiarity. Certainly, the residential parts of the Casbah were poor, and living in the crowded buildings of the center was a marker of class. However, the area was not considered dangerous, nor were its inhabitants considered "external" to Mazara.

"A Frontier Land": The Appearance of the Casbah

All of this would change by the early 1980s, when Mazarese Sicilians began to associate the old center with Tunisian migrants and to cast it as a space of "backwardness," danger, and difference from the rest of Mazara. This change corresponded with the boom of the city's fishing sector, supported in part by national subsidies for the development of the South, which in turn allowed its working-class inhabitants to radically improve their standard of living. Growing labor needs in the fishing sector, in turn, attracted a growing number of Tunisian migrant workers.

Capital accumulated through the fishing sector led to transformation of the old center. This transition emerges clearly in Calogero's memories of the time: "People were moving because . . . they bought a piece of land and built new houses, more comfortable, bigger ones: it was the time of the economic boom. Before that there were ten people to a house, even a donkey! But things began to change, people began to earn money: progress arrived!"

A Mazarese Catholic priest with a long history of social work with Tunisian migrants provided a similar account: "Slowly the Mazarese fishermen left. No one wanted to live in these houses, they were small, uncomfortable, and cars could not reach them. As soon as one could, one would build a house outside the old center."[6]

The earthquake of June 7, 1981, accelerated Sicilians' gradual abandonment of the area (Cole 2003; Sbraccia and Saitta 2003), with many homeowners using the government's earthquake-relief subsidies to build new houses on the outskirts of town. This meant that they either abandoned their houses in the old center or leased them to Tunisian migrants.[7] In this context, Mazarese Sicilians began to associate the decrepit state of the old center's buildings with the "backward" state of the area's new inhabitants. This emerges clearly in memories of business owners of the old center about post-earthquake development. A shopkeeper who used to run his business in the area, but who had moved it to a wealthier section of the old center, recounted: "The 1981 earthquake was a catastrophe for the old center! Apart from the physical decay, immigration also had a huge effect because the houses ended up in the hands of Tunisians. I lived close by there, but it became unlivable. It was really a frontier land, so we left."[8]

Another shopkeeper, his former neighbor, made a similar observation, but cast Tunisians themselves as the cause of the physical decay of the neighborhood: "The arrival of Tunisians was not a good thing because they took over the abandoned houses. A little at a time they began to occupy the streets, so they became more degraded. People were afraid to visit the zone, drugs also contributed to ruin the neighborhood."[9]

Some of Mazara's Tunisians also remember these tensions. Referring to her father's descriptions of that period, Hiba, the young Tunisian woman we met in the previous chapter, recalled: "Italians were afraid because the majority of the neighborhood's inhabitants were Arab. . . . There was a group of men who used to drink at night, so Italians had to run away because they didn't like that mess."[10]

In these years, the term *Casbah*, previously used sporadically to refer to the neighborhood's Arab heritage, became increasingly common for the area and carried with it a pejorative connotation. Preceding widespread usage of the term on a national scale in the 1990s to refer to migrant neighborhoods (Dal Lago 1999; Merrill 2006), both business owners and the press used *Casbah* to refer to physical decay, uncleanliness, and immigration (Betti 1979; Cavallaro 1981; *L'Unità* 1980; Migliardi 1980). This semantic shift is clear in the words of a business owner who had moved out of the old center in the early 1980s: "An invasion of foreigners occurred, so the neighborhood became a Casbah. It was already called Casbah before, with its ancient name, but it became a *real* Casbah when Tunisians arrived."[11] The essential alterity of the Casbah and its inhabitants in relation to Sicilian modernity was also apparent in a 1981 article covering racial tension between Tunisians and Sicilians around the allocation of earthquake aid:

> The earthquake has not erased the borders that Mazara has created everywhere for a community confined to the ghetto neighborhood. . . . Leaving via Bagno, a small street of the Casbah . . . means to come face-to-face with people [Sicilians] who clearly only tolerate them [Tunisians] reluctantly. . . . When someone [a Tunisian] arrives to Mazara, he looks for friends in the port and a place to sleep in the Casbah. Three falling rooms cost about 200,000 lire, but Abib Kesraoni . . . doesn't complain. "Eight of us live here, it is not that expensive." . . . Peacefully expelled from the rest of the city, they [Tunisians] survive in a Casbah from which Mazaresi attempt to flee. (Cavallaro 1981, 14)

The association between marginalized populations and poor, cramped, and unsanitary living conditions is a common trope. It characterized working-class neighborhoods in nineteenth-century Europe (Engels 1968), native ones in colonial contexts (Fanon 1965; Gandy 2008; Kooy and Bakker 2008), and immigrant neighborhoods in late twentieth-century Europe (Ross 1995). In these contexts, differences in infrastructure development between different parts of the city both reflected and produced notions of different levels of "cleanliness," and thus of "civilization," associated with different populations. The term *Casbah* itself of course reactivated assumptions of racial and cultural difference at the core of colonial urbanism. Throughout the dual-city structure that characterized North Africa, colonial planners considered the Arab *medina* or *casbah*, often separated from the European quarters by a cordon sanitaire, as a space of frozen tradition, representing the alterity of the native population from European modernity (Abu-Lughod 1980; Wright 1991). As we saw in chapter 2, in colonial Tunisia, where many working-class Sicilians lived either in the Arab medina or in close proximity to it, both French colonial intellectuals and Italian diplomatic authorities considered this as an indicator of Sicilians' cultural similarity to Arabs, and thus their lack of "modernity."

In Mazara del Vallo, however, prior to the early 1980s, cramped living conditions and rudimentary infrastructural connections had not racialized inhabitants of the Casbah nor cast them as different from the rest of the city's population. Paradoxically, Calogero's description of his childhood in the 1960s in the old center where "there were eight people, maybe even a donkey, for each house" is not that different from the conditions of eight Tunisians living in "three falling rooms" described by *Giornale di Sicilia* in the 1980s. However, by the 1980s, cramped living conditions had become a racializing characteristic that differentiated Tunisians from Sicilians, as the former lived "in houses where many Maza-resi would not even live for free" (Paturno 1980). For this change in perception to occur, Sicilian Mazaresi had to read the difference between the Casbah and the rest of the city through broader notions of racialized and economic differ-ence between southern Italy and North Africa. Until the early 1980s, however, Italy's internal North–South divide, and not the Mediterranean, had been the main focus of Italian debates around social economic difference, and overcom-ing internal territorial disparities was the focus of national economic planning (Ginsborg 1990). As chapter 1 has discussed, around 1980, just as some Sicilian politicians began to discuss immigration to the island, references to southern Mediterranean poverty began to appear in the press. As Italian politicians, intel-lectuals, and policymakers gathered in Palermo in 1980 for the first national con-ference on North African immigration, a series of newspaper articles underlined the paradox of the existence of an "even deeper South" from which people were emigrating to Sicily (Conti 1980; Hoffmann 1980; Mignosi 1980).[12]

Media references to North Africa as a site of extreme poverty were emerging just as class differences within Mazara del Vallo were becoming less significant. The boom of the fishing sector had made Mazara's wealth legendary, and income levels in the city meant that its citizens had little need to envy northern Italy. Some of this wealth had trickled down, allowing Sicilians who worked on fish-ing boats to greatly improve their living standards (Ben-Yehoyada 2018). In this context, associating the cramped living conditions of the Casbah with Tunisian migrants, and casting the neighborhood as an "Arab" space, allowed Sicilians to geographically displace their own recent history of poverty to North Africa and to depict ways of life that working-class Sicilians had once shared with Tunisians as now alien to Mazara. In other words, the difference produced through the built environment of the Casbah, once a marker of class, was reinterpreted as a deeper marker of racialized difference that reechoed broader territorial divisions between Italian progress (which now included Mazara) and Tunisian poverty. In this sense, casting the Mediterranean as a key developmental divide in Mazara predated a similar national discourse by about a decade.

The racialization of Tunisians in Mazara occurred despite the strengthening of the city's economic, cultural, and political ties with Tunisia. The early 1980s saw both the completion of the Algeria–Tunisia–Italy gas line that joined the Italian mainland in Mazara and a spike in the ongoing Fish War between Mazara del Vallo and Tunisia. This low-level conflict around fishing rights often led to Mazarese vessels fishing in Tunisian territorial waters being seized by the Tuni-sian authorities, which then required diplomatic negotiations for their release (Ben-Yehoyada 2014; Ben-Yehoyada et al. 2016). To support the fleet, Mazara's political elite engaged in a series of diplomatic initiatives with Tunisia. In 1981, for instance, the Christian Democrat mayor of the city, Nicolò Vella, supported the opening of a Tunisian government-run elementary school for the children of the local Tunisian community—a unique institution for a small town, because these sorts of schools are usually only present in national capitals.[13] The mayor also revitalized a twinning agreement between the municipality of Mazara and the Tunisian coastal town Mahdia that had been signed a decade earlier, when the mayor of Mahdia was also the Tunisian foreign minister—and thus a key player in the Fish War (Ben-Yehoyada 2018). When promoting these initiatives, the town's political class often wielded Mediterraneanist language, rhetorically invoking a long history of connection and shared heritage between Mazara del Vallo and Tunisia (Ben-Yehoyada 2014). This Mediterranean enthusiasm was also shared by the city's intellectuals, who organized a range of cultural activities, such as Arabic courses in the city's Liceo Classico,[14] and symposia bringing together writers and artists from around the Mediterranean rim.[15]

These declarations of proximity, friendship, and shared history with North Africa did not, however, translate into an inclusion of the city's Tunisian community in Mazara's public sphere. With the exception of a few families whose children attended the Tunisian school, the bulk of the community was made up of male laborers in the fishing fleet and in agriculture, who were essential to the city's economic boom but entirely absent from its public life. Indeed, just as the city's political class was strengthening its diplomatic ties with Tunisian authorities, Tunisian migrant workers were the target of mob violence on a couple of occasions, in retaliation for Tunisian coast guard attacks on Sicilian fishing vessels (Ben-Yehoyada 2014; Cusumano 1976). While these episodes were not common, they underline how the political importance of enhanced relations with North Africa did not translate into a valorization of the local Tunisian community, poor workers with little political and economic clout in Tunisia itself. Thus, despite public declarations of Mediterranean interconnectedness, affirming Sicilian modernity within Mazara meant underlining the difference between working-class Sicilians and Tunisian migrants.

"A Piece of North Africa in Italy": Reclaiming the Arab Casbah

In the first decade of the 2000s, the decline of Mazara's fishing sector, matched by a renewed Italian and European interest in cross-Mediterranean relations, led to an official reclaiming of Mazara's "Arabness." New tourism promotion materials, such as written guides and glossy maps of the city, celebrated the once-abandoned Casbah:

> Mazara del Vallo is an important example . . . of a multiethnic and multicultural city, where differences are resources. . . . A walk through the alleys and courtyards of its Islamic urbanism makes the visit to Mazara interesting and engaging. (Li Vigni and Mauro, n.d.)
>
> What makes this area [the Casbah] characteristic, in addition to its "Arabisant" structure, is that one of the largest North African communities in Europe lives there, that increases its fascination making it . . . a piece of North Africa in Italy.[16]

These texts were accompanied by photos of the newly renovated alleys of the old city center and of Tunisian businesses in the area, drawing an explicit connection between Mazara's Arab heritage and its contemporary Tunisian population.

Like other cases of postindustrial restructuring (Hoffman 2003), this change was part of a broader attempt at "branding of difference" (Leslie and Catungal 2009) to convert Mazara del Vallo's economy from industry to tourism and services. The city had decided on this as an alternative development strategy to its dwindling fishing sector, which had entered a profound crisis by the second decade of the twenty-first century, creating widespread unemployment among both Sicilian and Tunisian fishermen. This decline occurred in the context of the broader structural changes that accompanied the formation of the European Union, discussed in more detail in chapter 1, which led to cuts in government assistance to industries in the South, such as Mazara's fishing fleet. In this context, local governments throughout southern Italy turned to independent fundraising. The European Union was a key source of these funds, often through the intermediary of Sicily's regional government. Drawing on this funding, in 2009 Mazara del Vallo's municipal government commissioned a strategic plan from two consulting firms, the locally based EURES Group and the Turin-based Avventura Urbana, which worked together to suggest possible development alternatives to the city's fishing-based economy.[17]

The consultants advised the city to rebrand itself as a tourist destination and as a strategic location for cross-Mediterranean relations—in other words, to adopt Mediterraneanist language and to promote Mediterraneanist projects as an avenue for local development. Following the 1995 Barcelona Declaration, which created a framework for cooperation between the European Union and countries of the Mediterranean's southern rim, extensive funding was available for cross-border cooperation projects.[18] In this context, local governments throughout southern Europe, such as Marseille, Granada, and Málaga, embarked on operations of what Hackworth and Rekers (2005) call "ethnic packaging"—an attempt to market their "exoticism" (in this case, as a Mediterranean borderland) to generate economic development (Lafi 2013; Rogozen-Soltar 2007). The strategic plan argued that Mazara should also adopt this strategy: "For Mazara . . . the emergence of the Euro-Mediterranean perspective, promoted by the Barcelona treaty . . . appears to be the most promising scenario. . . . [Mazara should] take advantage of the 'positional advantage' that the city acquires thanks to its close geographical proximity with the coast of North Africa" (Avventura Urbana and EURES Group 2009, 47–48).

The plan identified a range of social, environmental, and urban-planning initiatives that could serve to reorient the city's economy away from the dwindling fishing sector. The only recommendation that was carried out, however, was the renovation of the Casbah.[19] The initial moves to renovate the area had been spearheaded by the center-left coalition that had commissioned the strategic plan. However, the project was continued by a right-wing mayor who won the local elections in 2009. This continuity is unusual in Italy, since the celebration of Mediterranean multiculturalism is usually only embraced by the left, and the mayor's political party was known nationally for its nationalism, racism, and xenophobia. Indeed, the mayor himself had started his political career in the ranks of the Movimento Sociale Italiano, a far-right party that had mobilized against Tunisian migrant workers in Mazara del Vallo in the 1970s and 1980s. The fact that this very mayor would turn to promoting Mediterraneanist initiatives shows the extent to which use of this language was dictated by imperatives of economic development—just as it had been in the 1980s, when celebration of cross-Mediterranean connections served to protect the interests of the fishing fleet.

The renovation of the Casbah involved two main types of projects. The first were large-scale, with budgets ranging from several hundred thousand to more than a million euros, for which the municipality received substantial outside funding. Casa Tunisia, the contested cultural center mentioned at the beginning of the chapter, was one of these projects, and saw the collaboration of skilled artisans from the Tunisian town of Mahdia, as part of the long-standing twinning program between the two cities. Another similar project was the planned "multi-functional center for the dialogue between cultures of the countries that border the Mediterranean," across the street.[20] The second type of project did not involve substantial structural alterations to the old city but focused mainly on an aesthetic shift characterized by the whitewashing of walls and their decoration with ceramic tiles depicting Mazara's "traditions": its Arab past, its current connections to Tunisia, and its multicultural nature. Each of these mini-projects cost between 10,000 and 30,000 euros and was funded entirely by the municipality.[21]

Both city council officials and Sicilian business owners considered the physical renovation of the Casbah to have changed its Tunisian inhabitants. Evoking

FIGURE 7. Tiles celebrating multiculturalism. Source: Author.

FIGURE 8. Renovated courtyard with whitewashed walls and ceramic tiles. Source: Author.

FIGURE 9.   Tiles celebrating Arab history. Translation: The Arabs, having landed at Mazara with about 10,000 foot soldiers and 700 knights on June 17 827, took it within a year, the first Sicilian city to be occupied. Persistent traces of Arab domination remain in the maze of alleys and courtyards that still characterize the historic center. Source: Author.

tropes of "civilizing through cleanliness" (Gandy 1999; Lombardi-Diop 2013; McClintock 1995; Rabinow 1989; Ross 1995), a right-wing city council official who had spearheaded the renovation of the Casbah described it as a process not only of physical restoration but also of social and moral regeneration of its inhabitants: "The rehabilitation of the Casbah was an urban, social, and sociological rehabilitation. Before, the houses were basically caves. Immigrants who arrived were modest people who occupied these ruins—a material neglect that became social neglect. You could see this in their clothing, in their self-presentation. The restoration had a positive influence on them, you see a sociological change in this community, in the way they dress, they pay more attention to their appearance, they feel like full citizens."[22]

Similar views emerged from Sicilian business owners in the old center. For example, the owner of a clothing shop, who had moved away from his Porta Palermo location in the 1980s, assessed the socio-spatial change of the old center quite positively: "With the ceramic tiles, the mayor cleaned up the old city. Before him, you couldn't pass through there, it was unlivable. . . . Now it has changed radically, he involved the immigrants who lived there. You know, Tunisians at the beginning were not good for the area, they didn't do anything, they would just drink. But now they are integrated, there are even some Tunisian shops!"[23]

These quotes show the importance of the renovation of the built environment and of its Mediterraneanist rebranding in changing how Mazarese Sicilians perceived Tunisians. Despite the fact that people of Tunisian descent in Mazara were generally worse off in the first years of the 2000s than they had been in the 1980s and 1990s, due to the crisis in the fishing sector, many Sicilian business owners in the old center shared the perception that the once-lazy Tunisians had finally begun to work.

The municipality's attempts to rebrand the old center were somewhat successful in attracting outsiders. In the years following these projects, about a dozen wealthy northern Italians and northern Europeans purchased and renovated houses in via Porta Palermo and via Bagno as vacation homes. They chose Mazara thanks to its so-called exoticism and authenticity—classic attributes in the urban branding of "diversity" to attract young, alternative consumers (Zukin 2008). In the words of Fritz, a Dutch artist who bought a vacation home in via Bagno: "It was the African atmosphere that led us to choose Mazara. We liked the messiness, the authenticity!"[24] Many of these homeowners had previously spent time in Tunisia, or had considered buying property there, but had settled on Mazara because they considered it a safer alternative in the aftermath of the 2011 uprisings in Tunisia. These purchases were few, however, in relation to the available housing stock, and they failed to generate substantial economic or demographic change in the Casbah. While Mazara's strategic plan, as well as discussions in city council meetings,[25] had called for the creation of "characteristic" Arab businesses in Mazara's old center, by early 2013 no new Tunisian-owned business had opened.[26] Despite the strategic plan's emphasis on the development of entrepreneurship, the municipality had not been able to accompany the aesthetic renovation of the old center with any economic support or capacity-building program aimed at the creation of Tunisian, or indeed any, businesses. If anything, the economic crisis that was hitting Sicily in the 2010s was forcing many small businesses to shut down.

As a consequence, with the exception of a few statements by city officials and business owners, the old center's reputation had not substantially changed. "People from Mazara don't go to the old center," observed Fritz, the Dutch artist. "When talking to locals, there is the notion the Casbah is a dangerous place. We noticed that Italians don't like Tunisians!"[27] A real estate agent who dealt with the majority of the housing stock of the old center confirmed this perception, noting that Mazarese Sicilians would never buy houses in the old center to live there. Some Tunisians also considered the Casbah to be dangerous, in spite of its renovation and its revamped iconography that recognized and celebrated their presence. Despite their modest economic means, a few had chosen to leave the area. For instance, Bassma, a stay-at-home mother of three whose husband was on disability benefits, explained to me, "We lived in the old center for a few years. We really liked the house, but we left because the environment was not good." After a pause, she turned to warn me: "Don't go there, and don't walk there at night. You should be scared, because they might steal your purse."[28] Because the aesthetic renovation of the Casbah did little to address the everyday needs of people of Tunisian descent, such as their economic subsistence and everyday safety, they were largely indifferent to the "ethnic packaging" of the old center, despite the fact that it formally recognized their presence in and contribution to Mazara.[29]

In essence, apart from the aesthetic renovation of the Casbah and the structural restoration of a few buildings, not much had changed in the old center. While a couple of successful sales had prompted Mazaresi homeowners to put their old houses up for sale, the market remained weak. Though real estate was cheap in comparison to northern Italy or northern Europe, the agent who dealt with most of the housing stock in the old center confessed that he spent the majority of his days alone in his office.[30] To some extent, for Mazara's Tunisians the unsuccessful renovation of the Casbah had a silver lining, because, unlike other cities where "ethnic packaging" has led to gentrification or displacement (Hoffman 2003), the renovation of the neighborhood had failed to attract private capital to the old center and to raise the value of its buildings. Thus, it had not displaced Tunisians from their homes. However, as we saw earlier, the economic crisis was also affecting people of Tunisian descent in the city, inducing many of them to consider emigrating to France or Germany. Thus, despite the city of Mazara's claims to have a flourishing multicultural community, Tunisians were mainly visible as unemployed men clustering around Porta Palermo at the entrance of the Casbah in search of day labor—hardly the "full citizens" that the old center's restoration should have produced.

Valuing Tunisianness: The Contested Politics of Mediterraneanist Recognition

Despite producing little change, the municipality's Mediterraneanist projects were sparking unprecedented contestation within the Tunisian community. This paradox can be explained by a combination of economic and political reasons. From an economic point of view, if initiatives such as the renovation of the Casbah were unsuccessful in attracting private capital, celebrating diversity and cross-Mediterranean connections was very effective at attracting public funds. These streams of revenue were significant enough for the city of Mazara to hire two diversity consultants with the explicit aim of attracting national and European funding for migrant integration and cross-border cooperation.[31] The majority of people of Tunisian descent were indifferent to these initiatives, but a small group of educated Tunisians was paying close attention, because they aspired to potential jobs in migration and diversity management funded by the Italian government and the European Union. Many of these educated people of Tunisian descent were also Italian citizens and were well aware of their power as a small but significant voting bloc in local elections. They therefore felt emboldened to demand access to the benefits generated by celebration of their presence in Mazara.

This new political scenario disrupted long-established ways of carrying out Mediterraneanist politics in Mazara. As previously mentioned, political leaders in Mazara had a long history of embracing Mediterraneanist politics to safeguard the economic interests of the city by strengthening ties with Tunisian politicians and investors. Even projects that provided services for the Tunisian community, such as the opening of a Tunisian school, were part of a broader program of cross-Mediterranean diplomacy that privileged contacts with the Tunisian economic and political elite over policies of inclusion of local Tunisian workers.[32] In the early years of the twenty-first century, as the Italian government and the European Union incentivized programs of migrant integration, Mazara's political class simply adapted their previous mode of operation to the new framework. For example, under recommendation from the EU during this period, Mazara's municipality created an advisory position on the city council for a foreign national, who was supposed to voice the needs and concerns of the town's immigrant community. However, the representative was not elected by the Tunisian community. Instead, as he himself recalled: "The mayor nominated me, after the Tunisian consulate, the Caritas, and the unions identified me as the right person."[33] Beyond the lack of a democratic process, considering the Tunisian consulate as the de facto representative of Mazara's Tunisian community cast people of Tunisian descent as foreigners, represented by their consular authorities, as opposed to members of the local community with their own independent voice.

In 2013, Mazara's mayor—a right-wing nationalist with a long political experience—had employed a similar process to control the management of Casa Tunisia.[34] He had involved the Tunisian consulate, and the individuals it designated, as the official interlocutors representing Tunisian migrants. In particular, he had conferred the management of the cultural center on the Tunisian organization Friends Without Borders, which was headed by his diversity consultant, who was also very close to the Tunisian consulate and was well known for providing services to the community, such as passport renewals and fictitious work contracts to regularize people's immigration status.[35] While the consultant had considerable clout within Mazara's Tunisian community, he also had some opponents. In particular, some people of Tunisian descent accused him of having been a long-time informant to the Tunisian government, and they argued that Friends Without Borders was a made-up organization created so that the mayor and consulate could cherry-pick interlocutors representing the Tunisian community. Prior to 2011, allegations against the mayor's diversity consultant would have been whispered only in private. However, after the fall of President Ben Ali in 2011, Tunisians were no longer afraid of repercussions from the Tunisian consulate for their political organizing. This allowed new Tunisian voices to emerge in Mazara, challenging the status quo of the municipality's Mediterraneanist politics.

In the aftermath of the Tunisian revolution, a group of Tunisian students at the University of Palermo, some of the more educated and politicized migrants in Mazara, and a few Italian-born second-generation students had come together to create an independent, Italian-registered organization, The Voice of the Tunisian Migrant. Their initial activism focused on Tunisian elections, but they soon began to engage with local politics in Mazara, demanding more substantial economic support and political involvement for the Tunisian community. In particular, they accused the municipal authorities and the Tunisian nationals who collaborated with them of disregarding the material needs of the community while wasting money on events celebrating the city's multiculturalism.[36] This did not mean that they were opposed to monetary gains from the celebration of Tunisianness. Indeed, some members of the organization ran for local political office with the explicit aim of obtaining a salary. Instead, they denounced the municipality's politics of patronage when choosing spokespersons for the Tunisian community. For example, when discussing the municipality's policy of hiring diversity consultants, one of the members of The Voice of the Tunisian Migrant complained:

> That asshole of the consultant costs the city 50,000 euro a year . . . the mayor nominated him to that position, and I am sure that they divide up the money he makes. . . . The municipality needs to respect people who are breaking their back working on the boats, people who really work. . . . I told the consul: Do you really need to pay someone to run Casa Tunisia? And if you do, why him? How do you choose who speaks for our community? Why not the son or daughter of one of the fishermen?[37]

In brief, activists from The Voice of the Tunisian Migrant demanded transparency in accessing positions as spokespersons of the Tunisian community and the resources that these positions guaranteed.[38] The outcome of these demands, however, was limited to the formal inclusion of representatives of the organization in public events organized by the municipality and did not translate into attempts to improve transparency and fairness in access to public resources.

To a large extent, it is possible to interpret Mazara's Mediterraneanist rebranding during the early 2000s as a typical example of "ethnic packaging" initiatives undertaken throughout southern Europe. Around the same time, indeed, cities such as Marseille, Granada, and Málaga also rebranded themselves as hubs of Mediterranean cosmopolitanism and models of peaceful coexistence between people of European and of North African descent (Kutz and Giglioli 2021; Rogozen-Soltar 2017). In more general terms, this rebranding can be understood as an example of neoliberal politics of recognition—a superficial acknowledgment of the presence and contribution of marginalized populations, particularly when this facilitates the circulation of capital, which does not entail any sort of redistribution of power and resources (see Fraser 2000). According to this framework, national or local governments are open to embracing diversity and multiculturalism as long as doing so does not call into question the rules of the game (Coulthard 2014). In the context of Mazara, these rules were the municipality's well-consolidated politics of Mediterraneanism, focused on developing relations with the Tunisian political and business community while continuing to sideline local workers of Tunisian descent. Mazara's Mediterraneanist rebranding had effects that went beyond the intentions of its proponents, however—suggesting that, at the right conjuncture, projects of neoliberal recognition may open the door for more radical forms of politics. In Mazara, this rebranding occurred in a historical moment characterized by a growing number of educated people of Tunisian descent, many of whom had Italian citizenship, who were becoming active in the city's political life, and by the aftermath of the Tunisian revolution, which had allowed for political organizing among the Tunisian diaspora without fear of repercussions. Thus, formal celebrations of the town's Mediterranean multiculturalism opened a window of opportunity for some people of Tunisian descent to demand access to resources and representation, thus calling into question long-consolidated politics of Mediterraneanist patronage. In other words, activists from Voice of the Tunisian Migrant were able to transform a depoliticized celebration of ethnicity, typical of ethnic packaging and of multicultural city branding (Davila 2004; Goonewardena and Kipfer 2005; Leslie and Catungal 2009), into a political claim to resources and representation.

The municipality, however, was not the only public actor embracing Mediterraneanist politics in Mazara. The Catholic Church had its own Mediterraneanist agenda, also focused on migrant integration and cross-Mediterranean cooperation, but with different strategic aims. The next chapter will analyze the social and political implications of these Catholic Mediterraneanist projects.

5

THE NEW CHURCH OF AFRICA

Catholic Mediterraneanism and the Negotiation
of Religious Difference

The bishop of Mazara del Vallo, Domenico Mogavero, visited North Africa in
January 2011, where he would meet the bishops of Tunis and Algiers to discuss
Mazara del Vallo's model of integration and coexistence. He explained his objec-
tive in the following terms:

> Our city, Europe's closest point to Africa . . . can be a model for peace-
> ful coexistence between people from different cultural and religious
> backgrounds. This model is the result of a migratory movement that
> used to flow towards Tunisia between the late 1800s and the early 1900s.
> In the mid 20th Century, this movement changed direction, coming
> towards our coasts. We returned the welcoming we had once received
> with the same attitude. . . . Perhaps this is the secret of our unusual
> situation! However . . . we do not really have inter-religious dialogue
> here . . . alongside its general difficulties, in Mazara we do not have a
> stable interlocutor who can promote it. (Firrieri 2011, 22)[1]

This was not the bishop's first visit to the southern Mediterranean. Mogavero
was a strong advocate for cross-Mediterranean cooperation between Catholic
churches, and since becoming bishop he had revitalized a decade-old twinning
program between the dioceses of Mazara del Vallo and Tunis. He was also a
prominent public commentator on migration to Mazara and to Italy (Ben-Yehoyada 2015), openly criticizing policies that criminalized rescuing migrants at sea.
Mogavero was not the only Catholic Mazarese voice framing the conversation

about migration and cross-Mediterranean cooperation. Other Catholic institutions, including Caritas and individual religious orders, as well as individuals with strong ties to the Catholic Church, were key service providers to migrants and had become important voices in the public debate about Tunisian migration. Catholic actors were thus key proponents of Mediterraneanist visions and projects.

Catholic Mediterraneanist projects were considerably different from those promoted by the municipality, which were mainly focused on city branding to attract national and EU funding. Catholic institutions instead invoked Mediterranean coexistence while providing much-needed services to the Tunisian community, such as financial and in-kind support, after-school programs, professional training, and support in finding housing—key social services that the public sector did not have the capacity to provide. However, when intervening in the public debate about Tunisian migration, they also reinforced symbolic hierarchies between Sicilians and Tunisians. They did so by framing Sicilians as modern Mediterranean subjects, open to cultural and religious diversity, and thus different from closed-minded Tunisians, for whom religion had a totalizing role.

Catholic voices did not reference Sicilians' openness to interreligious and intercultural dialogue only in terms of their Catholicism. As the bishop's 2011 interview suggests, they also invoked historical connections between Sicily and North Africa, in particular Sicilians' southward migration to colonial Tunisia at the turn of the twentieth century, discussed in chapter 2. However, deploying the history of Sicilian settlement in colonial Tunisia as explanation for and proof of Sicilian open-mindedness required Catholic figures to make a series of assumptions. The first was that a history of poverty and emigration had inoculated Sicilians against racism. The second was that Sicilians' positionality as European settlers in colonial Tunisia was structurally equivalent to that of contemporary Tunisian migrants in Italy. The third was that, in colonial Tunisia, relations between Sicilians and Tunisians were peaceful ones between equals. In sum, Catholic figures needed to ignore the uneven power relations that had characterized the long history of interconnection between Sicily and Tunisia—a characterization that also limited their analysis of contemporary structural inequalities between Sicilians and Tunisians.

How was it possible for Catholic institutions to simultaneously recognize and attempt to mitigate the social marginalization and economic precariousness of Mazara's Tunisian community while simultaneously glossing over structural inequalities and reproducing deeply rooted symbolic hierarchies between Sicilians and Tunisians? To fully understand the politics of Catholic Mediterraneanism in Mazara, it is necessary to ground them in the broader Italian public debate on Islam, Muslim immigration, and Catholic–Muslim relations.

Islam, Catholicism, and Secularism

Religion had been the last of my concerns when I began my fieldwork. Having come of age in the aftermath of 9/11, I intentionally wanted to avoid "culture talk" explanations (Mamdani 2002) of difference between Europeans and North Africans. Thus, I had decided to avoid studying religion as an arena of boundary-drawing between Sicilians and Tunisians. My interlocutors in the field, however, had a different opinion. Only a few weeks into my research, as I was wrapping up an interview with a former Christian Democrat mayor of Mazara, I had paused on my way out of his office to observe one of the many photos from the 1980s that depicted him shaking hands with Italian and Tunisian politicians. Walking me toward the door, with my recorder now turned off, he suddenly inquired: "Miss, I presume that you are Catholic?" Taken aback by this question, especially from a public figure well versed in cross-Mediterranean cooperation, I tried to hide my unease by mumbling something about my family being culturally Catholic. This answer, however, was clearly insufficient. "But miss," he persisted, "you must be baptized?" Cornered, I confessed reluctantly that I was not, but that sometimes people told me I should be, just to be on the safe side. The former mayor chuckled as he showed me out the door: "Listen to them, they are right! You really should get baptized!"

A little unsettled by this interaction, as I walked home, I brushed it off as a typical example of pressure to conform to a norm. In a way, it was not that different from the snide comments made by my teachers at an Italian public elementary school about my "breaking group unity" when I opted out of Catholic religion classes. However, I would not be able to forget about religion for long. A couple of days later, as I was watching the news in my Tunisian landlady's living room, her gaze shifted from the TV to the sofa where I was sitting playing with her baby kitten. "I don't want to offend you," she started, testing the waters, "but can I ask you a question?" "Go ahead!" I answered, unsure of the direction of the conversation. "You speak Arabic, you have traveled to many Arab countries, and you have been living with us for a few months. I was wondering if you ever thought about becoming Muslim?" Less surprised by the question this time, I answered carefully, to close the subject. "Honestly, I have not. But don't worry about offending me. Please feel free to ask me these types of questions!"

I made a brief note of this interaction in my fieldnotes, but continued to bracket it as an entertaining anecdote. Over the course of the year, however, the topic of religion became inescapable. My knowledge of Arabic sparked many Tunisian acquaintances to inquire about my possible conversion to Islam. Similarly, when I interacted with representatives of Catholic institutions and other Sicilian inter-locutors, they either assumed my Catholicism as a consequence of my Italianness, or—more rarely—explicitly questioned me. I did not interpret these questions as a sign of individual piousness. Instead, I began to understand that in many circles in Mazara, people interpreted religious affiliation as a marker of belonging and sympathies. In other words, religion was a central theme that shaped conversations about borders, citizenship, and cross-Mediterranean relations.

Much of the critical literature on European Islamophobia highlights how the European public debate juxtaposes Islam to secularism (Dakhlia 2005; El-Tayeb 2011). Certainly, some scholars claim that European models of secularism are based on the secularization of Christianity and thus derive from a specific, localized religious history (Mahmood 2009; Sayyid and Dabashi 2015). This interpretation remains confined to specialized scholarship, however, and Christianity is rarely mentioned in public debates about secularism in northwestern Europe. In Mazara del Vallo, on the contrary, public discussions about Islam inevitably revolved around the juxtaposition of Islam to Catholicism. Secularism was conspicuously absent.

The nature of the conversation in Mazara del Vallo is not unique but rather emblematic of how the Italian public debate juxtaposes Catholicism to Islam. Two reasons can explain this Italian peculiarity. First, at the national level, just as in Mazara, Catholic institutions have historically provided services to migrants, filling a need that national and local public institutions were unable to meet. As a consequence, Catholic voices played a major role in framing the debate about Muslim immigration to Italy. Second, the Italian state adopted a "weak secular" model (Frisina 2010, 2011) characterized by an incomplete division between church and state, with a privileged relationship between the state and the Catholic Church. An example of this weak secularism can be found in debates about the role of religion in public institutions. In France and Germany, this debate focuses on the right of public employees to wear the hijab (Dakhlia 2005; El-Tayeb 2011). In Italy, discussions about the hijab are rare.[2] Instead, the debate about secularism has focused on whether schools and other public buildings should display the crucifix, as they traditionally have, or remove it in the name of religious pluralism.

Despite the centrality of Catholicism, Italy's public debate reproduces many of the tropes that characterize the discussion on Muslim immigration elsewhere in Europe. Juxtapositions such as "Western democracy" versus "Eastern despotism," or the notion that Europe guarantees individual rights while the Muslim world denies individual freedom, are also common in Italy. However, the Italian public debate uses Catholicism—and not secularism—as an emblem of the West's progressiveness. The high-profile conversion story of Egyptian-born journalist Magdi Allam illustrates the specificities of the Italian debate, as it adds a Catholic tone to the "escape narrative" trope invoked by some people of Muslim descent in

Europe (El-Tayeb 2011). According to this narrative, a person of Muslim heritage publicly renounces Islam due to its "oppressive nature" and embraces the secular state as a guarantor of individual rights. This trope is widespread and has been employed by high-profile politicians and public figures such as the Dutch Ayaan Hirsi Ali and the French Fadela Amara (El-Tayeb 2011). Magdi Allam's story has a different twist. Historically a progressive commentator on immigration and Islam in the Italian media, he became increasingly critical of Islam and of Italian Muslim organizations in the 1990s and eventually converted to Catholicism in the early years of the next century through a high-profile public baptism by the pope. In brief, Allam's escape narrative ends not in a conversion to secularism but in a conversion to Catholicism.

Despite the consistency of its Catholic undertones, the Italian public debate about Islam has evolved considerably over time as a consequence of shifting immigration flows and changes to national migration policies. Let us turn to examining these changes, both in Italy as a whole and in Sicily.

Immigration and Islam in the Italian Public Debate

Prior to the 1990s, Islam received limited public and political attention in Italy. When it did, this was mainly in the context of cross-Mediterranean diplomacy initiatives spearheaded by the Italian government or by national political parties. After World War II, interest in cross-Mediterranean diplomacy cut across the political spectrum, with Catholic visions playing a prominent role.[3] Catholic Mediterraneanism, championed by the Christian Democrat mayor of Florence, Giorgio la Pira,[4] was based on an ecumenical approach that saw Christians, Muslims, and Jews as three Abrahamic peoples that could bring together the whole "family of mankind" by coexisting peacefully (Muci 2009).[5] The Mediterranean Sea was a central meeting point between these peoples and thus a strategic area within which to mediate both regional and global conflicts (Giovannoni 2014; La Pira and Giovannoni 2006). This political vision was informed by the Catholic Church's position following the Second Vatican Council, which officially advocated and celebrated dialogue with non-Christian religions.[6] It was also aligned with Italian foreign policy's "neo-Atlantic" orientation, according to which Italy should play a pivotal role in countering Soviet influence in the Mediterranean by mediating between NATO and newly decolonized Arab countries (Giovannoni 2014).

Sicilian public debate of the period also addressed Islam in the context of the island's cross-Mediterranean relations. Newspaper coverage was minimal until the 1980s. When a few articles on Islam appeared, they focused almost entirely on the opening of mosques in the island's two major cities, Palermo and Catania. These mosques were not founded through the mobilization of Sicily's immigrant Muslim community, however, and—particularly in the case of Catania—were little frequented by believers. Instead, they were promoted by Sicilian politicians and public intellectuals to strengthen their political connections with North Africa and to launch urban regeneration initiatives.[7] This intent emerges clearly in news coverage of the inauguration of the mosques, which focused on their potential to highlight the island's Islamic history as a way to strengthen contemporary cross-Mediterranean relations. In a 1980 article titled "Allah Returns after Eight Centuries with a Mosque," for instance, *Giornale di Sicilia* reported that "a mosque, the first in modern Italy, has been built in Catania, a city that has recently re-directed its traditional dynamism in commerce towards Mediterranean Africa" (Quatriglio 1980, 3). Similarly, a 1990 article in *L'Ora* explained that through this initiative, "Sicily can have a unique role in the Mediterranean area, both from a political and economic perspective, and from a cultural one. An island/bridge between Europe and North Africa" (Merosi 1990, 14).

By the late 1990s, however, Islam in Italy had taken a central role in public debate, in the context of a broader discussion on immigration as migration flows to Italy became more substantial.[8] The heart of the debate revolved around Islam's compatibility with Italian and European values and the consequent ability of Muslim immigrants to successfully integrate into Italian society. Both the Catholic Church and Italian political parties debated this question extensively. Within the Church, Pope John Paul II and Catholic grassroots organizations that had been providing services to migrants since the 1980s embraced an explicitly pro-dialogue position. The pope, in particular, framed Catholicism and Islam as a common "front" against the decline of religiosity in Europe.[9] In contrast, more conservative bishops critiqued the Church's "excessive" opening to interreligious dialogue and to immigration from Muslim countries. Some cited incompatibility between Catholicism and Islam to justify their position and argued that the Italian state should privilege the recruitment of Christian immigrants.[10] Other bishops claimed that Muslim conflation of religion and politics represented a threat to Europe's secularism and enlightened tradition (Guolo 2003).[11] Tensions between the conservative and the prodialogue positions exploded at the 1998 national episcopal conference (Politi 1998), which ended up adopting a conservative stance, discouraging mixed marriages between Catholics and Muslims out of fear that this would lead to conversions to Islam (Guolo 2003).[12]

The Italian political sphere was similarly divided. In general, the far left adopted a multicultural position and the center left a secular-liberal one, while the right espoused openly Islamophobic views. However, these differences were not always clear-cut. In the late 1990s, traditionally center-left voices such as the newspaper *La Repubblica* expressed fears of Muslim fundamentalism, often associating Islam with the lack of women's rights.[13] At the same time, while most of the right adopted a "clash of civilizations" position, some centrist politicians schooled in La Pira's Christian Democrat vision of cross-Mediterranean dialogue were open to the presence of Muslims in Italy.[14] The Northern League was the most openly and unapologetically Islamophobic party (Guolo 2003; Massari 2006), expressing its opposition to Islam as a form of protecting regional identity against transnational flows of people and capital.[15]

In Sicily, the public debate around Islam in the 1990s also shifted from addressing cross-Mediterranean diplomacy to a focus on Muslim immigration and, in the early years of the twenty-first century, on associating Islam with possible terror attacks. Regional specificities characterized this debate, with public commentators often underlining Sicily's geographic and cultural proximity to North Africa. On a few occasions, they highlighted the island's vulnerability to a terrorist attack due to this proximity, its significant Muslim population, and the presence of NATO bases (Lauria 2001; Lopapa 2001a, 2001b). More frequently, they cast Sicily as a model of dialogue and coexistence with the Muslim southern Mediterranean. An editorial in *La Repubblica* by high school teacher Maurizio Barbato exemplifies this rhetoric. Writing in the immediate aftermath of 9/11, he pondered: "What meaning can expressions such as . . . 'a war on western civilization' have for us, Mediterraneans of the South? . . . Living in an in-between zone . . . allows us . . . to be Americans and Arabs at the same time, and to choose a future of coexistence . . . being cosmopolitan and capable of coexistence are the most distinctive signs of western civilization" (Barbato 2001, i, xv). This type of discourse was hegemonic enough to be adopted by politicians across the political spectrum, including the center-right president of the Sicilian region, Salvatore Cuffaro, who had made similar claims in the immediate aftermath of 9/11 (Lopapa 2001a).

Sicilian newspaper articles of this period often pointed to Mazara del Vallo as an example of Sicilian traditions of hospitality and orientation toward peaceful coexistence and interreligious dialogue (Giacalone 2002; Transirico 2002). However, the version of this debate in Mazara del Vallo was more complex.

Immigration, Catholicism, and Islam in Mazara del Vallo

On one of my first visits to Mazara, as I was strolling through the streets of the old Casbah, I was startled by the call of the *adhan* interrupting the silence of the afternoon siesta. A customary part of the soundscape of the Middle East and

North Africa, it caught me by surprise; the call to prayer is hardly ever heard in Italy or elsewhere in Europe, regardless of the number of mosques present in an area. Despite its audible adhan, Mazara del Vallo does not have a mosque. In the 1980s, when Christian Democrat Nicolò Vella was mayor, there had been some talk of constructing one. Vella, a strong advocate of cross-Mediterranean diplomacy, had pushed for it and had sought to donate a municipally owned piece of land on the outskirts of the town for this purpose. Multiple explanations exist for why the mosque was never built, such as insufficient funding (Corleo 1981), lack of political will of the following administration,[16] indifference of the Tunisian community,[17] or the opposition of the bishop.[18] Regardless of the reason, by the early 2000s the call to prayer was emitted from a storefront converted into a prayer room on a small side street of the Casbah, marked only by a small Arabic and Italian sign reading "Masjed Al Taqwa / Moschea Ettakwa." It was managed by an Islamic cultural association, founded by a Moroccan national and two Italian converts to Islam, and—unlike the publicly celebrated mosque of Palermo—received no funding from the municipality.[19]

If contemporary Islam is hardly visible in Mazara's built environment, this is not the case for historic Catholic/Muslim relations. A five-minute walk from Masjed Al-Taqwa, in the main square of the city's historic center, a marble statue of Roger of Altavilla, the Norman count who defeated Sicily's Arab rulers in 1071, decorates the door of the cathedral. The triumphant count is depicted on horseback, trampling a cowering Moor as he completes his "*reconquista*" of Sicily.

Pope John Paul II invoked this history of reconquista in his visit to Mazara del Vallo in 1993. In his homily during Mass on May 8 at Lungomare San Vito on the Mediterranean seafront, he celebrated Mazara's medieval return to Christianity, while also declaring the city's "natural" propensity to interreligious and intercultural dialogue:

> During the last nine centuries, various events have marked the destiny of these lands: there have been multiple dominations and civilizations . . . of which the memory lies impressed . . . in the monuments of this City . . . ever since, nine centuries ago, the great Count Roger of Altavilla put an end to almost three hundred years of Islamic presence . . . and founded this Church, the Gospel has continued to echo on these shores. True crossroads of the history between two civilizations, your frontier Church has always represented, and continues to represent, the natural point of contact and dialogue between the Christian and the Muslim world, contributing . . . to a culture of tolerance and peace.[20]

FIGURE 10.   Statue of Roger of Altavilla on the facade of the cathedral of Mazara del Vallo. Source: Author.

It may appear to be a paradox that the pope's celebration of dialogue, tolerance, and peace in the Mediterranean began by celebrating a bloody reconquest of Sicily from Muslim rulers. However, it follows a clear logic of mapping religion onto territory, in which Europe is clearly Christian, North Africa is Muslim, and the Mediterranean Sea represents a religious dividing line. According to this logic, Islam is out of place in Europe; it is thus necessary for Sicily to be Christian to ensure peace and dialogue with North Africa. This does not mean that Muslims cannot live in Sicily, but that coexistence with Muslims is possible, and desirable, as long as they are a minority and do not call into question the hegemony of Christianity on the island.

Similar assumptions characterized the Mediterraneanist projects promoted by the diocese of Mazara del Vallo. Certainly, Catholic voices in Mazara were strong advocates for migrant integration, interreligious dialogue, and cross-Mediterranean

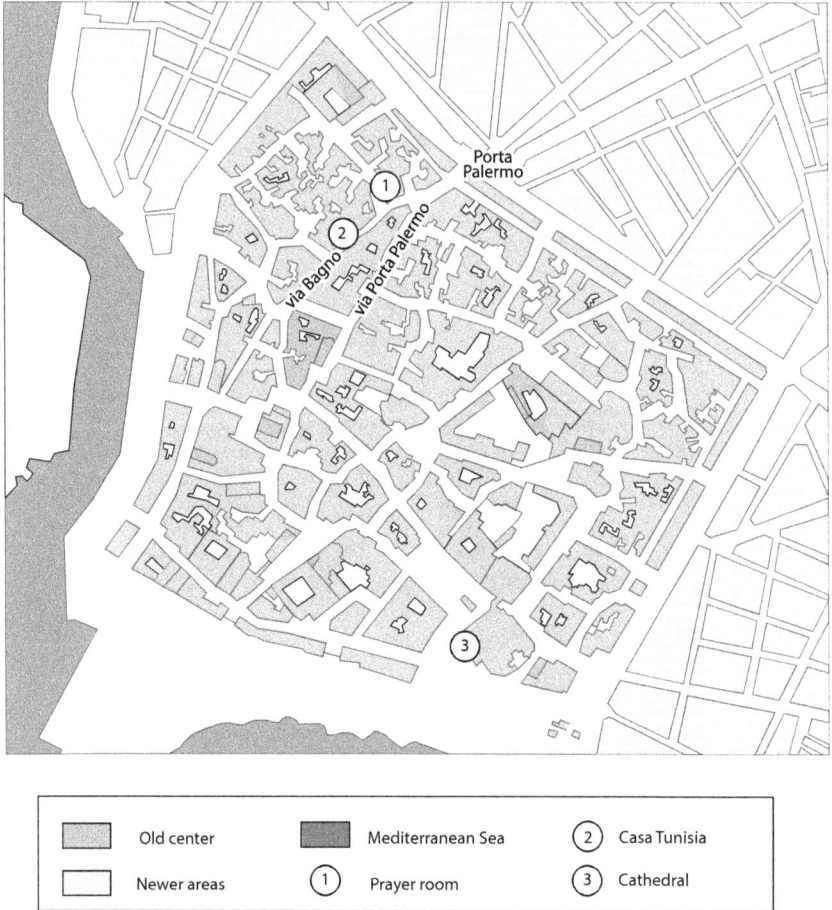

FIGURE 11. Locations of the prayer room and the cathedral of Mazara del Vallo. Source: Author.

cooperation. However, they did not cast Sicily as a meeting ground where Islam and Catholicism could come together on equal footing. Instead, they framed coexistence as a partial incorporation of Muslims into a Catholic framework, inasmuch as they saw Catholicism (sometimes conflated with Italianness and Europeanness) as a modern and open-minded religion, able to accommodate diversity in a way that Islam could not.

Three main Catholic voices articulated this discourse. The first were intellectual voices, such as the bishop of Mazara del Vallo and the diocese's office for ecumenical dialogue. They operated primarily at the political level, with little grassroots contact with Mazara's Tunisian community—or for that matter with the Sicilian one. Second, there were Catholic organizations providing fundamental social services to migrants, such as after-school programs and financial and in-kind assistance. Franciscan nuns had been offering these services since the 1970s and had been joined in the early part of the next century by the Fondazione San Vito, a Catholic foundation connected to Caritas.[21] These organizations were well embedded in the Tunisian community and often hired volunteers or staff of Tunisian descent to help with their day-to-day operation. Finally, there were religion teachers in Mazara's public schools, who played a prominent role in discussing the "integration" of Tunisian children.

Relationships between these Catholic actors were not always smooth. Grassroots Catholic organizations sometimes accused the office for ecumenical dialogue of framing interreligious dialogue in abstract terms, with no sense of actual daily interactions between Christians and Muslims in Mazara. In addition, Catholic grassroots organizations had differing politics when dealing with the municipality, ranging from collaboration to outright criticism. Despite their differences, however, they expressed similar tropes about interreligious dialogue and the possibilities of Muslim immigrants to successfully "integrate" into Sicily. Let us now turn to analyzing how these Catholic actors articulated their vision of Sicilian/Tunisian relations through two types of Mediterraneanist projects: those focused on migrant integration and those focused on cross-Mediterranean cooperation.

Catholic Mediterraneanism: Migrant Integration and Dialogue

"We . . . live among Tunisians . . . in the Casbah . . . we try to help them in their needs . . . but we stay away from teaching them Catechism, or from pushing them to baptize. We encourage them to be good Muslims, to observe Ramadan and to pray" (M. M. Fortuna, personal communication, May 5, 1984). With a letter sent to the Catholic newspaper *Nigrizia*, Franciscan nuns explained the mission for which the bishop had invited them to Mazara del Vallo in the late 1970s. The letter was written in 1984, yet the message of interreligious coexistence invoked by the nuns remained remarkably similar in the early 2000s. Interreligious and intercultural dialogue was the central narrative animating Catholic Mediterraneanist projects, whether focused on migrant integration within Mazara del Vallo or on cross-Mediterranean cooperation. This celebration of dialogue was, however, somewhat ambiguous. Catholic voices were careful to publicly distance themselves from explicit efforts to convert Muslim Tunisians, while quietly celebrating individual conversions.[22] At the same time, Catholic voices celebrated dialogue and coexistence while also creating symbolic hierarchical relationships between (Catholic) Sicilians and (Muslim) Tunisians.

The creation of these symbolic hierarchies was particularly clear in Mediterraneanist projects focused on migrant integration in Mazara de Vallo. In this case, all three Catholic voices—from the bishop, to Catholic grassroots organizations, to Catholic religion teachers—echoed the trope that Catholicism was more open to interreligious dialogue than Islam. Intellectual voices, such as the diocese's office for ecumenical dialogue and the bishop, were the strongest proponents of this narrative, lamenting the lack of will to engage in interreligious dialogue by Muslims in Mazara del Vallo and in Tunisia.[23] However, Catholic figures working closely with Tunisian migrants would often echo similar sentiments. For instance, a Catholic priest who ran after-school programs told me that he promoted interreligious dialogue in his programs but found this challenging due to the "totalizing" role of religion for Tunisian migrants: "For them," he explained to me, "Islam is not a choice, but a culture. Since for them religion and culture are connected, if you convert you are a traitor."[24]

Catholic religion teachers invoked similar ideas to explain the lack of "integration" of Tunisian children in schools. Speaking of the situation in her middle school, for instance, Alessandra, a Catholic religion teacher, explained:

> There is integration at school, but . . . outside . . . roads are separated. This is due to the cultural process of Tunisian children: religion, tradition. At school they live in a Western framework, but at home they are immersed in Arab and Islamic culture. At school they enter Western culture, and they participate in religious activities. At the beginning, if we organized a visit to a Church—as a cultural, not a religious activity—they would refuse to go. But then they realized that they could visit it, nothing would happen to them![25]

These words assume that Tunisian children are not mixing with their Italian peers due to the totalizing role or their religion, a hypothesis that creates a symbolic hierarchy between a "Western/Christian culture," open to interreligious dialogue, and a purportedly closed-minded Arab-Islamic one. This assumption implicitly suggests that proximity to Catholic institutions and interaction with Catholic students is a way to open the minds of Muslim students to dialogue—a trope that parallels assumptions elsewhere in Europe that Muslim migrants can become more open to coexistence through their acculturation to the secular state (El-Tayeb 2011).

This type of analysis was also echoed by "intellectual" voices of the Catholic Church to explain not only the dynamics of migrant integration in Mazara but also broader political and cultural dynamics in the MENA region. Reflecting on the difficulties of interreligious dialogue in Mazara and in the Mediterranean, for instance, the bishop of Mazara del Vallo explained to me in an interview:

The contact with Islam is provocative, because the religious element is in its DNA. . . . We come from an evolution in which the civil and the religious . . . have found a distinction and an equilibrium . . . in the Islamic world this distinction between civil and religious . . . does not exist. So everything that they live is three or four centuries behind our cultural standards. . . . The West—and Europe in particular—is the land of law and rights . . . in the Muslim world there is no culture of participation . . . so it is difficult to understand the value of a democratic system in that cultural context.[26]

The analysis developed by Mazarese Catholic voices is not surprising. The bishop's words echo well-rehearsed tropes juxtaposing a democratic West to a "despotic" East (Hall 1992; Said 1979), as well as the position adopted by some Catholic bishops at the 1998 episcopal conference, opposing Muslim immigration as a threat to Europe's tradition of secularism and enlightenment. Alessandra's identification of "Islamic culture" as the reason for the marginalization of Tunisian immigrant children is also common. Fatima El-Tayeb (2011) and Salman Sayyid (2015) underline how in the European public debate a frequent explanation for the marginalization of youth of immigrant descent is their "culture," rather than limited employment opportunities or systemic racism. More generally, both of these tropes create a static and monolithic picture of Muslim communities, which can only become open to democratic participation and multicultural coexistence through their gradual approximation to "European culture."

The commonality of this analysis is, however, matched by its lack of attention to historical and political developments, as well as the complexities of social and political debates, within Mazara's Tunisian community and across the Mediterranean. Neither the bishop nor other Catholic voices took into account processes of secularization that have occurred over the previous century throughout the Middle East and North Africa, including Tunisia itself (El-Tayeb 2011). They also ignored vivid debates about politics and religious practice within Mazara del Vallo's Tunisian community. Indeed, following the 2011 revolution, these discussions were frequent. Far from being a monolith, Mazara's Tunisians debated their support for different Tunisian political parties, from the Islamist Al-Nahda to the secular Nidaa Tunis (prominent in the initial years after the Tunisian revolution), and voted in Tunisian elections from Mazara. As noted earlier, people of Tunisian descent were also active in local politics and, if they had Italian citizenship, would sometimes run for office. This political activism was new, since prior to 2011 political organizing on Tunisian or Mazarese issues had been rare. However, Tunisian activists from the local The Voice of the Tunisian Migrant organization explained to me that this was mainly due to their fear of surveillance from the

Tunisian consulate during President Ben Ali's rule, rather than a lack of a "culture of participation."[27] They simply feared repercussions if they were seen to oppose the Ben Ali regime, which was at the time supported by the Italian government and the European Union (Cassarino 2014).

Support for political Islam was not the only religious theme debated within Mazara's Tunisian community. Throughout my fieldwork, daily conversations between Tunisian friends and neighbors in Mazara often addressed questions of what it meant to be a Muslim, what differences existed between Catholicism and Islam, and what relationships between these religious communities should look like. In the families of Farah, Hiba, and Ons, whom we met in previous chapters, conclusions were quite varied and nuanced. For instance, when discussing marriages between Christian men and Muslim women—a form of union not legally recognized by the Tunisian state until 2017—both Farah and Hiba were careful to justify these unions through references to love or practical class considerations, such as:

> Of course, our religion prefers that you marry someone from the same religious background. But what if you fall in love with someone else? We also have to respect that.[28]
>
> I would rather see my daughter marry an educated Italian than an unemployed Tunisian.[29]

Ons, in turn, explained the infrequency of mixed marriages in Mazara del Vallo by referencing racism as much as religion:

> Of course, it is forbidden for a Muslim woman to marry a non-Muslim man. But there are also other reasons—a mother might tell her daughter, "Think carefully about marrying an Italian. At the end of the day, his family will never really respect you or consider you an equal."[30]

While mixed marriages in Mazara del Vallo were rare, they did exist. Two of the most prominent people of Tunisian descent in Mazara—the former director of the city's Tunisian school and the daughter of the owner of the Casbah's only Tunisian restaurant—were married to Italians.

Relationships between Tunisian women and Italian men did provoke some sense of unease. One of the members of The Voice of the Tunisian Migrant, whose teenage daughter had a budding relationship with an Italian schoolmate, explained that some of Mazara's Tunisians disapproved of these relationships and she was looking for a religious interpretation that would condone her daughter's relationship. However, these discussions show the diversity of views and practices that existed within Mazara's community, where issues such as religion, gender, and politics were widely debated.

Despite the proximity of some Catholic grassroots organizations to Mazara's Tunisian community, these debates were generally absent from Catholic discourses about interreligious dialogue, which assumed that Catholicism—due to its intrinsic nature or to a European history of secularization of Christianity—was more open to interreligious dialogue. This framing created a symbolic hierarchy between a "European Christian Culture," which could represent a neutral terrain of dialogue and exchange, and a "North African Muslim Culture" that could not. It followed that Tunisians would have to adapt to European Christian Culture to successfully integrate into Italy—the Catholic version of tropes elsewhere in Europe that considered Muslim adaptation to secularism as the prerequisite for successful "integration." While this framing was most visible in Catholic Mediterraneanist projects focused on migrant integration, it also emerged in Catholic cross-Mediterranean cooperation projects. Mazarese Catholic institutions' advocacy for intercultural and interreligious dialogue was itself connected to a broader vision of cross-Mediterranean relations.

Catholic Mediterraneanism: Cross-Mediterranean Cooperation and "Models" of Coexistence

"For more than a millennium, Sicily has been a meeting place and a bridge between civilizations and cultures. . . . The vocation of this land is to provide a cultural basis for the Italian government's vision of the Mediterranean as a development opportunity. . . . This draws on the political tradition of great enlightened men of the past, such as La Pira, who . . . saw the Mediterranean as a site of peace and a model for new ways of being between people: a Mediterranean humanism."[31] With these words, Bishop Mogavero explained to me his vision of cross-Mediterranean cooperation in an interview I conducted with him in early 2014. His language was not unusual; his emphasis on Sicily's vocation as a bridge between civilizations echoed the words of John Paul II's 1993 homily in Mazara del Vallo, and his reference to La Pira is a classic Catholic Mediterraneanist trope. However, unlike La Pira, who had cast the Mediterranean as a large "Lake Tiberias" that could bring together people from different religious backgrounds, the bishop's vision of cross-Mediterranean cooperation focused exclusively on Catholic institutions (Ben-Yehoyada 2011). Drawing on this vision, the bishop promoted a twinning program between the dioceses of Tunis and of Mazara del Vallo and organized a periodic meeting of North African bishops in Mazara.

To some extent, a focus on cross-Mediterranean Catholic connections is to be expected by a Catholic bishop. However, Mogavero explained his choice by drawing on similar tropes about Islam's closure to interreligious dialogue invoked in discussions about migrant integration in Mazara. According to his vision, intercultural dialogue between churches was a necessary intermediate step to achieve interreligious dialogue, which was fraught with difficulties. His vision also emphasized the historic Christian character of North Africa. When speaking of Catholic churches of the southern Mediterranean, he described their presence as a "return to Christianity's origins." Catholic institutions operating in majority-Muslim contexts, he argued, represented as a return to the "simple" Catholicism of St. Cyprian and St. Augustine, who had evangelized North Africa under the Roman empire in the first century AD.

While the bishop invoked the millennia-old history of North African Catholicism, he made no mention of the more recent history of Catholic institutions in Tunisia. This history is worth examining to understand the work of contemporary Catholic institutions in the territory. The institutional presence of the Catholic Church in Tunisia dates back to the mid-nineteenth century, when the growth of the local European population led to the creation of an Apostolic Vicariate (Soumille 1977; Sugiyama 2007).[32] Following the establishment of the French protectorate, this was transformed into a full diocese. Thanks to an 1893 agreement between the Vatican and the French state, the Vatican placed the French Bishop Charles Lavigerie, former bishop of Algiers and supporter of the French colonial project in North Africa, at the head of the diocese. Over the years of the protectorate, the Catholic population in Tunisia surged, thanks in part to Sicilian immigration, and the Church established a network of parishes throughout Tunisian territory (Soumille 1975). French Catholic circles applauded the expansion of the Catholic Church in Tunisia in a language not that different from Bishop Mogavero; they celebrated the establishment of a "New Church of Africa" as part of a broader reaffirmation of the "Latin" character of North Africa and a return to the Catholicism of the first century AD (Soumille 1975). Following Tunisian decolonization in 1954, the status of Catholic institutions changed dramatically. The departure of the majority of European settlers meant that the number of Catholics in the territory dwindled. At the same time, the independent Tunisian state curbed the Catholic Church's power, obliging it to return the majority of its properties to the state. Catholic institutions were allowed to operate but were forbidden from intervening in politics (Tartamella 2011). This meant that by the early years of the twentieth century, the activities of the diocese of Tunis were limited, as were Catholic communities in the territory, mainly comprising descendants of European settlers and sub-Saharan African migrants.

The presence of small yet deeply rooted Catholic communities was, however, central to the twinning program between the dioceses of Mazara del Vallo and of Tunis. The bishop was a strong advocate for the program, but its operational side was managed by the Fondazione San Vito, one of the Catholic grassroots organizations that provided services to Mazara's Tunisian community. The foundation organized a range of activities. First, and most important, it provided services to the families of Mazara's Tunisian migrants, such as helping them access the Italian pensions of deceased relatives, thus supplementing the work of Italian and Tunisian public institutions that did not provide easy access to these types of benefits. Second, it supported Catholic institutions in Tunisia through regular volunteer trips for Mazarese Catholics to work on projects such as the restoration of buildings owned by the diocese. Finally, it supported a small community of elderly descendants of Sicilian settlers who had migrated to Tunisia at the turn of the twentieth century and were living their last years in Tunisia with little family or public economic, medical, or social support. This included both in-kind support to charitable organizations serving the community and the organization of cultural initiatives such as trips to Sicily for them to reconnect with their "homeland."

The Fondazione San Vito had not originally planned to engage with Sicilians of Tunisia. Prior to his trips to Tunisia, the director of the foundation did not even know that they existed, since—as chapter 2 has discussed—this community was fairly invisible in Tunisia, as indeed were the Sicilians of Tunisia who had settled in Mazara following decolonization. However, this little-known history would soon become crucial to Catholic visions of coexistence within Mazara and across the Mediterranean. In an interview with me in early 2014, the director of the foundation described how the existence of Sicilians of Tunisia was proof that the Mediterranean had long been a space of migration and exchange. More importantly, he argued, this history could serve as a model for contemporary multicultural Europe:

> During one of our trips, we realized that there was still a Sicilian community in Tunisia, mainly elderly people. . . . In Tunis, you can still see the signs of their historic presence: there is still a church in the [formerly Sicilian neighborhood of] the Petite Sicile. . . . Relationships were easier back then . . . Sicilians were closer to Tunisians than to the French. On the day of the Assumption, August 15, Muslims and Jews would participate in the procession for the Virgin Mary. People would celebrate together; it was a lot more natural than today—as it should be! This has all become more complicated with the emergence of Al Nahda [the Tunisian Islamist party].[33]

The bishop of Mazara del Vallo also invoked this history, often stating publicly that the model of peaceful coexistence between Sicilians and Tunisians in Mazara was "the result of a migratory movement that used to flow towards Tunisia between the late 1800s and early 1900s" (Firrieri 2011, 22). In an interview with me in 2014, Mogavero argued that the history of Sicilian southward migration had made Sicilians open to interreligious and intercultural dialogue: "When Tunisians arrived to Mazara . . . the welcoming that Sicilians received in Tunisia taught us how to handle the situation. At the beginning of the last century, migration used to flow in the opposite direction! Sicilians did not go to Tunisia to colonize, but to work, and they brought a large part of our civilization and our Christianity with them. So they were not treated like invaders, but like friends— despite their differences. This is the reason why, when migration changed direction, it was not difficult for us to welcome Tunisians here!"[34]

At the heart of both of these invocations of the past is a commitment to peaceful coexistence between Sicilians and Tunisians and an implicit critique of restrictive immigration policies and the fortification of the Mediterranean border. However, like much of the academic and public scholarship on colonial Tunisia discussed in chapter 2, neither the director of the Fondazione San Vito nor the bishop address uneven power relations between Sicilians and Tunisians. Their celebration of Tunisia at the turn of twentieth century as a space of coexistence does not mention that this was a colonial context, marked by hierarchies and inequalities. Thus, both the priest and the bishop celebrate colonialism as a motor of intercultural exchange while glossing over its structural violence—a trope denounced by Aimé Césaire in his *Discourse on Colonialism* (Césaire 1972). To some extent, the bishop's quote does implicitly acknowledge French colonialism in Tunisia. However, by explicitly distancing Sicilians from the role of the colonizer, and by ignoring Sicilians' privileged position as European settlers in a colony (Memmi 1965), he is able to cast contemporary Tunisian migration to Sicily and historic Sicilian southward migration to Tunisia as structurally equivalent. Sicilians thus emerge out of this narrative as Mediterranean subjects par excellence, thanks to their long history of migration unscathed by the legacies of colonialism.

In addition to ignoring the colonial nature of nineteenth-century Tunisia, these narratives reevoke the symbolic hierarchies between Catholicism and Islam that characterized discussions about migrant integration in Mazara. The director of the Fondazione San Vito, in fact, mentioned Muslims and Jews participating in a Catholic procession as an example of religious coexistence. This framing was similar to Catholic religion teachers' statement that Muslim students' visits to churches were proof of their integration. Both these accounts frame interreligious dialogue as Muslims participating in Christian rituals and thus becoming more open to religious diversity—a classic "modern" characteristic. However, they do not mention Catholics participating in Muslim holidays, even if they do not necessarily oppose it. This framing implicitly reinforces the notion that Christianity is more "open-minded" concerning dialogue than Islam and thus casts Christianity as the universalist basis into which religious diversity can be incorporated.

Mediterraneanism and Boundary-Drawing

Overall, Catholic celebrations of Mediterranean interconnection did not receive any pushback from people of Tunisian descent in Mazara. This may be because grassroots Catholic organizations did indeed attend to the material needs of the Tunisian community, providing fundamental cultural, educational, and social services and employing staff of Tunisian descent. This service work did not, however, prevent Catholic voices in Mazara from falling into similar paradoxes as the municipality—namely, celebrating Mediterranean coexistence while drawing symbolic boundaries between Sicilians and Tunisians.

In particular, Catholic celebrations of coexistence in late nineteenth-century Tunisia served to simultaneously naturalize notions of difference between Sicilians and Tunisians and to portray the former as open Mediterranean subjects, different from the latter. Catholic references to colonial Tunisia thus do not refer to privileges that Sicilians had access to in this space, such as higher salaries, better access to employment, and the possibility of acquiring French citizenship (Memmi 1965). These policies served to differentiate Sicilians from Tunisians, despite the fact that they shared many spaces of everyday life. By assuming that differences between Sicilians and Tunisians lie in the realm of religion and culture, and are thus longstanding and innate, Catholic actors were instead able to frame colonial Tunisia as a space of coming together of difference, and therefore as a model of coexistence to be reproduced in the present. In addition, while claims about a propensity of coexistence due to their history of living together could be made of all populations descendant of residents of colonial Tunisia, the Catholic actors described in this chapter primarily attributed this legacy to Sicilians, claiming that Tunisians are more closed to this dialogue because of the alleged "totalizing" role of their religion.

Symbolic borders also emerge in Catholic celebrations of Sicily as a Mediterranean borderland. Statements about Sicily's open and multicultural character and its long history of interconnection with the southern Mediterranean went hand in hand with references to Sicily as fundamentally Christian and Catholic, both in the past and in the present. This mapping of religion onto territory creates a clear symbolic boundary between Catholic Sicily, in which Muslims may coexist as long as they are a minority, and Muslim Tunisia.

The previous three chapters have discussed the limits of celebrations of Mediterranean interconnection that emerge out of Sicilian borderlands as political projects that create social, political, and economic belonging for people of Tunisian descent in Mazara del Vallo. They have also discussed the limits of Mediterranean borderlands such as Mazara as spaces of economic stability for people of Tunisian descent, because of their own status as internally economically marginalized peripheries. Does this mean that Mediterranean borderlands as a model of inclusion and an alternative to nationalism are simply an intellectual fantasy of a few progressive scholars, activists, and political commentators? Might it be possible to reclaim celebrations of Mediterranean interconnection and coexistence as a project of cross-Mediterranean solidarity and an alternative model of belonging to exclusionary forms of nationalism? The conclusion will explore these questions in more detail.

Conclusion

RECLAIMING THE MEDITERRANEAN

Mediterraneo	Mediterranean
Tra me e te il Mediterraneo	**Between me and you the Mediterranean**
Il volto familiare di un estraneo	**The familiar face of a stranger**

Ghali, Bayna, 2024

Every Friday, bustling crowds at the port of Palermo board the ferry to Tunis. Cars packed with used Italian goods crowd the lower area of the ship, headed to Tunisian street markets or to makeshift warehouses in the empty homes built by remittances of the Tunisian diaspora. A mixed chatter of Italian and Arabic fills the air—symbolic of the daily circulation of people, money, and goods across the Mediterranean Sea. The strictest of EU border controls cannot prevent this integration of the two shores of the Mediterranean, just as the most outspoken nationalist movements could not stop the single "Casa Mia" (My Home) by Tunisian-Italian rapper Ghali from achieving fourth place at the 2024 Italian San Remo music festival. Every day, in the alleys of Mazara del Vallo, the lecture halls of the University of Palermo, and the corridors of the World Social Forum, youth of Italian and Tunisian descent mingle, make lifelong friendships, and fall in love. Their children's family heritage will span both shores of the Mediterranean, a mixed identity shared by many youths of Tunisian descent settled in Italy, whose lived history, multilingualism, and thick web of family and friends weave together the two shores of this sea. While not routed to a specific place, these daily relations and networks of family, friendship, and solidarity have much in common with what some theorists have described as key characteristics of borderland culture and politics: an alternative understanding of membership and belonging from that of nationalism, produced through a rich web of cross-border interconnections (Anzaldúa 1987; Chambers 2008; Dear 2013).

At a time of rising nationalist movements throughout Europe, the intention of this book is to analyze alternative models of belonging that reframe the

Mediterranean Sea from a militarized border to a rich space of exchange and interconnection, one that celebrates past and present movement of people across this sea and thus naturalizes the presence of people of North African descent in Europe. It hypothesized that southern European borderlands such as Sicily might be home to such a model, thanks to their long history of interconnection with North Africa, the official framing of local identity as mixed and hybrid, and their long history of internal marginalization within the nation-state. However, the analysis of the lives and livelihoods of people of Tunisian descent in Mazara del Vallo, as well as different strands of local Mediterraneanist politics, has shown that these borderlands are not necessarily sites of social inclusion and economic opportunity for people of North African descent, and indeed that celebrations of Mediterranean interconnection and local culture as a hybrid may paradoxically create new symbolic hierarchies between people of Italian and Tunisian descent. Thus, the book cautions against searching for specific "intermediate" and "mixed" locations as models for alternative understandings of belonging to rising nationalisms, or as epicenters of solidarity politics between people of European and North African descent.

But might it be possible to look elsewhere in for examples of cross-border collaboration and solidarity that bind together the northern and the southern shores of the Mediterranean, advocating that this sea and the lands that border it become spaces of belonging for all? After discussing the limits of Mediterranean borderlands as models of coexistence and political laboratories at a time of rising nationalisms, these concluding pages will explore the potential to reclaim notions of Mediterranean mixing and interconnection to develop solidarity between people of European and North African descent in the Mediterranean region.

Limits of Mediterranean Borderlands

At a first glance, it is tempting to idealize Mediterranean borderlands such as Mazara del Vallo as models for the social and economic inclusion of people of North African descent and as laboratories for hybrid understandings of identity that call into question fortified borders. Mazara's long history of economic, cultural, and migratory connections with Tunisia, as well as Sicily's history of internal racialization within Italy, have in fact created a distinct articulation of local identity as "Mediterranean" and "mixed," suggesting a local propensity toward the incorporation of difference and toward the development of solidarity initiatives with racialized populations hailing from the southern Mediterranean.

However, due to structural limits determined by Sicily's subordinate incorporation within Italian and European geographies of uneven development, in the 2010s Mazara was hardly a space of economic, social, and political inclusion for people of Tunisian descent. Long histories of incorporation at the bottom of the labor market, often in the informal economy, coupled with the decline of the local fishing economy since the first decade of the twenty-first century, rendered the lives, livelihoods, and immigration status of people of Tunisian descent extremely precarious. In other southern European countries, such as Greece, some studies have shown that following the 2008 financial crisis, new forms of solidarity developed between citizens and migrant workers, as the former began to experience forms of insecurity previously only experienced by noncitizens or by racialized populations of migrant descent (Cabot 2016). However, while both Sicilians and Tunisians experienced economic precariousness in Mazara, its implications on immigration status were such that Tunisian nationals experienced much more profound effects on their stability. In addition, this moment actually saw increased labor competition between these two populations in the fishing and agricultural sectors.

We have also seen that histories of internal marginalization and internal racialization within Italy do not necessarily translate into a politics of solidarity with populations hailing from the southern Mediterranean. A long legacy of Sicilian declarations of proximity and similarity with the southern Mediterranean has in fact coexisted with attempts to differentiate Sicilians from Tunisians to assert the former's full Italianness and Europeanness. This occurred at the urban scale in the context of Mazara del Vallo, when in the 1980s Mazarese Sicilians affirmed their own modernity by associating the poverty and decaying infrastructure of the Casbah with Tunisian migrant workers. This type of association was also present in regional media, particularly in the context of immigration debates of the 1990s, in which the Sicilian press associated poverty and underdevelopment—two traits long used to characterize the island in the Italian public debate—squarely with Tunisia. Adopting a longer historical lens, chapters 1 and 2 show how Italian colonial educational policy explicitly sought to affirm the modernity and Europeanness of Sicilian settlers in Tunisia by differentiating them from Tunisian colonial subjects with whom they shared many spaces of everyday life. In essence, then, occupying a position of precarious Europeanness may mean similar experiences of racialization to those of colonial subjects historically, or present-day migrants, but this may actually lead to an intensified drawing of symbolic borders to affirm the Europeanness of internally racialized subjects (Newman 2006).

But what of the widespread celebrations of cross-Mediterranean interconnection and the framing of Mazarese identity as "hybrid" and "mixed"? Does this not represent a political discourse that calls into question material and symbolic borders and advocates local policies of multicultural belonging? Certainly, Mazara del Vallo represents a unique example of an Italian small town where the celebra-

tion of local identity is based on emphasizing its historic and contemporary connections with North Africa (for a similar discussion of Palermo, see Neil 2024;
Palma 2021). This language does provide an alternative discourse to the vision
of the Mediterranean Sea as a fault line in a broader "clash of civilizations" or as
a dangerous border in need of fortification. However, the celebrations of mixing
embraced by municipal authorities and various Catholic voices in Mazara del
Vallo paradoxically both reified notions of cultural difference between Sicilians
and Tunisians and created symbolic hierarchies between these two populations.
While some Catholic organizations in Mazara did provide material support to
people of Tunisian descent, thus recognizing their material needs, in general both
Catholic voices and Mazarese municipal authorities identified culture, rather
than economic precariousness, as the primary barrier to Tunisian "integration" in Mazara. Thus, they described successful Tunisian integration as cultural
approximation to Italianness. This meant that Catholic visions of Mediterranean
coexistence, and also municipal celebrations of Mazara's Mediterranean nature,
were based on a partial incorporation and celebration of some Tunisian elements
in Mazara (such as cuisine, architectural motifs, or some religious practices) but
certainly did not advocate for notions of mixing that would call into question
what it meant to be Italian or Sicilian. This was based on a symbolic hierarchy,
particularly explicit in Catholic discourses, that Sicilian (Catholic) culture was
particularly suitable as a basis for peaceful coexistence between difference, as
opposed to Tunisian (Muslim) culture.

These contradictions are not unique to Mazara del Vallo. In other southern
European borderlands, official discourses celebrating Mediterranean multiculturalism and cross-Mediterranean interconnections show similar limits in tack-
ling economic precariousness faced by people of North African descent, as well
as in calling into question the symbolic bordering of the Mediterranean. The
southern Spanish region of Andalusia is home to many such projects. The city
of Granada, for instance, has long embraced its legacy as a site of multireligious
coexistence dating back to the Caliphate of Al-Andalus as an attempt not only to
assert a distinct regional identity from the Spanish state but also to attract tourism
(Rogozen-Soltar 2017). The city of Málaga, in the same region, has also adopted
the strategy of highlighting its Arab legacy in order to facilitate investments from
the city's private sector in neighboring Morocco (Kutz and Giglioli 2021). In
France, the city of Marseille in 2013 launched the Museum of the Civilizations
of Europe and the Mediterranean (MUCEUM) as part of a broader project of
urban redevelopment, which involved the gentrification of various working-class
neighborhoods (Cartelli 2020). In all these cases, the celebration of Mediterranean interconnection and coexistence was primarily a regional development
strategy that was unable to address continuing racialized inequalities faced by

North African communities in these southern European borderlands, despite recognizing the presence and contribution of people of North African descent to their respective cities (Boursiquot 2014). As was the case for Mazara del Vallo's urban regeneration projects discussed in chapter 3, this may be explained by the fact that some of these local initiatives were connected to national and EU projects of cross-Mediterranean diplomacy, which were primarily geostrategic initiatives aimed at facilitating access to natural resources, supporting the off-shoring of European production, or controlling undocumented migration (Ben Hamouda and Bouchard 2012; Ben-Yehoyada 2014; Mourlane 2012).

Across the Mediterranean Sea, some celebrations of Mediterranean intercon-nection and coexistence in Tunisia—particularly prominent in the richer coastal regions of the country—also reproduce symbolic hierarchies between the north-ern and southern shores of the Mediterranean. While it has never become a wide-spread popular or political discourse, over the past thirty years Tunisian busi-ness leaders and politicians have occasionally embraced a language celebrating cross-Mediterranean interconnections as a strategic move to facilitate economic integration with the European Union. Starting in the mid-1990s, for instance, the Tunisian government began to celebrate the country's "Mediterranean" identity to rhetorically position it as an ideal business partner for Europe (Abbassi 2005), paving the way for the association agreement the country would soon sign with the EU.[1] Similarly, Tunisian entrepreneurs who did business with Italy would often mention the country's Mediterranean nature to underline its similarity to Europe and to rhetorically distance it from other parts of the MENA region.[2] In both cases, embracing a Mediterranean rhetoric meant claiming a Tunisian hybrid identity that framed the country as "modern" through its proximity to Europe.

Celebrating Tunisia's Mediterranean nature was also part of broader debates about national identity in the post–2011 revolution period, in which framing Tunisia as a Mediterranean borderland served to trace symbolic boundaries between a (Euro)Mediterranean space inclusive of Tunisia and the rest of the Arab/Muslim world, or sub-Saharan Africa. Tunisian President Ben Ali, ousted by the January 2011 uprising, had been a strong advocate for initiatives celebrating Mediterranean interconnection. In the aftermath of the revolution, the symbolic role of the Mediterranean within Tunisian national identity was up for discus-sion, as the constitutive assembly debated whether to include a clause on Tunisia's Mediterranean heritage in the preamble of the 2014 constitution (AlFatlahi 2014; Alkakli 2014). As is the case elsewhere in North Africa, such as Algeria, high-lighting a Mediterranean identity is a common counterargument to an Islamist vision that highlights the country's relationship with the rest of the MENA region and the Muslim world (Sayyid and Dabashi 2015). In 2014, proponents of the

Mediterraneanist vision lost the debate, and the final version of the preamble situated Tunisia as belonging to the Arab and Muslim Ummah, also affirming its affinity to the rest of the African continent. However, symbolic borders between Tunisia and sub-Saharan Africa reemerged in the Tunisian political discourse in summer 2023, as EU policies of border externalization coupled with a profound economic crisis created fertile terrain for popular hostility toward sub-Saharan African migration to the country. In this context, invocations of Tunisia's long history of cross-Mediterranean interconnection have served to cast African migrants and asylum seekers as invaders of a Euro-Mediterranean space.[3]

Overall, I have argued in this book against idealizing Mediterranean borderlands as mixed "intermediate" locations that call into question the symbolic boundaries of the nation, and against popular assumptions that borderland subjects—thanks to their own long history of marginalization—are intrinsically in solidarity with their cross-border counterparts. We have seen in several contexts how celebrations of cross-Mediterranean interconnection and multicultural coexistence do not necessarily call into question material and symbolic borders, but may indeed reproduce long-standing symbolic hierarchies between the northern and southern shores of the Mediterranean. But what prospects does this leave for creating political alternatives to rising nationalisms throughout Europe? Might it be possible to create "mixed" or "hybrid" spaces that are open and welcoming to people of both European and North African descent, and to reclaim the language of Mediterranean interconnection as a cross-borders solidarity project and a challenge to the material and symbolic bounding of Europe?

Reclaiming the Mediterranean

The years since the turn of the century have witnessed the building of many networks of activists from the northern and southern shores of the Mediterranean who embrace ideas of Mediterranean mixing and interconnection as a means to develop transnational solidarity initiatives, as well as to advocate for symbolic decolonization and political transformation in the Euro-Mediterranean region. Some initiatives are based in southern European borderlands, such as Lampedusa's Askavusa collective mentioned in chapter 1 of this book, and frame their work as a form of "south-south" solidarity between internally marginalized subjects and those excluded by Europe's borders. However, many are not based in borderland locations. Thus, they do not frame their politics as a natural outcome of their "intermediate" positionality, but around their commitment to address long-standing inequalities in the Euro-Mediterranean region. Among many such projects, Milano Mediterranea and the Maydan association, two initiatives that originated in Tunisia in the aftermath of the 2011 revolution, particularly exemplify how celebrations of Mediterranean mixing and interconnection can be mobilized to recognize and address material inequalities, to build bridges of solidarity between subjects experiencing similar conditions of economic precariousness with very different levels of opportunity, and to question symbolic hierarchies produced by a "clash of civilizations" discourse.

Milano Mediterranea is a self-defined postcolonial participatory art project founded by an Italo-Tunisian couple who met in Tunis in the aftermath of the 2011 revolution, where they had been involved with the activist theater group Corps Citoyens. Resettled in Milan, they founded an art center in the traditionally working-class and now primarily immigrant neighborhood Giambellino, in the southwest of the city, with the objective of creating space for artists of African descent in Milan. The project combines the sponsorship of artist residencies for southern Mediterranean and local artists with public-facing activities targeted to neighborhood youth. While artistic initiatives bringing together youth of North African and Italian descent are many, Milano Mediterranea is unique in explicitly embracing a postcolonial optic, organizing events such as debates on art and decolonization. In addition, the project produces all of its promotional materials in Arabic and Italian, thus fully recognizing the different backgrounds of all participants.

From its location in the northern Italian city of Milan, embracing language celebrating the Mediterranean is a strong political statement. While in Sicily, claims to a Mediterranean nature have long been part of official place-making strategies, Milan is located in a part of Italy in which long-standing antisouthern sentiments have morphed into antimigrant ones. In this context, claiming Milan as Mediterranean can be perceived as a direct challenge to the city's "modernness" and "Europeanness." For instance, a proposal to place palm trees in the square adjacent to the Duomo (the city's main cathedral) was met with a heated debate, with some public commentators claiming that these trees would have "Africanized" the city (Hawthorne 2022). In this context, then, embracing a Mediterranean identity signifies claiming Italy as a postcolonial space, home to people of both North African and European descent.

The Maydan association, in turn, embraces the notion of the Mediterranean as a space of interconnection to develop transnational solidarity between activists and civil society members on both shores of the Mediterranean. This association originated out of conversations and relationships built during the two iterations of the World Social Forum held in Tunisia in 2013 and 2015. Initially a loose, transnational network of activists who came together to organize a recurring political and artistic festival in the southern Italian cities of Messina and Reggio Calabria, they eventually founded the formal association Maydan, based on guiding principles of a shared Manifesto for Mediterranean Citizenship drafted by participants from southern Europe and the MENA region at one of the festivals.

Central to Maydan's work is a rejection of culturalist understandings of difference between Europe and the MENA region and a focus on economic questions, including both long-standing material inequalities between the northern and southern shores of the Mediterranean and their common yet differentiated experiences of neoliberal austerity. Similarly to urban-scale solidarity movements that emerged throughout southern Europe in the aftermath of the 2008 financial crisis, it treads the delicate balance of building solidarity on common conditions, while recognizing difference in power and privilege between those experiencing austerity on the two shores of the Mediterranean (Arampatzi 2017; Cabot 2016; Carastathis 2015). This framework of analysis means that while Maydan does engage with EU projects in the Mediterranean region, it departs from the European Union's depoliticized language, focused on dialogue and multicultural exchange, which frames dialogue as the main solution to tensions in the region. By arguing that the main dividing line between the northern and southern shores of the Mediterranean is a "clash of opportunity" (i.e., difference in wealth and access to mobility) rather than a "clash of civilizations" (Solera 2013), Maydan reframes "dialogue" from an objective in itself to a means to develop relationships of trust and collaboration between activists on both shores of the Mediterranean to support each other in solidarity or joint struggles, such as that against neoliberal austerity. The "clash of opportunities" analysis also means that the Maydan association clearly identifies and recognizes uneven power relations between the northern and the southern shores of the Mediterranean, visible in disparities of freedom of movement or in the subordinate status of the southern Mediterranean with regard to economic relationships with the European Union and collaboration on migration and security issues.

A detailed analysis of the internal organization and political practice of Milano Mediterranea and Maydan lies beyond the scope of this book. However, the language and the type of projects promoted by these two organizations highlight the potential of building cross-Mediterranean networks that call into question the material and symbolic bordering of Europe and—by so doing—of reclaiming the language of Mediterranean interconnection as a transformative political project that challenges the status quo of uneven power relations between people of European and North African descent. Reclaiming mixing created through colonial violence into a form of emancipatory politics is not unique to the Mediterranean. Speaking from the Caribbean, Martinican writer Edouard Glissant embraced *creolization* as the coming together of people of different backgrounds in a manner that broke with French colonial projects that celebrated coexistence under the politico-economic domination and cultural hegemony of France. The creolization he envisaged instead involved copresence, coexistence, and recipro-cal influence in a nonhierarchical manner, with the aim of collective emancipa-tion (Glissant 1989). The examples of Milano Mediterranea and Maydan suggest that this vision may be put into practice in the Mediterranean, but efforts to do so must grapple with several considerations.

First, it is fundamental to recognize and address historic and contemporary inequalities between the northern and southern shores of the Mediterranean and between people of European and North African descent. Maydan does so by clearly identifying inequalities in opportunities between citizens of European and North African countries as one of the main challenges in the Mediterra-nean region. Milano Mediterranea does so more implicitly, by recognizing the inequalities that have led people of North African descent to migrate to Milan.

Second, and a related point, it is important to not idealize "coexistence" and "dialogue" as the main objectives of cross-Mediterranean collaboration projects. At a conceptual level, celebrating coexistence runs the risk of reifying difference as an inherent characteristic, as opposed to the product of historical processes. At a more practical level, focusing on dialogue as the key challenge in the Euro-Mediterranean region means ignoring the substantial differences in opportu-nities between EU citizens and those of southern and eastern Mediterranean countries. The Maydan association explicitly questioned this framing by con-sidering dialogue as a first step toward more substantial collaboration on social, economic, and political campaigns and as a necessary step toward developing relationships of solidarity and costruggle.

Third, it is important to question symbolic hierarchies between the north-ern and the southern shores of the Mediterranean. Maydan members do so by developing relationships of costruggle and solidarity. This approach breaks with diffusionist models that see Europe as the default location of democratic prac-tices to be copied by activists on the southern shore of the Mediterranean—a common framing in EU-funded sociopolitical cooperation projects with the MENA region. In addition, the very origins of both the Maydan association and the Milano Mediterranea project question this hierarchy, because both devel-oped out of North African social movements. Beyond these examples, looking to the southern Mediterranean as a site of political innovation can prove crucial to developing a new political language to tackle long-standing social and economic issues within southern Europe. For instance, to address long-term regional inequalities, southern Italians could look for inspiration to activists from the Tunisian interior, who revolutionized discussions about regional inequalities by advancing claims for reparations for decades of state policies that privileged the development of the coastal regions at their expense (Salman 2017).

Finally, a critical look at the past is crucial to envisage emancipatory Mediterranean futures. This allows us to break with forms of colonial amnesia that prevent serious grappling with the inequalities of the past and their current legacies, as well as with claims to "innocence" by minor colonial powers such as Italy. In particular, this book has shown how a critical analysis of processes of colonial differentiation can shed light on how the symbolic borders of Europeanness came to be, and thus how they might be dismantled. For instance, understanding that Sicilians were "modernized and civilized" into Europeans in colonial Tunisia implies that there is nothing natural or intrinsic about Sicilians belonging to Europe, nor about Tunisians' exclusion from it. In addition, this analysis allows us to see how colonial boundary tracing between different populations allowed some (of European descent) to have access to opportunities at the expense of others (colonial subjects). As geographer Reece Jones argues, contemporary European borders continue to play a similar role, as they maintain access to opportunity for a few privileged insiders (Jones 2016). Recognizing the colonial origin of the material and symbolic borders we take for granted can allow us to advocate for freedom of movement in the Mediterranean as a form of reparations (Nevins 2019).

As migrants continue to die while trying to cross the Mediterranean Sea and right-wing nationalist movements are gaining strength across Europe, it is easy to lose hope in the possibility of developing a political alternative in this space. Yet daily relationships of friendship, love, and solidarity are forming across the waters of the Mediterranean, crafting new forms of transnational belonging that undermine the fortification of this sea. At the same time, activists on both its shores are embracing the celebration of Mediterranean interconnection as a platform for collaboration and solidarity to prevent deaths at borders, to reclaim Europe as a postcolonial space that belongs to all, and to struggle together against neoliberal austerity. It is precisely this intentional reckoning with long-standing injustices, and the attempt to build solidarity across difference, that can lead to a form of shared political practice that sees the unmaking of borders as reparations for the injustices of the past and as a means to construct a new emancipatory future.

Notes

INTRODUCTION

1. Interview with a board member of the Maydan association, March 2022.

1. MEDITERRANEAN INTERCONNECTIONS

1. This symbolism is not limited to the European context. The island appears as a symbol of the dangers of emigration in North African novels and popular music. Examples of this are the two homonymous novels by the Tunisian Saʿīd Luṭfuy (2012) and the Moroccan ʿAbd Al-Raḥman ʿAbīd (2011), as well as the Tunisian political singer Bendir Man (see his 2011 "Hbiba Ciao," https://www.youtube.com/watch?v=eq4DINMjBGc).

2. The description of the episode and all quotes are based on ethnographic research carried out in Lampedusa in January 2014.

3. In some contexts, such as France, the religious aspect may be framed as a predisposition toward secularism.

4. In 1937, the Fascist state embraced Aryanism, casting Jews as external to Italy and disavowing theories of Mediterranean mixing. The 1937 *Manifesto della Razza*, signed by more than 180 scholars, clearly articulated this position.

5. These numbers come from French government records, which tended to underestimate the number of Italians (Davi 2000).

6. Interview with Tunisian migrants, Mazara del Vallo, March 2014.

7. Interview with Nicolò Vella, Mazara del Vallo, February 2014.

8. *L'Ora* closed in the early 1990s, and the local edition of the national center-left paper *La Repubblica* took over its readership and some of its journalists.

9. The EU's Dublin Regulation required asylum claims to be heard in the EU country in which asylum seekers first arrive. This created a heavy burden on southern European countries with a Mediterranean coastline—countries that had also been hardest hit by the 2008 recession and subsequent austerity measures.

10. As a consequence of Italian and Greek pressure, the EU adopted a "hotspot" approach, according to which candidates for asylum were screened on their arrival on EU territory, and those whose asylum claims were likely to be successful were transferred to other EU countries (Guiraudon 2018). Migrant rights advocates criticized this approach, however, arguing that it hampered full and fair consideration of individual asylum claims (Garelli and Tazzioli 2013).

2. FUSING THE RACES OR TRACING THEIR BOUNDARIES?

1. Interview with Giuseppina, Florence, November 2013.

2. See, for instance, the justice system (Lewis 2014), French naturalization policies (Loth 1905; Pasotti 1979), and colonial urban-planning policies (Beguin 1983).

3. The capitulations regime was in place throughout the Ottoman empire and was aimed at avoiding trial of non-Muslims in an Islamic justice system. In the context of Tunisia, the capitulation system was also a means by which European imperial powers could spread their influence over the territory (Clancy-Smith 2010).

4. This dual system was also created to maintain a formal authority of the Tunisian ruling family, alongside a parallel system of French rule. Tunisia's status was different from that of Algeria, which had been directly annexed to France.

5. The term *bey* refers to the monarch of Tunisia, under the Husainid dynasty that ruled the country from 1705 till 1957.

6. Estimates of the exact number of illiterate Italians vary. According to the Italian consul to Tunis Carletti, at the turn of the twentieth century, 45% of this population was illiterate (Carletti 1903). According to French statistics, in 1911 this number was higher—59.2% of the population (Direction Générale de l'Agriculture 1915).

7. These included the Petite Sicile and the suburb of Halq-el-wad (La Goulette) in Tunis and the neighborhoods of Cappaci Grande and Cappaci Piccola in Sousse (Melfa 2007).

8. Despite having their own class prejudice toward poor Sicilian migrants, the Italian bourgeoisie resented French descriptions of "uncivilized" Sicilians. In 1901, the Institut de Carthage (a French cultural institute in Tunis) published an article titled "Our Sicilian Migrants in Their Own Land," which described the deep poverty of late nineteenth-century Sicily (Germain 1901). The article was met by such outrage from the Italian bourgeoisie in Tunis that the magazine was forced to publish the following disclaimer: "Some sentences . . . in the last issue of *La Revue Tunisienne* have irritated a part of Tunis's Italian colony. The translator . . . made a point to declare . . . that his thoughts had been wrongly interpreted, and that . . . no one could imagine associating the population of an entire country with a fraction of it that has remained in a savage state" (Germain 1902, 61). The content of the offending article was not the product of its French author, however, but the translation of Franchetti and Sonnino's 1876 Italian parliamentary report investigating the cause of Sicilian "backwardness." This incident shows that despite hostilities between French and Italian elites, their descriptions of working-class Sicilians were remarkably similar.

9. Positivist criminology was a school of thought spearheaded by the Italian criminologist Cesare Lombroso. As a type of biological determinism and racial thinking, it focused on the hereditary transmission of physical and psychological traits, linking them to criminal behavior. One of the most famous scholars operating in this tradition, Alfredo Niceforo, deployed these notions to theorize racial difference between northern and southern Italians (Caglioti 2017). In Tunisia, some French descriptions of Sicilians also appear to draw on this language. Noureddine (2001) recounts how, in the criminal court of Sousse, prosecutors of Sicilians sometimes described them as "born criminals."

10. The concept of atavism emerges directly from Italian positivist criminologist Cesare Lombroso's theories. He argued that criminals reproduced traits of more "primitive" human beings.

11. The 1899 final report of the director of the Principe di Napoli boys' elementary school (Sironi 1899).

12. Italian schools included three kindergartens, five elementary schools, a teachers' college, two secondary schools, and a boarding school for Italians living outside of the capital. French schools included twenty-seven elementary schools (a mix of private, public, and religious), a professional school, four secondary schools (a mix of private and public), and a teachers' college (Machuel 1906).

13. In 1905, 5,921 Italian students attended French schools, only slightly less than the 6,224 Italian students in Italian schools (Machuel 1906).

14. In his 1899 year-end report, the director of the Principe di Napoli boys' elementary school underlined that only two of his students came from "professional" families (one lawyer and one engineer), compared to 96 children of construction workers, 53 children

of day laborers, and more than 300 children of skilled and semiskilled laborers, artisans, or small-scale merchants (Sironi 1899).

15. The only exceptions were the Margherita di Savoia girls' elementary school and the Garibaldi kindergarten, situated in the new French quarters of the city. Most of the other schools were located in the area immediately south of the medina. The only school situated north of it was the Umberto I elementary school (Machuel 1906).

16. 1906 final report of the Margherita di Savoia girls' elementary school (Castagnetti 1906).

17. 1895 final report of the director of the night school (D'Alessandro 1895).

18. Various teachers emphasized that school represented a means of keeping children out of trouble and providing basic day care for them. For instance, the director of the Umberto I school noted in his 1903 end-of-year report that he was obliged to accept a wide range of students at the night school, because "If I had sent them away they would have learned nothing, and would have remained in the streets . . . committing all sorts of pranks" (Sironi 1903). Similarly, the director of the Crispi preschool observed in a 1905 trimestral report, "This kindergarten is almost entirely working class . . . it is also a place in which the dear name of Italy is blessed . . . by many poor families that, constrained by their work, can send us their children . . . without worries" (Paroni Brasi 1905).

19. 1896 Final Report of Director of Commercial School (Cybeo 1896b).

20. The only exception to this were three weekly hours of Arabic instruction included in the high school curriculum (Mascia 1897).

21. According to the 1881 final report of the Margherita di Savoia girls' elementary school, hygiene was included in the third-grade General Knowledge class (Mascia Merolli 1896).

22. From the 1896 final report of the director of the Margherita di Savoia Girls' elementary school (Mascia Merolli 1896).

23. 1898 Final Report of the Fourth Grade, Margherita di Savoia girls' elementary school (Canterini 1898).

24. 1896 Final Report, director of the Scuola Commerciale Italiana (Cybeo 1896b).

25. 1899 final report, Principe di Napoli boys' elementary school (Sironi 1899).

26. 1879 Final report, director of the Collegio Italiano (Agra 1879).

27. 1903 letter from the Italian consul general in Tunis to the Italian minster of foreign affairs (Console Generale 1903).

28. Transcript of speech in *La Depeche Tunisienne*, cited in Loth (1905, 447).

29. In Tunisia, proponents of the biological version of the fusion des races primarily understood this as a fusion between Italians and French, to create a unified Latin race (Bonurra 1922). Members of the French settler lobby supported this version. For instance, Louis Bertholon, a French military doctor stationed in Tunisia since the mid nineteenth century, member of the Committee for French Settlement, and president of the Institut de Carthage, underlined how Italians were "an extremely useful aid to the French, and regardless much more capable of assimilation than the natives. . . . They blend fairly quickly with the French component" (Loth 1905, 435). The promotion of intermarriage between French men and Arab women was supported in neighboring Algeria by some French intellectuals and colonial authorities, with the objective of creating a single "Mediterranean race" (Abbassi 2009; Gastaut 2001; Streiff-Fénart 1990). Eventually, a similar vision of the fusion des races would be adopted by French socialists in Tunisia. This vision led to their clash with the Tunisian independence movement, which considered this to be a French assimilationist project (Ben Hamida 2000; Soumille 1977).

30. This program also had the objective of limiting Italian influence, an aim clearly expressed in the words of Gaston Loth, who observed that "the natives . . . will learn Ital-

ian . . . spoken by a large part of the population. Italians, once they find that the natives speak their language, will be less open to learning French. Instead, if we drown the Italian influence in a native population that speaks French . . . Italians will learn French" (Loth 1905, 449).

31. These schools were created with the support of the newly created Tunisian bilingual elite. In some areas of the interior, French agricultural colonizers were actively opposed to the opening of these schools because they saw them as an obstacle to the availability of cheap Tunisian agricultural labor. This meant that many Franco-Arab schools eventually closed in the interior and in the south of the country (Ayadi 1986).

32. This was true for both Muslim and Jewish Tunisians. In this sense, French authorities adopted a different policy in Tunisia from that in Algeria, where they provided preferential avenues to citizenship for Jewish Algerians (Lewis 2014).

33. Celebrations of this victory made their way into daily interactions between Sicilians and Tunisians, with the former taunting the latter through expressions such as "Today we took Tarablus [Libya], tomorrow Costantinople or Mecca" and "Italy raped the Turkish girl" (Sghaier 1999, 18).

34. Interviews with descendants of Italians of Tunis, Bologna, and Florence, November 2013; Tunis, April 2014.

35. Interview with Sarah (pseudonym), Tunis, July 2012.

36. Interview with Italians of Tunisia, Tunis, April 2014.

37. See the film project *Vento*, directed by Enrico Montalbano (https://filmvento.blog spot.com).

38. Interview with Leila Al Houssi, February 2021.

3. MEDITERRANEAN OR "NOT EUROPEAN ENOUGH"?

1. In Milan, for example, 12.4 percent of the population are non-EU nationals (Ministero del Lavoro e delle Politiche Sociali 2020, 6). These numbers—of course—account only for foreign citizens and not descendants of immigrants.

2. The description of this episode and all cited quotes are based on ethnographic fieldwork carried out in Mazara del Vallo in March 2014.

3. The descriptions of these three families are based on ethnographic fieldwork carried out in Mazara del Vallo between December 2013 and August 2014.

4. Interview with Imen, Mazara del Vallo, March 2014.

5. The 2007 European enlargement had given Eastern European workers—primarily Romanian nationals—the same labor and residency rights as Italians, which meant that employers ran lower risks in employing them. In addition, by virtue of being able to move easily between Italy and Romania, Romanian workers were able to reduce the cost of reproduction for themselves and their families just as Tunisian workers used to do in the 1970s and 1980s, when they needed no visa.

6. Interview with Rami, Mazara del Vallo, March 2014.

7. Unione Italian dei Lavoratori, http://www.italuil.it/jsps/216/Attivita/573/Immigra zione/786/Le_procedure_per_il_rilascio_rinnovo_dei_titoli/787/Permesso_di_sog giorno.jsp.

8. Istituto Nazionale per la Prevenzione Sociale (INPS), https://www.inps.it/it/it.html? itemdir=50184.

9. In practice, there was some level of overlap between these categories, as sometimes people who had been providing these services as employees of Catholic service organizations or unions would then start their own for-profit agencies and bring their clientele with them.

10. Istituto Nazionale di Statistica (ISTAT), Statistiche Flash, Anno 2013, Occupati e Disoccupati, https://www.istat.it/it/files/2014/02/media_20131.pdf.

11. Interview with Aziz, Mazara del Vallo, March 2014.

12. These quotes and the description of the episode are based on ethnographic fieldwork carried out in Mazara del Vallo in March 2014.

13. Interview with Ahmad, Mazara del Vallo, March 2014.

14. Interview with Mehdi, Tunis, April 2014.

15. Interview with Majd and Khaled, Mahdia, April 2014.

16. Cole and Booth's (2007) ethnography of West African migrant communities in Sicily's capital, Palermo, found this vision to be quite common.

4. MEDITERRANEAN REDEVELOPMENTS

1. The description of this episode and all cited quotes are based on ethnographic fieldwork carried out in Mazara del Vallo in December 2013.

2. Women also pass through the area. However, its use as a social space is almost exclusively male.

3. Interview with Calogero, Mazara del Vallo, February 2014.

4. Interviews with business owners, Mazara del Vallo, February 2014.

5. Interview with Calogero, Mazara del Vallo, February 2014.

6. Interview with Catholic priest, Mazara del Vallo, February 2014.

7. Interviews with city council member and with NGO worker, Mazara del Vallo, February 2014.

8. Interview with business owner, Mazara del Vallo, February 2014.

9. Interview with business owner, Mazara del Vallo, February 2014.

10. Interview with Hiba, Mazara del Vallo, March 2014.

11. Interview with business owner, Mazara del Vallo, February 2014.

12. Interview with Agostino Spataro, Ioppolo Giancaxio, February 2014.

13. Interview with Nicolò Vella, Mazara del Vallo, March 2014. Interview with director of Tunisian school, Mazara del Vallo, February 2014.

14. Liceo Classico is a type of Italian high school focused on the study of the humanities.

15. Interview with Antonino Cusumano, Mazara del Vallo, March 2014.

16. "Mazara Del Vallo. Storia, Cultura, Leggenda." n.d. City map.

17. Some 94 percent of the funding for the strategic plan, which had a total cost of 260,000 euros, had come from the European Regional Development Fund, channeled through the Sicilian Region. Città di Mazara del Vallo: Deliberazione della Giunta Municipale [hereafter CMVDGM], March 5, 2010, n. 31.

18. Interview with Sicilian regional government employee, Palermo, January 2013.

19. Interview with studio employee, Marsala, February 2014.

20. Of the 200,000 euro budget to restore Casa Tunisia, 90 percent came from the Regional Department for Family, Social Policy and Local Autonomy (CMVDGM, January 29, 2010, n. 6); 85 percent of the total budget (1,400,000 euros) for the "multi-functional center for dialogue between the cultures of countries that border the Mediterranean" was funded by the Regional Department of Infrastructure and Transport (CMVDGM, September 3, 2010, n. 172).

21. The individual projects, usually involving one or two small alleyways, were approved in individual city council meetings starting in 2010 (CMVDGM, December 6, 2010, n. 239; CMVDGM, September 10, 2010, n. 176; CMVDGM November 21, 2011, n. 163; CMVDGM, May 13, 2013, n. 75). An older 1,500,000 euro project, dating back to 2006, had involved more substantial restructuring, including the renovation of water and sewage networks, as well as the artistic lighting of the old center (CMVDGM, July 10, 2009, n. 110).

22. Interview with member of Mazara del Vallo's City Council, Mazara del Vallo, March 2014.

23. Interview with business owner, Mazara del Vallo, March 2014.

24. Interview with Fritz, Mazara del Vallo, March 2014.

25. CMVDCC, March, 26, 2012, n. 44. "Mozione: Problematiche attività commerciali extracomuntari."

26. Data provided informally by an employee at the municipality of Mazara del Vallo.

27. Interview with Fritz, Mazara del Vallo, March 2014.

28. Interview with Bassma, Mazara del Vallo, February 2014.

29. Multiple interviews with people of Tunisian descent, Mazara del Vallo, February and March 2014.

30. Interview with a real estate agent, Mazara del Vallo, March 2014.

31. "We pay a consultant very well. . . . I imagined that . . . this would have facilitated access for the city . . . to privileged channels, sources of external funds." Mauro in CMVDCC, March 26, 2012, n. 44.

32. By the early 2000s, this school was highly criticized, since its curriculum was an exact copy of that used Tunisian elementary schools in the national territory and thus did not include the study of Italian. Many Italian teachers and Tunisian social workers criticized the school, because—with the Tunisian community more stably settled in Italy—they considered that it set up Tunisian children for failure when they eventually would move into the Italian school system. At the same time, this was the only avenue for Tunisian children to be able to learn Arabic and maintain an official connection to their parents' roots.

33. Eventually the position did become an elected one, but this happened only during the council member's second mandate. Interview with former additional city council member, Mazara del Vallo, February 2014.

34. The mayor had served as president of the Sicilian Regional Assembly and as a European Parliament delegate.

35. In the municipality's initial plan, Casa Tunisia was supposed to be managed directly by the Tunisian consulate in Palermo (CMVDGM, March 3, 2013, n. 44; CMVDGM, April 11, 2013, n. 60). This decision was later amended to confer the management of the center on the Tunisian association Friends Without Borders (CMVDGM, May 9, 2013, n. 72; CMVDGM, December 19, 2013, n. 193).

36. On the day of the opening of Casa Tunisia, for instance, activists from Voice of the Tunisian Migrant posted a photo of two homeless Tunisian men on a Facebook group for Tunisians abroad with the caption: "100 meters away from the inauguration of Casa Tunisia, members of the Tunisian community who have been without shelter for months denounce their situation to social services representatives from the Tunisian consulate in Palermo."

37. Interview with a member of the organization The Voice of the Tunisian Migrant, Mazara del Vallo, March 2014.

38. Article 2 of the memorandum of understanding between the City of Mazara del Vallo and the association Friends Without Borders stipulated that the municipality would give the association 10,000 euros a year to manage the center. Some activists interpreted this as a monthly salary that would go to the president of the association (Città di Mazara del Vallo and Associazione Amici Senza Frontiere. 2013. "Protocollo di intesa istituzionale tra l'associazione 'Amici Senza Frontiere' e la città di Mazara del Vallo per la gestione delle attività da svolgersi presso la Casa Tunisia.")

5. THE NEW CHURCH OF AFRICA

1. From a January 27, 2011, interview in *Giornale di Sicilia*, as quoted in Firrieri (2011).

2. This may be partially explained by the limited number of Muslim women employed by state institutions.

3. An example of this is the work of the National Cultural Association for Italo-Arab Cooperation active in the 1970s and 1980s, which brought together Communists, Social-

ists, and Christian Democrats (interview with Agostino Spataro, Ioppolo Giancaxio, March 2014).

4. Giorgio la Pira's influence went well beyond the city of Florence. Professor of Roman law at the University of Florence, he had been part of the Italian constitutive assembly following World War II. He was an active voice in Cold War Mediterranean diplomacy and tensions around decolonization in the southern and eastern Mediterranean (Giovannoni 2014; La Pira and Giovannoni 2006).

5. *Ecumenical dialogue* refers to the dialogue between different Christian denominations. In this context, however, it incorporates a more universalist meaning to embrace interreligious dialogue. Catholic figures in Mazara del Vallo also used the term with this broader meaning.

6. Pope John XXIII's 1964 encyclical *Nostra Aetate* laid out the Church's position on relating to non-Christian religions. While the document refers to many different religions, its main focus is to establish commonalities between Christianity, Judaism, and Islam—the three Abrahamic religions. Originally, the focus of the document was supposed to be on the relationship between Christianity and Judaism. It was broadened to include Islam to address tensions around the creation of the state of Israel.

7. Catania's first mosque was founded in 1980, as a private initiative of Michele Papa, a lawyer and advocate for cross-Mediterranean cooperation. He received funding from the Libyan government to restore a building in the historic center of Catania to house the mosque (Allievi 2003; Bolzoni 1980). Palermo's first mosque was opened in 1990, in a former church in the historic center of the city, through collaboration with the Tunisian consulate (Allievi 2003). Leoluca Orlando, the city's mayor, promoted it as part of an urban regeneration initiative focused on highlighting monuments from Palermo's Arab and Islamic past (Merosi 1990; *L'Ora* 1990).

8. While the debate on Islam emerged in the context of discussions about immigration, it did not characterize these debates. In the Italian newspaper *La Repubblica*, for instance, only thirty articles discussed Islam in the first years of the 2000s, compared with two hundred articles on immigration issues.

9. John Paul II had an open position toward Islam. However, he also coined the concept of a "cultural balance of a territory," according to which the state should respect and protect minority religions as long as they did not question the religious majority (Guolo 2003).

10. Giacomo Biffi, bishop of Bologna between 1984 and 2003, adopted this position.

11. Carlo Maria Martini, archbishop of Milan between 1979 and 2002, adopted this position.

12. Cardinal Ratzinger (later Pope Benedict XVI between 2005 and 2013) adopted this position.

13. *La Repubblica* gave ample space to Magdi Allam's commentaries on these issues; he wrote articles titled "The Islamic Menace in Italy" (Allam 1998a), "Italy Is Ready for the Challenge of Islamic Terror" (Allam 1998b), and "The Other Half of Islam: Voyage to Italian Harems" (Allam 1998c).

14. Some right-wing intellectuals who took this position included Oriana Fallaci and Giovanni Sartori (Sciortino 2002).

15. The party's 1998 statement *Padania, Identity and Multi-Racial Societies* expresses this position clearly. See http://www.network54.com/Forum/151860/message/999783871.

16. Interview with Nicolò Vella, Mazara del Vallo, March 2014.

17. Interview with a Sicilian activist for Tunisian migrant rights, Mazara del Vallo, January 2014.

18. Interview with a Mazarese journalist for *L'Ora* and *La Repubblica*, Mazara del Vallo, February 2014.

19. Interview with a Tunisian social worker, Mazara del Vallo, February 2014.

20. John Paul II, Mass on the Lungomare San Vito, Mazara del Vallo, Saturday, May 8, 1993, https://www.vatican.va/content/john-paul-ii/it/homilies/1993/documents/hf_jp -ii_hom_19930508_mazara-del-vallo.html.

21. The Franciscan nuns and the Fondazione San Vito provided similar services but had slightly different politics. The Franciscan nuns, who had been called to Mazara del Vallo by Bishop Costantino Trapani in the 1970s (Marusso 1980), worked closely with the municipality, from which they received funding (*Giornale di Sicilia* 2011). The Fondazione San Vito had instead a conflictual relationship with the municipality, because its director was a vocal critic of municipal authorities' disinterest in the material condition of Tunisian migrants; he accused the authorities of marketing Mazara as a cosmopolitan Mediterranean borderland while offering no public services to migrants (interview with an employee of the Fondazione San Vito, Mazara del Vallo, February 2014).

22. Interview with a Catholic clergy member, Mazara del Vallo, February 2014.

23. In an interview in February 2014, the bishop of Mazara explained to me how "we attempted to foster intercultural dialogue as a premise for interreligious dialogue, which is very difficult and far from happening organically."

24. Interview with a Catholic clergy member, Mazara del Vallo, February 2014.

25. Interview with a Catholic religion teacher, Mazara del Vallo, February 2014.

26. Interview with the bishop of Mazara del Vallo, Mazara del Vallo, February 2014.

27. Interview with an activist from The Voice of the Tunisian Migrant, Mazara del Vallo, March 2014.

28. Interview with Hiba, Mazara del Vallo, February 2014, in which she was describing her cousin's mixed Tunisian/German family.

29. Interview with Farah, Mazara del Vallo, March 2014.

30. Interview with Ons, Mazara del Vallo, March 2014.

31. Interview with the bishop of Mazara del Vallo, Mazara del Vallo, February 2014.

32. An apostolic vicariate is a form of territorial jurisdiction of the Catholic Church in contexts characterized by a minority of Catholics, where other structures of the Catholic Church are not present. It is usually part of the infrastructure of missionaries.

33. Interview with the director of the Fondazione San Vito, Mazara del Vallo, February 2014.

34. Interview with the bishop of Mazara del Vallo, Mazara del Vallo, February 2014.

CONCLUSION

1. See https://ec.europa.eu/trade/policy/countries-and-regions/countries/tunisia.

2. Interviews with Tunisian entrepreneurs active in Mazara del Vallo, Tunis, April 2014.

3. See, for instance, the letter published anonymously in the French-language paper *La presse* in the coastal Tunisian city of Sousse in June 2023, which set the civilizing cosmopolitanism of colonial Tunisia against forms of alleged cultural and moral degradation represented by the presence of Black sub-Saharan African migrants: "During the colonial era, in Sfax there were Jewish and Christian communities, French, Maltese, Greeks . . . Norwegians . . . it was an enriching and coherent human and cultural mosaic that reflected an elevated way of life. . . . Today this society has clearly been degraded with the presence of these migrants that are, far from any racial or ethnic discrimination, the mere residues of Black Africa, a source of violence, criminality . . . a source of disease." https://web .archive.org/web/20230610181844/https://lapresse.tn/160815/lettre-ouverte-dun-groupe -duniversitaires-et-de-journalistes-de-sfax-au-president-de-la-republique-la-tunisie-ne -doit-pas-etre-le-bouc-emissaire-des-tensions-en-afrique-subsaharie.

References

ʿAbīd, ʿAbd Al-Raḥman. 2011. *Lambīdūzā. Riwāyah*. Beirut: al-Markaz al-Ththaqāfī al-ʿArabī.

Abbassi, Driss. 2005. *Entre Bourguiba et Hannibal: Identité tunisienne et histoire depuis l'indépendance*. Paris: Karthala.

Abbassi, Driss. 2009. *Quand la Tunisie s'invente: Entre Orient et Occident, des imaginaires politiques*. Paris: Autrement.

Abu-Lughod, Janet L. 1980. *Rabat: Urban Apartheid in Morocco*. Princeton, NJ: Princeton University Press.

Agnew, John. 1994. "The Territorial Trap: The Geographical Assumptions of International Relations Theory." *Review of International Political Economy* 1 (1): 53–80. https://doi.org/10.1080/09692299408434268.

Agra, Giuseppe. 1879. "Collegio italiano di Tunisi nell'anno scolastico 1878–1879," September 10. Archivio Scuole 1868–1881. Archivio Storico, Ministero degli Affari Esteri, Rome.

Alexandropoulos, Jacques, and Patrick Cabanel. 2000. *La Tunisie mosaïque: diasporas, cosmopolitisme, archéologies de l'identité*. Toulouse: Presses Universitaires du Mirail.

Al-Faṭlaḥī, Ḥassān. 2014. "Āms fī al-majlis al-taʾāsīsī al-intilāq fī munāqashat al-dustūr: tasiq baṭiʾ qad yuʾaṭil al-muṣādaqah ʿalā al-dustūr fī al-mwāqthat al-muhaddad." *Le Maghreb*.

Al-Kaklī, ʿAbd-al-Salām. 2014. "Munāqashat al-dustūr: hiyn taghraq al-jālisah fī mīāh al-baḥr al-mutawassiṭ." *Astrolabe Tv*.

Allam, Magdi. 1998a. "L'altra metà dell'Islam. Viaggio negli harem italiani." *La Repubblica*, November 29.

Allam, Magdi. 1998b. "L'Italia pronta alla sfida contro il terrorismo islamico." *La Repubblica*, August 29.

Allam, Magdi. 1998c. "Pericolo islamico in Italia." *La Repubblica*, August 24.

Allievi, Stefano. 2003. *Islam italiano: Viaggio nella seconda religione del paese*. Torino: Einaudi.

Ansaldo, Marco. 1998. "La Tunisia pronta a trattare, ma 'Roma ci ha offesi.'" *La Repubblica*, August 1.

Anzaldúa, Gloria. 1987. *Borderlands: The New Mestiza = La Frontera*. San Francisco: Spinsters/Aunt Lute.

Arampatzi, Athina. 2017. "The Spatiality of Counter-Austerity Politics in Athens, Greece: Emergent 'Urban Solidarity Spaces.'" *Urban Studies* 54 (9): 2155–2171. https://doi.org/10.1177/0042098016629311.

Avallone, Gennaro. 2017. "The Land of Informal Intermediation: The Social Regulation of Migrant Agricultural Labour in the Piana Del Sele, Italy." In *Migration and Agriculture: Mobility and Change in the Mediterranean Area*, edited by Alessandra Corrado, 217–230. New York: Routledge.

Avventura Urbana and EURES Group. 2009. "Mazara città porta del Mediterraneo." Piano Strategico.

Ayadi, Taoufik. 1986. *Mouvement réformiste et mouvements populaires à Tunis: 1906–1912*. Tunis: Université de Tunis.

Bachrouch, Taoufik. 1985. "Co-instruction et géographie de la scolarisation primaire élementaire en Tunisie, 1883–1909." *Les Cahiers de Tunisie* 33 (133–134): 71–112.

Banfield, Edward C. 1958. *The Moral Basis of a Backward Society*. Chicago: Free Press; Research Center in Economic Development and Cultural Change, University of Chicago.

Barbato, Maurizio. 2001. "Noi Siciliani tra l'America e i paesi arabi." *La Repubblica*, September 15, Palermo edition.

Barrera, Mario. 1979. *Race and Class in the Southwest: A Theory of Racial Inequality*. Notre Dame, IN: University of Notre Dame Press.

Bassel, Leah, and Emejulu Akwugo. 2017. *Minority Women and Austerity: Survival and Resistance in France and Britain*. Bristol: Bristol University Press.

Bayly, Christopher A. 2004. *The Birth of the Modern World 1780–1914: Global Connections and Comparisons*. Oxford: Blackwell.

Ben Hamouda, Houda. 2012. *La construction d'un espace euro-méditerranéen: Genèses, mythes et perspectives*. Bruxelles: P. Lang.

Ben Hamouda, Houda, and Mathieu Bouchard. 2012. "Introduction." In *La construction d'un espace euro-méditerranéen: Genèses, mythes et perspectives*, edited by Houda Ben Hamouda, 15–22. Bruxelles: P. Lang.

Ben Hamida, Abdesselem. 2000. "Les socialistes français de Tunisie à l'époque coloniale entre assimilationnisme et antiracisme." *Cahiers de La Méditerranée* 61 (1): 59–67.

Ben-Yehoyada, Naor. 2011. "The Moral Perils of Mediterraneanism: Second-Generation Immigrants Practicing Personhood Between Sicily and Tunisia." *Journal of Modern Italian Studies* 16 (3): 386–403. https://doi.org/10.1080/1354571X.2011.565641.

Ben-Yehoyada, Naor. 2014. "Transnational Political Cosmology: A Central Mediterranean Example." *Comparative Studies in Society and History* 56 (4): 870–901. https://doi.org/10.1017/S0010417514000437.

Ben-Yehoyada, Naor. 2015. "'Follow Me, and I Will Make You Fishers of Men': The Moral and Political Scales of Migration in the Central Mediterranean." *Journal of the Royal Anthropological Institute* 22:183–202. https://doi.org/10.1111/1467-9655.12340.

Ben-Yehoyada, Naor. 2018. *The Mediterranean Incarnate: Region Formation Between Sicily and Tunisia since World War II*. Chicago: Chicago University Press.

Ben-Yehoyada, Naor, Salvatore Cusumano, Vito Pipitone, Tiziana Polizzi, and Raul Sanchez de la Sierra. 2016. "L'economia della pesca di Mazara Del Vallo in prospettiva storica." *Strumenti RES—Rivista Online Della Fondazione RES* 8 (1).

Bessis, Julie. 2006. "Communautés méditerranéennes et cosmopolitisme tunisien dans la première moitié du 20eme siècle." In *Les communautés méditerranéennes de Tunisie*, edited by Doyen Mohamed Hédi Cherif. Tunis: Centre de Publication Universitaire.

Betti, P. G. 1979. "Il clandestino Alì sulla barca di Mazara." *L'Unità*, April 23.

Bialasiewicz, Luiza. 2012. "Off-Shoring and Out-Sourcing the Borders of EUrope: Libya and EU Border Work in the Mediterranean." *Geopolitics* 17 (4): 843–866. https://doi.org/10.1080/14650045.2012.660579.

Bialasiewicz, Luiza, Paolo Giaccaria, Alun Jones, and Claudio Minca. 2013. "Re-Scaling 'EU'Rope: EU Macro-Regional Fantasies in the Mediterranean." *European Urban and Regional Studies* 20 (1): 59–76. https://doi.org/10.1177/0969776412463372.

Blandi, Franco. 2012. *Appuntamento a La Goulette: Le assenze senza ritorno Dei 150,000 emigrati italiani in Tunisia*. Marsala: Navarra.

Blauner, Robert. 1969. "Internal Colonialism and Ghetto Revolt." *Social Problems* 16 (4): 393–408. https://doi.org/10.2307/799949.

Bolzoni, Attilio. 1980. "S'è inventato una moschea l'avvocato del 'Billygate.'" *L'Ora*, October 2.

Bonurra, Francesco. 1922. *Gli Italiani in Tunisia ed il problema della naturalizzazione.* Roma: Tiber.

Boudreau Morris, Katie. 2017. "Decolonizing Solidarity: Cultivating Relationships of Discomfort." *Settler Colonial Studies* 7 (4): 456–473. https://doi.org/10.1080/2201473X.2016.1241210.

Boughedir, Férid. 2004. "Orphelin d'une enfance plurielle." In *Les lycées français du soleil: Creusets cosmopolites de la Tunisie, de l'Algérie et du Maroc*, edited by Effy Tselikas and Lina Hayoun, 51–63. Paris: Autrement.

Boursiquot, Fabienne. 2014. "Ethnographic Museums: From Colonial Exposition to Intercultural Dialogue." In *The Postcolonial Museum: The Arts of Memory and the Pressures of History*, edited by Iain Chambers, Alessandra De Angelis, Celeste Ianniciello, and Mariangela Orabona. London: Routledge.

Brambilla, Chiara. 2015. "Exploring the Critical Potential of the Borderscapes Concept." *Geopolitics* 20 (1): 14–34. https://doi.org/10.1080/14650045.2014.884561.

Bromberger, Christian. 2007. "Bridge, Wall, Mirror; Coexistence and Confrontations in the Mediterranean World." *History and Anthropology* 18 (3): 291–307. https://doi.org/10.1080/02757200701389030.

Brown, Wendy. 2010. *Walled States, Waning Sovereignty.* London: Zone Books.

Buscarino, Giuseppe, Nicolò Campanella, Benedetto Parisi, and Mario Tumbiolo. 1980. "Persistenza della cultura islamica nell'urbanistica di Mazara del Vallo." Undergraduate Thesis, Università di Palermo, Facoltà di Architettura.

Cabot, Heath. 2016. "'Contagious' Solidarity: Reconfiguring Care and Citizenship in Greece's Social Clinics." *Social Anthropology* 24 (2): 152–166. https://doi.org/10.1111/1469-8676.12297.

Caglioti, Angelo Matteo. 2017. "Race, Statistics and Italian Eugenics: Alfredo Niceforo's Trajectory from Lombroso to Fascism (1876–1960)." *European History Quarterly* 47 (3): 461–489. https://doi.org/10.1177/0265691417707164.

Caldanu, Giampaolo. 2011. "Immigrati, la UE gela il governo 'I permessi validi solo in Italia.'" *La Repubblica*, April 17.

Canal, Albert, Maximilienne Heller, and Raymond Marival. n.d. *L'Afrique du nord et sa littérature.* Tunis: Pascal Campo.

Canterini, Adele. 1898. Letter to Adria Mascia Merolli, June 20, "Relazione finale della classe quarta." Archivio Scuole 1888–1920. Archivio Storico, Ministero degli Affari Esteri, Rome.

Carastathis, Anna. 2015. "The Politics of Austerity and the Affective Economy of Hostility: Racialized Gendered Violence and Crises of Belonging in Greece." *Feminist Review* 109 (1). https://doi.org/10.1057/fr.2014.50.

Carletti, T. 1903. "La Tunisia e l'emigrazione italiana (Rapporto del Gar. T. Carletti, Regio Console a Tunisi." *Bollettino Dell'emigrazione* 2.

Carney, Megan. 2021. *Island of Hope. Migration and Solidarity in the Mediterranean.* Oakland: University of California Press.

Cartelli, Philip. 2020. "The 'Euro-Mediterranean' City: Transnational Difference and Belonging on the Marseille Waterfront." *Ethnologie Française* 50 (3): 501–512.

Casas-Cortes, Maribel, Sebastian Cobarrubias, and John Pickles. 2013. "Re-Bordering the Neighbourhood: Europe's Emerging Geographies of Non-Accession Integration." *European Urban and Regional Studies* 20 (1): 37–58. https://doi.org/10.1177/0969776411434848.

Casas-Cortes, Maribel, Sebastian Cobarrubias, and John Pickles. 2015. "Riding Routes and Itinerant Borders: Autonomy of Migration and Border Externalization." *Antipode* 47 (4): 894–914. https://doi.org/10.1111/anti.12148.

Casas-Cortes, Maribel, Sebastian Cobarrubias, and John Pickles. 2016. "'Good Neighbours Make Good Fences': Seahorse Operations, Border Externalization and Extra-Territoriality." *European Urban and Regional Studies* 23 (3): 231–251. https://doi.org/10.1177/0969776414541136.

Cassano, Franco. 2005. *Il pensiero meridiano*. Roma-Bari: GLF Editori Laterza.

Cassano, Franco. 2009. *Tre modi di vedere il Sud*. Bologna: Il Mulino.

Cassarino, Jean-Pierre. 2014. "Channeled Policy Transfers: EU-Tunisia Interactions on Migration Matters." *European Journal of Migration and Law* 16 (1): 97–123. https://doi.org/10.1163/15718166-00002050.

Castagnetti, Alberta. 1906. Letter to Adria Mascia, direttrice della scuola femminile Margherita di Savoia, June 27, "Relazione finale dell'anno scolastico 1905–1906." Busta 332, Archivio Scuole 1888–1920. Archivio Storico, Ministero degli Affari Esteri, Rome.

Castles, Stephen. 2011. "Migration, Crisis, and the Global Labour Market." *Globalizations* 8 (3): 311–324. https://doi.org/10.1080/14747731.2011.576847.

Cavallaro, Felice. 1981. "Mazara paralizzata dalla paura. E a chi è tunisino niente tenda." *Giornale di Sicilia*, June 11.

Césaire, Aimé. 1972. *Discourse on Colonialism*. New York: MR.

Chambers, Iain. 2008. *Mediterranean Crossings: The Politics of an Interrupted Modernity*. Durham, NC: Duke University Press.

Choate, Mark I. 2007. "Identity Politics and Political Perception in the European Settlement of Tunisia: The French Colony versus the Italian Colony." *French Colonial History* 8 (1): 97–109. https://doi.org/10.1353/fch.2007.0003.

Choate, Mark I. 2008. *Emigrant Nation: The Making of Italy Abroad*. Cambridge, MA: Harvard University Press.

Choate, Mark I. 2010. "Tunisia, Contested: Italian Nationalism, French Imperial Rule, and Migration in the Mediterranean Basin." *California Italian Studies* 1 (1). https://doi.org/10.5070/C311008861.

Clancy-Smith, Julia A. 2010. *Mediterraneans: North Africa and Europe in an Age of Migration, c. 1800–1900*. Berkeley: University of California Press.

Cobarrubias, Sebastian, Paolo Cuttitta, Maribel Casas-Cortes, Martin Lemberg-Pedersen, Nora El Qadim, Beste Isleyen, Shoshana Fine, Caterina Giusa, and Charles Heller. 2023. "Interventions on the Concept of Externalization in Migration and Border Studies." *Political Geography*. https://doi.org/10.1016/j.polgeo.2023.102911.

Cole, Jeffrey. 1997. *The New Racism in Europe: A Sicilian Ethnography*. Cambridge: Cambridge University Press.

Cole, Jeffrey. 2003. "Borders Past and Present in Mazara del Vallo, Sicily." *European Studies: A Journal of European Culture, History and Politics* 19 (1): 195–216. https://doi.org/10.1163/9789401201391_010.

Cole, Jeffrey, and Sally S. Booth. 2007. *Dirty Work: Immigrants in Domestic Service, Agriculture, and Prostitution in Sicily*. Lanham, MD: Lexington Books.

Colloca, Carlo, and Alessandra Corrado. 2013. *La globalizzazione delle campagne: Migranti e società rurali nel Sud Italia*. Milano: FrancoAngeli.

Console Generale. 1903. Letter to Ministro degli Affari Esteri, January 29, "Le nostre scuole alla scadenza dei trattati colla Francia." Archivio Scuole 1888–1920. Archivio Storico, Ministero degli Affari Esteri, Rome.

Conti, Natale. 1980. "500 mila 'clandestini' alimentano il racket della manodopera." *Giornale di Sicilia*, July 29.

Coppola, Paola, and Vladimiro Polchi. 2011. "Immigrati, scontro Italia-Fancia. Parigi: Non subiremo l'ondata, Il Viminale: allora esca da Schengen." *La Repubblica*, April 8.

Corleo, N. 1981. "Una moschea a Mazara per gli immigrati tunisini." *Giornale di Sicilia*, December 2.

Corrado, Alessandra, Domenico Perrotta, and Carlos De Castro. 2016. "Introduction. Cheap Food, Cheap Labour, High Profits: Agriculture and Mobility in the Mediterranean." In *Migration and Agriculture: Mobility and Change in the Mediterranean Area*, edited by Alessandra Corrado, 1–24. New York: Routledge.

Coulthard, Glen. 2014. *Red Skin, White Masks: Rejecting the Colonial Politics of Recognition.* Minneapolis: University of Minnesota Press.

Curtis, L. Perry. 1968. *Anglo-Saxons and Celts: A Study of Anti-Irish Prejudice in Victorian England.* Bridgeport, CT: New York University Press.

Cusumano, Antonino. 1976. *Il ritorno infelice: I Tunisini in Sicilia.* Palermo: Sellerio.

Cybeo, T. 1896a. Letter to ispettore generale delle scuole all'estero, February 20, "Relazione trimestrale." Archivio Scuole 1888–1920. Archivio Storico, Ministero degli Affari Esteri, Rome.

Cybeo, T. 1896b. Letter to Ministro degli Affari Esteri, July 8, "Relazione scolastica." Busta 334, Archivio Scuole 1888–1920. Archivio Storico, Ministero degli Affari Esteri, Rome.

Dakhlia, Jocelyne. 2005. *Islamicités.* Paris: PUF.

D'Alessandro, Luigi. 1895. Letter to ispettore generale delle scuole italiane all'estero De Luca Aprile, July 18, "Relazione scuola festiva." Busta 334, Archivio Scuole 1888–1920. Archivio Storico, Ministero degli Affari Esteri, Rome.

Dal Lago, Alessandro. 1999. *Non-persone: L'esclusione dei migranti in una società globale.* Milano: G. Feltrinelli.

Daly, Faïçal. 2001. "The Double Passage: Tunisian Migration to the South and North of Italy." In *The Mediterranean Passage: Migration and New Cultural Encounters in Southern Europe*, edited by Russell King, 186–205. Liverpool: Liverpool University Press.

Danewid, Ida, Angelica Pesarini, Camilla Hawthorne, Timothy Raeymaekers, P. Khalil Saucier, and Vivian Gerrand. 2021. "Introduction." In *The Black Mediterranean: Bodies, Borders and Citizenship.* New York: Palgrave Macmillan.

D'Arrigo, Maria. 2006. "'La Mérica è qua': Emigrazione di Siciliani in Tunisia (1890–1938)." Undergraduate thesis, Palermo: Università degli Studi di Palermo.

Davi, Laura. 2000. "Entre colonisateurs et colonisés: les Italiens de Tunisie (XIX-XXe siècle)." In *La Tunisie Mosaïque: Diasporas, Cosmopolitisme, Archéologies de l'identité.* Toulouse: Presses universitaires du Mirail.

Davila, Arlene. 2004. *Barrio Dreams: Puerto Ricans, Latinos, and the Neoliberal City.* Berkeley: University of California Press.

Davis, John. 1998. "Casting Off the 'Southern Problem': Or the Peculiarities of the South Reconsidered." In *Italy's "Southern Question": Orientalism in One Country*, by Jane Schneider, 205–224. Oxford: Berg.

Dear, M. J. 2013. *Why Walls Won't Work: Repairing the US-Mexico Divide.* New York: Oxford University Press.

De Donno, F. 2006. "La razza ario-mediterranea." *Interventions* 8 (3): 394–412. https://doi.org/10.1080/13698010600955958.

De Genova, Nicholas. 2017. *The Borders of "Europe": Autonomy of Migration, Tactics of Bordering.* Durham, NC: Duke University Press.

De la Cadena, Marisol. 2005. "Are Mestizos Hybrids? The Conceptual Politics of Andean Identities." *Journal of Latin American Studies* 37 (2): 259–284. http://www.jstor.org/stable/3875686.

Del Boca, Angelo. 2005. *Italiani, brava gente? Un mito duro a morire.* Vicenza: N. Pozza.

De Luca, Viviana. 2014. "La fatica della resilienza: i lavoratori immigrati di fronte all'esperienza della disoccupazione." In *Perdere e ritrovare il lavoro: L'esperienza della disoccupazione al tempo della crisi.* Bologna: Il Mulino.

Dimitriadis, Iraklis. 2021. "Onward Migration Aspirations and Transnational Practices of Migrant Construction Workers Amidst Economic Crisis: Exploring New Opportunities and Facing Barriers." *International Migration* 59 (6): 128–141. https://doi.org/10.1111/imig.12803.

Dines, Nick. 2022. "After Entry: Humanitarian Exploitation and Migrant Labor in the Fields of Southern Italy." *Society and Space* 41 (1). https://doi.org/10.1177/026 37758221117161.

Direction Générale de l'Agriculture. 1915. *Statistique générale de la Tunisie, année 1914.* Tunis: Société Anonyme de l'Imprimerie Rapide.

Du Bois, W. E. B. 1989. *The Souls of Black Folk.* New York: Bantam Books.

El Houssi, Leila. 2014. *L'urlo contro il regime: Gli antifascisti italiani in Tunisia tra le due guerre.* Roma: Carocci.

El-Tayeb, Fatima. 2011. *European Others: Queering Ethnicity in Postnational Europe.* Minneapolis: University of Minnesota Press.

Engels, Friedrich. 1968. *The Condition of the Working Class in England.* Stanford, CA: Stanford University Press.

Fanon, Frantz. 1965. *The Wretched of the Earth.* New York: Grove.

Farinella, Domenica. 2013. "Tra formale ed informale. Lavoro precario e strategie di sussistenza nel Mezzogiorno." *Etnografia e Ricerca Qualitativa* 1:13–34. https://doi.org/10.3240/73065.

Favell, Adrian. 2001. "Integration Policy and Integration Research in Europe: A Review and Critique." In *Citizenship Today: Global Perspectives and Practices,* edited by T. Alexander Aleinikoff and Douglas Klusmeyer, 349–400. Washington, DC: Carnegie Endowment for International Peace.

Ferguson, Kennan. 2007. *William James: Politics in the Pluriverse.* Lanham, MD: Rowman & Littlefield.

Fernando, Mayanthi L. 2014. *The Republic Unsettled: Muslim French and the Contradictions of Secularism.* Durham, NC: Duke University Press.

Filetto, Giuseppe. 1998. "Ecco il campo dei clandestini. Al di là del filo spinato: Un giorno tra i disperati." *La Repubblica,* July 29.

Firrieri, Max. 2011. "Mogavero parte oggi per Tunisia e Algeria." *Giornale di Sicilia,* January 27.

Floriani, Giorgio. 1974. *Scuole italiane all'estero: Cento anni di storia.* Roma: A. Armando.

Focardi, Filippo. 2016. *Il cattivo Tedesco e il bravo Italiano: La rimozione delle colpe della Seconda Guerra Mondiale.* Bari: Laterza.

Foderà, R., and Vito Pipitone. 2016. "Approcci integrati nello studio dei movimenti degli immigrati. I Tunisini in Italia come caso di studio." *Working Papers Fondazione RES,* 1..

Fortuna, Margherita Maria. 1984. Letter to Nigrizia, May 5, "L'Africa Da Noi.", Franciscan Nuns' Archive, Mazara del Vallo.

Fraser, Nancy. 2000. "Rethinking Recognition." *New Left Review* 3 (June): 107–120.

Frazzetta, Federica, and Gianni Piazza. 2020. "The Protests of Migrants in Sicily: Why Are There Few and Only Single-Issue?" *Geopolitics* 27 (4): 1284–1307. https://doi.org/10.1080/14650045.2020.1716737.

Frisina, Annalisa. 2010. "Young Muslims' Everyday Tactics and Strategies: Resisting Islamophobia, Negotiating Italianness, Becoming Citizens." *Journal of Intercultural Studies* 31 (5): 557–572. https://doi.org/10.1080/07256868.2010.513087.

Frisina, Annalisa. 2011. "The Making of Religious Pluralism in Italy: Discussing Religious Education from a New Generational Perspective." *Social Compass* 58 (2): 271–284. https://doi.org/10.1177/0037768611402611.

Frusciante, Alessandra. 2012. "Taviani e la nascita del centro per le relazioni Italo-Arabe." In *La politica araba dell'Italia democristiana: Studi e richerche sugli anni cinquanta*, edited by Matteo Pizzigallo. Milano: FrancoAngeli.

Fuller, Mia. 2007. *Moderns Abroad: Architecture, Cities and Italian Imperialism.* New York: Routledge.

Galemba, Rebecca B. 2012. "Remapping the Border: Taxation, Territory, and (Trans) National Identity at the Mexico–Guatemala Border." *Environment and Planning D: Society and Space* 30 (5): 822–841. https://doi.org/10.1068/d7710.

Gandy, Matthew. 1999. "The Paris Sewers and the Rationalization of Urban Space." *Transactions of the Institute of British Geographers* 24 (1): 23–44. https://doi.org/10.1111/j.0020-2754.1999.00023.x.

Gandy, Matthew. 2008. "Landscapes of Disaster: Water, Modernity, and Urban Fragmentation in Mumbai." *Environment and Planning A* 40 (1): 108–130. https://doi.org/10.1068/a3994.

Garelli, Glenda, and Martina Tazzioli. 2013. "Arab Springs Making Space: Territoriality and Moral Geographies for Asylum Seekers in Italy." *Environment and Planning D: Society and Space* 31 (6): 1004–1021. https://doi.org/10.1068/d15812.

Garnaoui, Wael. 2021. "Harga et désir d'Occident au temps du Jihad. Frontières et subjectivités migrantes des jeunes tunisiens." PhD dissertation, Paris: Université Paris Diderot.

Gastaut, Yvan. 2001. "Relations interculturelles dans les villes du Maghreb colonial: Peut-on parler de solidarités?" *Cahiers de la Méditerranée* 63. https://doi.org/10.4000/cdlm.13.

Germain, V. 1901. "Nos émigrants siciliens chez eux." *Revue tunisienne* IX: 428–444..

Germain, V. 1902. "Nos émigrants siciliens chez eux." *Revue tunisienne* IX: 61–75.

Getachew, Adam. 2019. *Worldmaking after Empire.* Princeton, NJ: Princeton University Press.

Giacalone, S. 2002. "'Mazara esempio di integrazione': gli studenti incontrano i giornalisti." *Giornale di Sicilia*, December 3.

Giaramidaro, Nino. 1975. "Il raro caso d'essere più povero di noi." *L'Ora*, October 17.

Gibson, Mary. 1998. "Biology or Environment? Race and Southern 'Deviancy' in the Writings of Italian Criminologists, 1880–1920." In *Italy's "Southern Question": Orientalism in One Country*, edited by Jane Schneider. Oxford: Berg.

Giglioli, Ilaria. 2017a. "Producing Sicily as Europe: Migration, Colonialism and the Making of the Mediterranean Border between Italy and Tunisia." *Geopolitics* 22 (2): 407–428. https://doi.org/10.1080/14650045.2016.1233529.

Giglioli, Ilaria. 2017b. "From 'a Frontier Land' to 'a Piece of North Africa in Italy': The Changing Politics of 'Tunisianness' in Mazara Del Vallo, Sicily." *International Journal of Urban and Regional Research* 41 (5): 749–766. https://doi.org/10.1111/1468-2427.12544.

Giglioli, Ilaria. 2021. "On Not Being European Enough: Migration, Crisis and Precarious Livelihoods on the Periphery of Europe." *Social and Cultural Geography* 22 (5): 725–744. https://doi.org/10.1080/14649365.2019.1601248.

Ginsborg, Paul. 1990. *A History of Contemporary Italy: Society and Politics, 1943–1988.* New York: Penguin Books.

Giornale di Sicilia. 1990a. "Dieci Nordafricani respinti al porto di Trapani," November 22.

Giornale di Sicilia. 1990b. "Gli immigrati respinti al porto di Trapani bloccano un aliscafo," August 30.

Giornale di Sicilia. 1990c. "Trapani, respinti sessanta Nordafricani," April 27.

Giornale di Sicilia. 2011. "Il sindaco regala tre computer alle suore," March 10.

Giovannoni, Macro Pietro. 2014. "La visione e la strategia mediterranea in Giorgio La Pira." *Egeria* 6 (3): 59–78.

Giudice, Christophe. 2006. "La construction de Tunis, "ville européenne" et ses acteurs de 1860 à 1945." PhD dissertation, Paris: Université Panthéon-Sorbonne.

Giuliani, Gaia, and Cristina Lombardi-Diop. 2013. *Bianco e nero: Storia dell'identità razziale degli italiani.* Firenze: Le Monnier Università.

Glissant, Édouard. 1989. *Caribbean Discourse: Selected Essays.* Charlottesville: University of Virginia Press.

Gonzales Casanova, Pablo. 1965. "Internal Colonialism and National Development." *Studies in Comparative International Development* 1:27–37. https://doi.org/10.10 07/BF02800542.

Goonewardena, Kanishka, and Stefan Kipfer. 2005. "Spaces of Difference: Reflections from Toronto on Multiculturalism, Bourgeois Urbanism and the Possibility of Radical Urban Politics." *International Journal of Urban and Regional Research* 29 (3): 670–678. https://doi.org/10.1111/j.1468-2427.2005.00611.x.

Goswami, Manu. 2004. *Producing India: From Colonial Economy to National Space.* Chicago: University of Chicago Press.

Graham, Stephen. 2010. *Cities under Siege: The New Military Urbanism.* London: Verso.

Gramsci, Antonio. 1971. "Alcuni temi della questione meridionale." In *La costruzione del Partito comunista, 1923–1926,* edited by Elsa Fubini, 137–158. Torino: G. Einaudi.

Grosfoguel, Ramón. 2003. *Colonial Subjects: Puerto Ricans in a Global Perspective.* Berkeley: University of California Press.

Gualini, Enrico. 2004. *Multi-Level Governance and Institutional Change: The Europeanization of Regional Policy in Italy.* Burlington, VT: Ashgate.

Guiraudon, Virginie. 2018. "The 2015 Refugee Crisis Was Not a Turning Point: Explaining Policy Inertia in EU Border Control." *European Political Science* 17:151–160. https://doi.org/10.1057/s41304-017-0123-x.

Guolo, Renzo. 2003. *Xenofobi e xenofili: Gli italiani e l'islam.* Roma: Laterza.

Hackworth, Jason, and Josephine Rekers. 2005. "Ethnic Packaging and Gentrification: The Case of Four Neighborhoods in Toronto." *Urban Affairs Review* 41 (2): 211–236. https://doi.org/10.1177/1078087405280859.

Hall, Stuart. 1992. "The West and the Rest: Discourse and Power." In *Formations of Modernity: Understanding Modern Societies,* edited by Stuart Hall and B. Gieben, 195–225. Cambridge: Polity.

Hall, Stuart. 2000. "Multi-Cultural Question." In *Un/Settled Multiculturalisms: Diasporas, Entanglements, "Transruptions,"* edited by Barnor Hesse. New York: Zed Books.

Haller, Dieter. 2004. "The Cosmopolitan Mediterranean: Myth and Reality." *Zeitschrift Für Ethnologie* 129 (1): 29–47.

Hawthorne, Camilla. 2022. *Contesting Race and Citizenship: Youth Politics in the Black Mediterranean.* Ithaca, NY: Cornell University Press.

Hawthorne, Camilla, and Pina Piccolo. 2016. "'Meticciato' o della problematicità di una parola." *La Macchina Sognante* 5. http://www.lamacchinasognante.com/meticciato -o-della-problematicita-di-una-parola-camilla-hawthorne-e-pina-piccolo/.

Hechter, Michael. 1975. *Internal Colonialism: The Celtic Fringe in British National Development, 1536–1966.* Berkeley: University of California Press.

Hernández, Roberto. 2018. *Coloniality of the US-Mexico Border: Power, Violence, and the Decolonial Imperative.* Tucson: University of Arizona Press.

Herzfeld, Michael. 1984. "The Horns of the Mediterraneanist Dilemma." *American Ethnologist* 11 (3): 439–454. https://doi.org/10.1525/ae.1984.11.3.02a00020.

Hess, Sabine. 2010. "De-Naturalizing Transit Migration: Theory and Methods of an Ethnographic Regime Analysis." *Population, Space and Place* 18:428–440. https://doi .org/10.1002/psp.632.

Hesse, Barnor, and Salman Sayyid. 2008. "Narrating the Postcolonial Political and the Immigrant Imaginary." In *A Postcolonial People: South Asians in Britain*, edited by Nasreen Ali, Virinder S. Kalra, and Salman Sayyid. New York: Columbia University Press.

Hibou, Béatrice, Hamza Meddeb, and Mohamed Hamdi. 2011. "Tunisia after 14 January and Its Social and Political Economy: The Issues at Stake in a Reconfiguration of European Policy." Report, Euro-Mediterranean Human Rights Network, Copenhagen.

Hill, Mark Lamont. 2018. "From Ferguson to Palestine: Reimagining Transnational Solidarity Through Difference." *Biography* 41 (4): 942–957.

Hoffmann, Alessandro. 1980. "A Trapani il miracolo economico si chiama 'duro lavoro tunisino.'" *Giornale di Sicilia*, May 4.

Hoffman, Lily M. 2003. "The Marketing of Diversity in the Inner City: Tourism and Regulation in Harlem." *International Journal of Urban and Regional Research* 27 (2): 286–299. https://doi.org/10.1111/1468-2427.00448.

Huntington, Samuel P. 1993. "The Clash of Civilizations?" *Foreign Affairs* 31 (May). https:// www.foreignaffairs.com/articles/united-states/1993-06-01/clash-civilizations.

IOM (International Organization for Migration). 2011. "First Migrants from Libya Arrive on the Italian Island of Linosa." Online article, March 27. International Organization for Migration, Geneva.

Jerfal, Kamal. 2001. *Al-jāliāt al-awrūbīa fī ẓill al-isti'mār al-faransī. Mujtamaʿ ʿalā hāmish al-mujtamaʿ: Madīnat Sūsa 1881–1939*. Sfax: Dār Muḥammad ʿAlī al-Ḥāmī.

Jones, Alun. 2006. "Narrative-Based Production of State Spaces for International Region Building: Europeanization and the Mediterranean." *Annals of the Association of American Geographers* 96 (2): 415–431. https://doi.org/10.1111/j.1467-8306.2006 .00484.x.

Jones, Reece. 2016. *Violent Borders: Refugees and the Right to Move*. London: Verso.

Kazdaghli, Habib. 1999. "Communautés européennes de Tunisie face à la décolonisation (1955–1962)." In *Actes Du IXe Colloque Sur: Processus et Enjeux de La Décolonisation En Tunisie (1952–1964)*, Tunis: Université de Tunis I, Institut superieur d'histoire du movement national, 321–338.

Kazdaghli, Habib. 2006. "La 'mosaïque' Tunisie dans le champ de la recherche." In *Les Communautés Méditerranéennes de Tunisie*, edited by Doyen Mohamed Hédi Cherif. Tunis: Centre de Publication Universitaire.

Khairallah, Chedly. 1934. *Le Mouvement évolutionniste tunisien: Notes et documents*. Tunis: Imprimerie de Tunis.

Khiari, Sadri. 2009. *La contre-révolution coloniale en France: De de Gaulle à Sarkozy*. Paris: Fabrique.

King-O'Rian, R., Stephen Small, Minelle Mahtani, M. Song, and P. Spickard. 2014. *Global Mixed Race*. New York: NYU Press.

Kipfer, Stefan. 2011. "Decolonization in the Heart of Empire: Some Fanonian Echoes in France Today." *Antipode* 43 (4): 1155–1180. https://doi.org/10.1111/j.1467-83 30.2011.00851.x.

Knight, Daniel, and Charles Stewart. 2016. "Ethnographies of Austerity: Temporality, Crisis and Affect in Southern Europe." *History and Anthropology* 27 (1): 1–18. https://doi.org/10.1080/02757206.2015.1114480.

Kooy, Michelle, and Karen Bakker. 2008. "Technologies of Government: Constituting Subjectivities, Spaces, and Infrastructures in Colonial and Contemporary Jakarta."

International Journal of Urban and Regional Research 32 (2): 375–391. https://doi
.org/10.1111/j.1468-2427.2008.00791.x.

Kutz, William, and Ilaria Giglioli. 2021. "Pour une géopolitique extrospective du développement urbain: Málaga et Mazara del Vallo, la coopération transfrontalière par le pragmatisme territorial." *L'espace Politique* 32 (3). https://doi.org/10.4000/espacepolitique.9299.

Labanca, Nicola. 2002. *Oltremare: Storia dell'espansione coloniale italiana.* Bologna: Il Mulino.

La Carta Di Lampedusa. 2014. https://www.meltingpot.org/2014/02/la-carta-di-lampedusa/.

Lafi, Nora. 2013. "Mediterranean Cosmopolitanism and Its Contemporary Revivals." *New Geographies (Journal of the Harvard School of Design)* 5:325–333.

La Pira, Giorgio, and Marco Pietro Giovannoni. 2006. *Il grande lago di Tiberiade. Lettere di Giorgio La Pira per la pace nel Mediterraneo: 1954–1977.* Firenze: Polistampa.

Largueche, Abdelhamid, Julia Clancy-Smith, and Caroline Audet. 2001. "The City and the Sea: Evolving Forms of Mediterranean Cosmopolitanism in Tunis, 1700–1881." *Journal of North African Studies* 6 (1): 117–128. https://doi.org/10.1080/13629380108718424.

Lauria, Emanuele. 2001. "Sicilia: Vigilanza sui siti archeologici." *Giornale di Sicilia*, September 14.

Lauria, Emanuele. 2011a. "La paura dell'invasione: la Sicilia non può assorbire una maxi-ondata di sbarchi." *La Repubblica*, February 24.

Lauria, Emanuele. 2011b. "Lombardo: I Tunisini se li prenda il nord." *La Repubblica*, February 22.

Leslie, Deborah, and John Paul Catungal. 2009. "Contesting the Creative City: Race, Nation, Multiculturalism." *Geoforum* 40:701–704. https://doi.org/10.1016/j.geoforum.2009.05.005.

Lewis, Mary Dewhurst. 2014. *Divided Rule: Sovereignty and Empire in French Tunisia, 1881–1938.* Berkeley: University of California Press.

Lewis, Oscar. 1966. La Vida: *A Puerto Rican Family in the Culture of Poverty—San Juan and New York.* New York: Vintage Books.

Li Vigni, Valeria, and Giovanna Mauro, eds. n.d. *Museo Del Satiro. Mazara del Vallo. Itinerari Cittadini.* Museo del Satiro, Mazara del Vallo.

Lombardi-Diop, Cristina. 2013. "L'Italia cambia pelle: La bianchezza degli italiani dal Fascismo al boom economico." In *Bianco e nero: Storia dell'identità razziale degli italiani*, edited by Gaia Giuliani and Cristina Lombardi-Diop. Firenze: Le Monnier università.

Lombardi-Diop, Cristina. 2021. "Preface." In *The Black Mediterranean: Bodies, Borders and Citizenship*, edited by Gabriele Proglio, Camilla Hawthorne, Ida Danewid, P. Khalil Saucier, Giuseppe Grimaldi, Angelica Pesarini, Timothy Raeymaekers, Giulia Grechi, and Vivian Gerrand. New York: Palgrave Macmillan.

Lombardi-Diop, Cristina, and Caterina Romeo. 2012. *Postcolonial Italy: Challenging National Homogeneity.* New York: Palgrave Macmillan.

Lopapa, Carmelo. 2001a. "Sicilia, la regione più a rischio." *La Repubblica*, September 14.

Lopapa, Carmelo. 2001b. "Sicilia nel mirino dei terroristi? D'Ali: 'Noi non siamo un obiettivo.'" *Giornale di Sicilia*, September 18.

L'Ora / الساعة.1979. "Perchè." November 20.

L'Ora. 1990. "Moschea a San Paolino. Zisa: Museo dell'Islam." September 10.

Lorello, Massimo. 2011. "Immigrati solo nel centrosSud? La Russa è suddito della Lega." *La Repubblica*, February 25.

Loth, Gaston. 1905. *Le peuplement italien en Tunisie et en Algérie.* Paris: Colin.

Loth, Gaston. 1907. *La Tunisie et l'oeuvre du Protectorat Français.* Paris: Delagrave.

L'Unità. 1976. "Il piccone ha fatto più del terremoto. A Trapani e nell'intera provincia i centri storici devastati dalla speculazione edilizia." October 17.

L'Unità. 1980. "Immigrati nella terra dell'emigrazione." June 24.

Lupo, Salvatore. 1990. *Il giardino degli aranci: Il mondo degli agrumi nella storia del Mezzogiorno*. Venezia: Marsilio.

Lupo, Salvatore. 2015. *La questione: Come liberare la storia del Mezzogiorno dagli stereotipi*. Rome: Donzelli.

Luṭfuy, Saʿīd. 2012. "*Lambīdūzā*": *Zawraq al-Ssaʿādah*. Tunis: Majmaʾ al-batrāʾ l-al-ṭṭabāʾah w-al-nnashr w-al-ttawzīʾ.

Machuel, Louis. 1906. *L'enseignement public en Tunisie (1883–1906)*. Tunis: Société Anonyme de l'Imprimerie Rapide.

Mahmood, Saba. 2009. "Feminism, Democracy, and Empire: Islam and the War on Terror." In *Gendering Religion and Politics: Untangling Modernities*, edited by Hanna Herzog and Ann Braude. New York: Palgrave Macmillan.

Mamdani, Mahmood. 2002. "Good Muslim, Bad Muslim: A Political Perspective on Culture and Terrorism." *American Anthropologist* 104 (3): 766–775. https://doi.org/10.1525/aa.2002.104.3.766.

Marusso, Irene. 1980. "Quattro Francescane, due assistenti, la benedizione del vescvovo, e il centro di servizio sociale è fatto." *Giornale di Sicilia*, February 5.

Mascia, Luigi. 1897. Letter to Ispettore Generale delle Scuole Coloniali, July 15, "Licenza liceale." Archivio Scuole 1888–1920. Archivio Storico, Ministero degli Affari Esteri, Rome.

Mascia Merolli, Adria. 1896. Letter to Aprile De Luca, Ispettore Generale delle Scuole Italiane, January 9, "Programmi didattici particolareggiati." Archivio Scuole 1888–1920. Archivio Storico, Ministero degli Affari Esteri, Rome.

Mascia Merolli, Adria. 1898. Letter to Ministero degli Affari Esteri, March, "Regia scuola femminile Margherita Di Savoia." Archivio Scuole 1888–1920. Archivio Storico, Ministero degli Affari Esteri, Rome.

Mas Giralt, Rosa. 2017. "Onward Migration as a Coping Strategy? Latin Americans Moving from Spain to the UK Post-2008." *Population, Space and Place* 23 (3). https://doi.org/10.1002/psp.2017.

Massari, Monica. 2006. *Islamofobia: La paura e l'Islam*. Roma: Laterza.

Massey, Doreen B. 1994. *Space, Place, and Gender*. Minneapolis: University of Minnesota Press.

McClintock, Anne. 1995. *Imperial Leather: Race, Gender, and Sexuality in the Colonial Contest*. New York: Routledge.

Meldolesi, Luca. 1998. "L'economia sommersa nel Mezzogiorno." *Stato e Mercato* 2:319–334. https://doi.org/10.1425/414.

Melfa, Daniela. 2007. "Regards italiens sur les Petites Siciles de Tunis." *IBLA* 199 (1): 3–27.

Melfa, Daniela. 2008. *Migrando a sud: Coloni italiani in Tunisia*. Roma: Aracne.

Memmi, Albert. 1965. *The Colonizer and the Colonized*. New York: Orion.

Merosi, Mauro. 1990. "Ora Allah abita qui." *L'Ora*, November 7.

Merrill, Heather. 2006. *An Alliance of Women: Immigration and the Politics of Race*. Minneapolis: University of Minnesota Press.

Mezzadra, Sandro, and Brett Neilson. 2013. *Border as Method, or, the Multiplication of Labor*. Durham, NC: Duke University Press.

Migliardi, G. 1980. "I centomila Arabi che vivono tra noi." *L'Unità*, June 23.

Mignosi, Enzo. 1980. "C'è un 'treno del sole' che porta in Sicilia." *Giornale di Sicilia*, March 1.

Mills, Amy. 2010. *Streets of Memory: Landscape, Tolerance, and National Identity in Istanbul*. Athens: University of Georgia Press.

Mingione, Enzo, and Fabio Quassoli. 2000. "The Participation of Immigrants in the Underground Economy in Italy." In *Eldorado or Fortress? Migration in Southern Europe*, edited by Russell King, Gabriella Lazaridis, and Charalambos G. Tsardanidis, 29–56. Basingstoke: Macmillan.

Ministero del Lavoro e delle Politiche Sociali. 2020. "La presenza dei migranti nella Città Metropolitana di Milano." Statistical report. https://integrazionemigranti .gov.it/it-it/Dettaglio-ricerca/id/1158/La-presenza-dei-migranti-nella-Citta -metropolitana-di-Milano.

Mitchell, Katharyne, and Matthew Sparke. 2018. "Hotspot Geopolitics versus Geosocial Solidarity: Contending Constructions of Safe Space for Migrants in Europe." *Environment and Planning D: Society and Space* 38 (6): 1046–1066. https://doi.org /10.1177/0263775818793647.

Moe, Nelson. 1998. The Emergence of the Southern Question in Villari, Franchetti and Sonnino. In *Italy's "Southern Question": Orientalism in One Country*, edited by Jane Schneider, 176–240. Oxford: Berg.

Moe, Nelson. 2002. *The View from Vesuvius: Italian Culture and the Southern Question*. Berkeley: University of California Press.

Montalbano, Gabriele. 2018 "Les Italiens de Tunisie: La construction de l'italianité dans un contexte colonial français (1896–1918)." PhD diss., École Pratique des Hautes Études and Università di Firenze

Mourlane, Stéphane. 2012. "Actions culturelles et coopération méditerranéenne: Le projet italien d'Eurafrica au début des années 1950." In *La construction d'un espace euro-méditerranéen: Genèses, mythes et perspectives*, edited by Houda Ben Hamouda, 23–32. Bruxelles: P. Lang.

Muci, Roberto. 2009. *L'Islam in Italia: Profilo Storico e Teologico, Possibilità Di Dialogo Interreligioso, Problematiche Dei Flussi Migratori*. Galatina: Congedo.

Neil, Margaret. 2024. "'We Welcome Migrants and the Tourists Come': Postmodern Hospitality in Palermo, Sicily." *Journal of the Royal Anthropological Institute*. https:// doi.org/10.1111/1467-9655.14093.

Nesticò, Massimo. 2011a. "Stop ai barconi carichi di immigrati: L'Italia da quattro motovedette alla Tunisia." *Giornale di Sicilia*, May 12.

Nesticò, Massimo. 2011b. "Tunisia-Italia, firmato l'accordo. Maroni: 'Faremo anche rimpatri.'" *Giornale di Sicilia*, April 6.

Nevins, Joseph. 2002. *Operation Gatekeeper: The Rise of the "Illegal Alien" and the Making of the U.S.-Mexico Boundary*. New York: Routledge.

Nevins, Joseph. 2019. "Migration as Reparations." In *Open Borders: In Defense of Free Movement*, edited by Reece Jones, 129–140. Athens: University of Georgia Press.

Newman, David. 2006. "The Lines That Continue to Separate Us: Borders in Our 'Borderless' World." *Progress in Human Geography* 30 (2): 143–161. https://doi.org/10 .1191/0309132506ph599xx.

Noureddine, Ali. 2001. *La justice pénale française sous le protectorat: L'exemple du tribunal de première instance de Sousse, 1888–1939*. Sousse: L'Or du Temps.

Orsini, G. 2015. "Lampedusa: From a Fishing Island in the Middle of the Sea to a Tourist Destination in the Middle of Europe's External Border." *Italian Studies* 70 (4): 521–536. https://doi.org/10.1080/00751634.2015.1120945.

Palma, Agatha Evangeline. 2021. "The Migrant, The Mediterranean, and the Tourist: Figures of Belonging in Post-Austerity Palermo." PhD diss., University of California, Los Angeles.

Panebianco, Stefania. 2022. "Human Security at the Mediterranean Borders: Humanitarian Discourse in the EU Periphery." *International Politics* 59:428–448. https:// doi.org/10.1057/s41311-021-00316-1.

Paoli, Simone. 2012. "The Cultural Issue from the Euro-Mediterranean Partnership to the Union for the Mediterranean, 1995–2010." In *La construction d'un espace euro-méditerranéen: Genèses, mythes et perspectives*, edited by Houda Ben Hamouda, 103–114. Bruxelles: P. Lang.

Papadopoulos, Dimitris, and Vassilis S. Tsianos. 2013. "After Citizenship: Autonomy of Migration, Organisational Ontology and Mobile Commons." *Citizenship Studies* 17 (2): 178–196. https://doi.org/10.1080/13621025.2013.780736.

Pappé, Ilan. 2006. *The Ethnic Cleansing of Palestine*. Oxford: Oneworld.

Paroni Brasi, Carlotta. 1905. Letter to Ispettore Generale, August 21. Archivio Scuole 1888–1920. Archivio Storico, Ministero degli Affari Esteri, Rome.

Pasotti, Nullo. 1979. *Italiani e Italia in Tunisia dalle origini al 1970*. Roma: Finzi editore.

Patriarca, Silvana. 1998. "How Many Italies? Representing the South in Official Statistics." In *Italy's "Southern Question": Orientalism in One Country*, edited by Jane Schneider, 77–97. Oxford: Berg.

Paturno, Roberto. 1980. "Faticano a Mazara con gli occhi all"altra sponda." *Giornale di Sicilia*, March 1.

Pecoraro, Alfredo. 2011. "A Lampedusa abitanti in rivolta: Donne in catena e porto bloccato." *Giornale di Sicilia*, March 29.

Pendola, Marinette. 2000. *La riva lontana*. Palermo: Sellerio.

Perini, Alessandro. 2011. "La Tunisia blocca i migranti. Maroni: l'accordo funziona." *Giornale di Sicilia*, May 8.

Perrotta, Domenico. 2014a. "Ben oltre lo sfruttamento: Lavorare da migranti in agricoltura." *Il Mulino* 2014 (1). https://doi.org/10.1402/75749.

Perrotta, Domenico. 2014b. "Vecchi e nuovi mediatori: Storia, geografia ed etnografia del caporalato in agricoltura." *Meridiana, Rivista Di Storia e Scienze Sociali* 79:193–220.

Petti, Alessandro. 2007. *Arcipelaghi e enclave: Architettura dell'ordinamento spaziale contemporaneo*. Milano: B. Mondadori.

Piro, Valeria. 2014. "What Is a Fair Wage? Negotiations of the Price of Labor in a Sicilian Greenhouse." *Etnografia e Ricerca Qualitativa* 2:219–244. https://doi.org/10.3240/77329.

Pisa, Massimo. 2011. "Immigrati, lo stop della Germania: 'I permessi violano Schengen." *La Repubblica*, April 9.

Politi, Marco. 1998. "Vescovi spaccati sull'immigrazione." *La Repubblica*, November 11.

Povinelli, Elizabeth A. 2002. *The Cunning of Recognition: Indigenous Alterities and the Making of Australian Multiculturalism*. Durham NC: Duke University Press.

Prefettura di Verona and CIR Rifugiati. 2023. "Guida alla cittadinanza italiana: Residenza, matrimonio e giovani." https://www.prefettura.it/FILES/AllegatiPag/1232/Guida_alla_cittadinanza_italiana.pdf.

Quatriglio, Giuseppe. 1980. "Allah dopo otto secoli torna con una Moschea." *Giornale di Sicilia*, December 10.

Quijano, Anibal, and Michael Ennis. 2000. "Coloniality of Power, Eurocentrism, and Latin America." *Nepantla: Views from South* 1 (3): 533–580. https://doi.org/10.1177/0268580900015002005.

Quijano, Anibal, and Sonia Therborn. 2007. "Coloniality and Modernity/Rationality." *Cultural Studies* 21 (2-3): 168–178. https://doi.org/10.1080/09502380601164353.

Rabinow, Paul. 1989. *French Modern: Norms and Forms of the Social Environment*. Cambridge, MA: MIT Press.

Rainero, Romain H. 2002. *Les Italiens dans la Tunisie contemporaine*. Paris: Publisud.

Rinelli, Lorenzo. 2016. *African Migrants and Europe: Managing the Ultimate Frontier*. London: Routledge.

Rogozen-Soltar, Mikaela. 2007. "Al-Andalus in Andalusia: Negotiating Moorish History and Regional Identity in Southern Spain." *Anthropological Quarterly* 80 (3): 863–886.

Rogozen-Soltar, Mikaela. 2017. *Spain Unmoored: Migration, Conversion and the Politics of Islam.* Bloomington: Indiana University Press.

Ross, Kristin. 1995. *Fast Cars, Clean Bodies: Decolonization and the Reordering of French Culture.* Cambridge, MA: MIT Press.

Rozakou, Katerina. 2012. "The Biopolitics of Hospitality in Greece: Humanitarianism and the Management of Refugees." *American Ethnologist* 39 (3): 562–577. https://doi.org/10.1111/j.1548-1425.2012.01381.x.

Rygiel, Kim, and Feyzi Baban. 2019. "Countering Right-Wing Populism: Transgressive Cosmopolitanism and Solidarity Movements in Europe." *American Quarterly* 71 (4): 1069–1076. https://doi.org/10.1353/aq.2019.0078.

Said, Edward W. 1979. *Orientalism.* New York: Vintage Books.

Salman, Lana. 2017. "What We Talk about When We Talk about Decentralization? Insights from Post-Revolution Tunisia." *L'Année Du Maghreb* 16 (1): 91–108. https://doi.org/10.4000/anneemaghreb.2975.

Saurin, Jules. 1899. *Peuplement français en Tunisie.* Paris: A. Challamel.

Saurin, Jules. 1900. *L'invasion sicilienne et le peuplement français de la Tunisie: Conférence faite par M. Jules Saurin, en mars et avril 1900, à Marseille, Lyon, Lille, Roubaix, Nancy, Le Havre, Amiens & St-Quentin.* Paris: A Challamel.

Sayyid, S., and Hamid Dabashi. 2015. *Fundamental Fear: Eurocentrism and the Emergence of Islamism.* London: Zed Books.

Sbraccia, Alvise, and Pietro Saitta. 2003. "Lavoro, identità e segregazione dei Tunisini a Mazara Del Vallo." CeSPI Occasional Papers no. 9, Centro Studi di Politica Internazionale, Rome.

Schapendonk, Joris. 2021. "Counter Moves: Destabilizing the Grand Narrative of Onward Migration and Secondary Movements in Europe." *International Migration* 59 (6): 45–58. https://doi.org/10.1111/imig.12923.

Schneider, Jane, ed. 1998. *Italy's "Southern Question": Orientalism in One Country.* Oxford: Berg.

Sciortino, Giuseppe. 2002. "Islamofobia all'italiana." *Polis* 16 (April): 103–123.

Sebag, Paul. 1998. *Tunis: Histoire d'une ville.* Paris: Harmanttan.

Sergi, Pantaleone. 1998. "Tunisia, la strada è libera per chi sogna le coste italiane." *La Repubblica*, July 26.

Sghaier, Amira Aleya. 1999. "Al-jālīa al-iṭālīya wa ʿalāqatuhā bil-tūnisīīn." In *Les relations tuniso-italiennes dans le contexte du protectorat*, 5–32. Tunis: Université Tunis I, Institut Supérieur d'Histoire du Mouvement National.

Shorrock, William I. 1983. "The Tunisian Question in French Policy toward Italy, 1881–1940." *International Journal of African Historical Studies* 16 (4): 631–651. https://doi.org/10.2307/218270.

Simpson, Audra. 2014. *Mohawk Interruptus: Political Life across the Borders of Settler States.* Durham, NC: Duke University Press.

Sironi, Renato. 1896. Letter from the director of the Principe di Napoli boys school in Tunis to Ispettore Generale delle Scuole Italiane all'Estero, July 28, "Relazione finale." Archivio Scuole 1888–1920. Archivio Storico, Ministero degli Affari Esteri, Rome.

Sironi, Renato. 1899. Letter from the director of the Principe di Napoli boys school in Tunis to Ispettore Generale delle Scuole all'Estero, July 28, "Relazione finale." Archivio Scuole 1888–1920. Archivio Storico, Ministero degli Affari Esteri, Rome.

Sironi, Renato. 1903. Letter from the director of the Principe di Napoli boys school in Tunis to Ispettore Generale delle Scuole all'Estero, May 1, "Relazione finale del corso serale." Busta 334, Archivio Scuole 1888–1920. Archivio Storico, Ministero degli Affari Esteri, Rome.

Solera, Gianluca. 2013. *Riscatto mediterraneo: Voci e luoghi di dignità e resistenza.* Portogruaro: Nuovadimensione.

Solomos, John, Bob Findlay, Simon Jones, and Paul Gilroy. 1982. "The Organic Crisis of British Capitalism and Race: The Experience of the Seventies." In *Empire Strikes Back: Race and Racism in 70s Britain*, edited by Centre for Contemporary Cultural Studies, University of Birmingham. London: Hutchinson.

Soumille, Pierre. 1975. *Européens de Tunisie et questions religieuses (1892–1901): Étude d'une opinion publique.* Paris: CNRS.

Soumille, Pierre. 1977. "Elie Cohen-Hadria: du protectorat français à l'indépendance tunisienne, souvenirs d'un témoin socialiste." *Revue de l'Occident Musulman et de La Méditerranée* 24:259–263.

Spataro, Agostino. 1980. "Centomila Arabi sfruttati." *L'Ora*, June 24.

Spataro, Agostino. 1986. *Oltre il canale: Ipotesi di cooperazione siculo-araba.* Roma: Edizioni delle Autonomie.

Spencer, Rainier. 2006. *Challenging Multiracial Identity.* Boulder, CO: Lynne Rienner.

Stoler, Ann Laura. 2002. *Carnal Knowledge and Imperial Power: Race and the Intimate in Colonial Rule.* Berkeley: University of California Press.

Streiff-Fénart, Jocelyne. 1990. "Catégories politiques et imaginaires à propos des mariages mixtes." *Annuare de l'Afrique Du Nord, CNRS Editions* 39:343–351.

Suárez-Navaz, Liliana. 2006. *Rebordering the Mediterranean: Boundaries and Citizenship in Southern Europe.* New York: Berghahn Books.

Sugiyama, Yoshiko. 2012. "Comment inculquer la modernité aux jeunes musulmans tunisiens sous le protectorat français (1896–1908)." *Oriental Archive* 80 (2): 167–182.

Sugiyama, Yoshiko. 2007. "Sur le même banc d'école : Louis Machuel et la rencontre franco-arabe en Tunisie lors du Protectorat français (1883–1908)." PhD diss., Université de Provence.

Tartamella, Enzo. 1975. "Aggredito un Tunisino a Mazara." *Giornale di Sicilia*, October 9.

Tartamella, Enzo. 2011. *Emigranti anomali: Italiani in Tunisia tra otto e novecento.* Trapani: Maroda.

Tazzioli, Martina. 2023. *Border Abolitionism: Migrants' Containment and the Genealogies of Struggles and Rescue.* Manchester: Manchester University Press.

Transirico, C. 2002. "Mazara del Vallo: Un Tunisino al comune." *Giornale di Sicilia*, December 14.

Trauner, Florian. 2020. "A Multifaceted Crisis as an Opportunity and a Risk: The EU's Long Struggle to Reform the Dublin System for Asylum Seekers." In *The State of the European Union: Fault Lines in European Integration*, edited by Stefanie Wöhl, Elisabeth Springler, Martin Pachel, and Bernhard Zeilinger, 257–274. Staat – Souveränität – Nation. Wiesbaden: Springer Fachmedien. https://doi.org/10.1007/978-3-658-25419-3_11.

Triandafyllidou, Anna, and Maurizio Ambrosini. 2011. "Irregular Immigration Control in Italy and Greece: Strong Fencing and Weak Gate-Keeping Serving the Labour Market." *European Journal of Migration and Law* 13:251–271. https://hdl.handle.net/1814/24734.

Tselikas, Effy, and Lina Hayoun. 2004. *Les lycées français du soleil: Creusets cosmopolites de la Tunisie, de l'Algérie et du Maroc.* Paris: Autrement.

Tsianos, Vassilis, and Serhat Karakayali. 2010. "Transnational Migration and the Emergence of the European Border Regime: An Ethnographic Analysis." *European Journal of Social Theory* 13 (3): 373–387. https://doi.org/10.1177/1368431010371761.

Valenzi, Lucia. 2008. "La formazione dei giovani antifascisti." In *Italiani e antifascisti in Tunisia negli anni trenta: Percorsi di una difficile identità*, edited by Lucia Valenzi, 1–40. Napoli: Liguori.

Vasile, V. 1979. "3000 pescatori allo sbaraglio." *L'Unità*, October 21.

Weber, Eugen. 1976. *Peasants into Frenchmen: The Modernization of Rural France, 1870–1914*. Stanford, CA: Stanford University Press.

Weizman, Eyal. 2007. *Hollow Land: Israel's Architecture of Occupation*. London: Verso.

Welch, R. 2010. "Intimate Truth and (Post)Colonial Knowledge in Shirin Ramzanali Fazel's *Lontano Da Mogadiscio*." In *National Belongings: Hybridity in Italian Colonial and Postcolonial Cultures*, edited by J. Andall and D. Duncan. Bern: Peter Lang.

Wright, Gwendolyn. 1991. *The Politics of Design in French Colonial Urbanism*. Chicago: University of Chicago Press.

Zaiotti, Ruben. 2016. "Mapping Remote Control: The Externalization of Migration Management in the 21st Century." In *Externalizing Migration Management: Europe, North America and the Spread of "Remote Control" Practices*, edited by Ruben Zaiotti, 3–30. New York: Routledge.

Zukin, Sharon. 2008. "Consuming Authenticity." *Cultural Studies* 22 (5): 724–748. https://doi.org/10.1080/09502380802245985.

Index

adhan, 109–10
agriculture, 33, 72–75, 136n31
Allam, Magdi, 106–7, 139n13
Amara, Fadela, 107
ambiguous identity, 14–18
Andalusia, 126
Apostolic Vicariate, created in Tunisia, 118
Arabic language, 14, 53, 55, 56, 59–60, 105
Arab Spring (2011), 41, 60, 127
Aryanism / Aryanists, 29, 133n4
Askavusa, 23, 128
assimilation: of migrants, 9; in settler-colonial versus non-settler-colonial states, 8–9. *See also* belonging; coexistence; incorporation; mixing; multiculturalism
asylum, 41–42, 128, 133nn9–10
atavism, 49, 134n10
austerity measures, 2, 17–18, 79, 130, 133n9
Avventura Urbana, 94, 95

Barbato, Maurizio, 109
Barcelona Declaration (1995), 94
belonging: alternative understanding of, 5–6, 123–24; religious affiliation as marker of, 106; of Sicilian migrants in Tunisia, 59; support for Italy's foreign interest through national, 29; of Tunisian migrant workers in Italy, 82. *See also* assimilation; coexistence; incorporation; mixing; multiculturalism
Ben Ali, Zine El Abidine, 101, 115–16, 127
Bertholon, Louis, 135n29
Biffi, Giacomo, 139n10
Black Mediterranean collective, 13
bordering: as process in multiple locations, 7–8; and racialization, 8; settler-colonial processes of, 8–9
borders: defined, 6–7; and other forms of spatial differentiation, 7–8; production of, 7; reframing of Southern Question in epoch of fortification of, 36–43; settler-colonial, 8–9

Cairoli, Benedetto, 47
Canal, Albert, 56

capitulations regime, 46–47, 133n3
Carletti, T., 134n6
Casa Tunisia, 84–85, 95, 100, 101, 137n20, 138nn35–36
Casbah (term), 90, 91
Casbah neighborhood: as case study, 84–86; change in, 89–93; everyday conviviality in, 87–89; map of, 88*f*; memories of familiarity and safety in, 87–89; renovation of, 93–99, 137nn20–21
Cassa per il Mezzogiorno (Fund for the South), 33–34
Catholic Mediterraneanism, 103–4; and boundary-drawing, 121–22; and cross-Mediterranean cooperation, 117–21; and immigration in Mazara del Vallo, 109–13; and Islam and secularism, 105–7; and Italian public debate about Islam, 107–9; and migrant integration and dialogue, 113–17; and Tunisian incorporation into Mazara del Vallo, 126
Césaire, Aimé, 120
Charter of Lampedusa, 22–24
citizenship, 76, 77, 78
"clash of opportunities" analysis, 130
coexistence: celebrations of Mediterranean, 3, 5, 6, 11, 121, 127; and colonial schools in Tunisia, 46, 54–57; in colonial Tunisia as model for modern-day Sicily, 5, 61, 63–64; idealization of intermediate spaces of, 6; implications of, in Mazara del Vallo, 66; and inequality in colonial Tunisia, 57–59; interreligious, in Mazara del Vallo, 111–12, 113, 114; limits of Mediterranean borderlands as models of, 124–28; Mazara del Vallo as model for, 71, 103; as objective of cross-Mediterranean collaboration projects, 131; in other southern European borderlands, 126–27; Sicily as model of, 109; Tunisia as space of, 119–20. *See also* assimilation; belonging; incorporation; mixing; multiculturalism
colonialism / coloniality, 9–11, 26–27, 29–31, 50, 120

coloniality of power, 9
colonial Mediterraneanism, 45–46; and
    coexistence and inequality in Tunisia,
    57–59; and colonial schools in Tunisia,
    49–50; and division of Tunisia's
    population between Europeans and
    Tunisians, 46–49; and French schools
    in Tunisia, 54–57; and Italian schools in
    Tunisia, 50–54; mobilization of, 61–64;
    remnants of, in Tunisia, 59–61
colonial schools, 46, 49–50; French schools,
    51*f*, 54–57, 134n13, 135n31; Italian
    schools, 50–55, 51*f*, 134nn12,14, 135n18
Common Agricultural Policy, 74
Common Fishing Policy (2002), 74
cosmopolitanism, 13–14, 102, 140n3
Craxi, Bettino, 60
creolization, 130–31
Cuffaro, Salvatore, 109

decolonization, 27, 58–61
differential inclusion, 78
disability pensions, 70, 78–79
Dublin Regulation, 133n9

earthquake of June 7, 1981, 90, 91
emigrant colonialism, 29–31, 50
emigration. *See* migration
employment: in Sicily versus northern Italy,
    81–82; of Tunisians in Mazara del Vallo,
    67–68, 69; of Tunisians in Sicily in
    1970s–1990s, 72–74; and vulnerability
    of Tunisians in Mazara del Vallo in early
    2000s, 74–79. *See also* agriculture; fishing
    industry; migrant labor
"ethnic packaging" initiatives, 94–95, 99, 102
EURES Group, 94
Euro-Mediterranean partnership (1995), 37
European Union: and government assistance
    to southern Italy, 36–37; intensification
    of border controls by southern
    Mediterranean countries and, 37–38; and
    post–Arab Spring migration, 41; refugee
    crisis (2015), 41–42

Fallaci, Oriana, 139n14
Fanon, Frantz, 31
Fascist regime, 29–30, 133n4
fishing industry: and change in Casbah
    neighborhood, 89–90, 92–93; in Mazara
    del Vallo, 3, 93–94, 95; and vulnerability
    of Tunisians in Mazara del Vallo in early
    2000s, 74, 75
Fish War, 92–93

Fondazione San Vito, 113, 118–19, 120,
    140n21
Fortuna, M. M., 113
France: and colonial schools in Tunisia, 49–50,
    51*f*, 54–57, 134n13, 135n31; "fusion of
    the races" policy, 44; and growing interest
    in history of Italian settlers in Tunisia,
    61–62; incorporation of rural populations
    in, 26; management and civilization of
    colonial populations, 26; perceptions
    of Sicilians in colonial Tunisia, 47–49;
    protectorate over Tunisia, 30; reform of
    Tunisian legal system, 46–47; and Sicilian
    migrants in Tunisia, 31–32
Franchetti, Leopoldo, 28–29
Franciscan nuns, 113, 140n21
Franco-Arab elementary schools, 56,
    135n31
French Protectorate, 46–49
French schools, 51*f*, 54–57, 134n13, 135n31
Friends Without Borders, 100–101,
    138nn35,38
Frontex, 38
fusion des races (fusion of the races), 44, 55,
    135n29. *See also* mixing

Ghali, 123
Giornale di Sicilia, 38–39, 72–73, 91, 108
Glissant, Edouard, 11, 130–31
Global Approach to Migration (2005), 38
Gramsci, Antonio, 28, 29, 82
Granada, 126
Great Britain, 26
Great Recession (2008), 68

hierarchies: celebrations of mixing as
    creating symbolic, 11–12, 56–57;
    between Europeans and non-Europeans,
    50; between French and Tunisians,
    50; French policies of coexistence
    as creating symbolic, 62; in mixed
    Mediterranean spaces, 12–13;
    questioning symbolic, between northern
    and southern shores of Mediterranean,
    131; between Sicilians and Tunisians,
    45–46, 104, 113–14, 126; symbolic
    religious, 113–14, 117, 120, 126
Higher Institute of the History of the National
    Movement, 61
hijab, 106
Hirsi Ali, Ayaan, 107
Huntington, Samuel, 1
hybridity, politics of, 11–14
hygiene, 52–53. *See also* living conditions